Paul Baylis • Philip Holmes
Sarah Holmes • Sally Jewers

Edexcel Diploma

Creative and Media

Level 2 Higher Diploma

A PEARSON COMPANY

Heinemann is an imprint of Pearson Education Limited, a company incorporated in England and Wales, having its registered office at Edinburgh Gate, Harlow, Essex, CM20 2JE. Registered company number: 872828

www.heinemann.co.uk

Heinemann is a registered trademark of Pearson Education Limited

Text © Paul Baylis, Phillip Holmes, Sarah Holmes and Sally Jewers 2008

First published 2008

12 11 10 09

10 9 8 7 6 5 4 3

British Library Cataloguing in Publication Data is available from the British Library on request.

ISBN 978 0 435499 28 0

Copyright notice

Edited by Julia Naughton

Cover and pages designed by Siu Hang Wong

Typeset by Wooden Ark Studio

Original illustrations © Pearson Education Ltd 2008

Illustrated by Dan Chernett at Bright Illustration

Picture research by Arnos Design Ltd

Cover photo/illustration © Fotosearch Stock Photography

Printed in China (GCC/03)

Websites

The websites used in this book were correct and up-to-date at the time of publication. It is essential for tutors to preview each website before using it in class so as to ensure that the URL is still accurate, relevant and appropriate. We suggest that tutors bookmark useful websites and consider enabling students to access them through the school/college intranet.

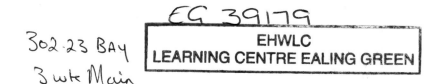

Contents

About the Diploma

Welcome to the Creative and Media Diploma. The Diploma is an exciting qualification that allows you to explore and develop your knowledge, skills and understanding of the creative and media industries. It will enable you to work across a wide range of disciplines and get a real feel for the sector.

> **Discipline** – A term used here to describe the different types of activities or subjects that are included in the creative and media industry.

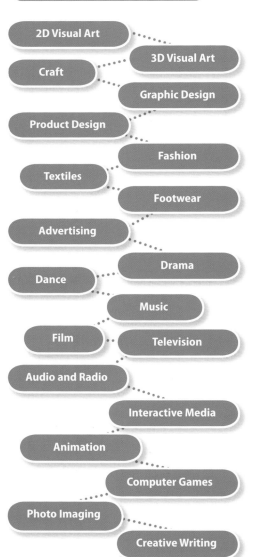

- 2D Visual Art
- 3D Visual Art
- Craft
- Graphic Design
- Product Design
- Fashion
- Textiles
- Footwear
- Advertising
- Drama
- Dance
- Music
- Film
- Television
- Audio and Radio
- Interactive Media
- Animation
- Computer Games
- Photo Imaging
- Creative Writing

Creative and Media industry

The creative and media industry encompasses a huge range of companies that do very different things, from broadcast journalism or theatre production to computer graphics or music technology. Throughout your Diploma, you will have the chance to learn how the creative processes can be applied to many of the types of organisations and careers that make up this exciting industry.

In each unit, you'll concentrate on at least two different disciplines. For example, when you do your Festival project, you may work on the creative processes leading up to performance and exhibitions, but also use advertising and graphic design skills to promote it.

Although the examples given in this book sometimes illustrate just one area of the creative arts, you may find that when you come to implement them you also encounter other areas. For instance, if you give a theatre presentation, it may also possibly need costume (fashion and textiles), props (3D visual arts), sets (2D visual arts) or even audio-visual back projection (film, audio). The possibilities for mixing different media elements are almost endless!

What you will cover

Your Diploma is made up of three elements. You will have to pass all three elements to achieve your qualification.

* **Principal learning** – this is the main part of the qualification and is organised into the units shown on the table on the right. The work you do here is directly related to the knowledge and skills required by the creative and media industries. Your teacher will make sure that the work you do is really relevant to your future career.

* **Generic learning** – during your course, you will also work on your Maths, English and ICT skills. These will be vital in getting the basics right for your career or further education. You'll also have the chance to develop your personal communication and thinking skills (Personal, Learning and Thinking Skills).

* **Additional and specialist learning** – in this part of your course, you can choose to broaden your experience by choosing qualifications from areas outside the creative industries, or specialise even further in the Creative and Media sector.

Principal Learning
Unit 1: Scene
Unit 2: Performance
Unit 3: Artefact
Unit 4: Record
Unit 5: Campaign
Unit 6: Festival
Unit 7: Project Report

These are the units that you must do. Your teacher will set projects and assignments for each of them.

Practical work

The Diploma will involve a lot of practical work. It is an active course in which you need to be an active learner. Your teacher will set up fantastic projects for you to work on, which may involve making videos, performing a play, putting on festival for your community, or creating an exhibition. You will have to take on a range of roles and responsibilities.

Most of this practical work will involve the following four stages:

1	**Investigating creative and media products**	Researching existing products and finding out how they are made, distributed and consumed
2	**Planning for production**	Developing and exploring ideas, planning and researching your own projects
3	**Production**	Working on your own or with a team to complete the actual production process
4	**Monitoring your production activity**	Continuously reviewing and refining your production activity

Your practical work will help you to explore the themes that are common across all the creative and media disiciplines and that are built into all the units:

* Creativity in Context
* Thinking and Working Creatively
* Principles, Processes and Practice
* Creative Business and Enterprise

Activity

Think about the creative work that you have been involved with in the past. Have you performed in a school play, taken some photographs, contributed to a student magazine or produced some posters? What sort of skills did you need to use to complete these tasks? Were some of them specific to the practical work that you were doing at the time and were some more generalised?

Think carefully about which disciplines of the Diploma you are interested in and discuss the options that are available to you with your teacher.

Your teacher will make sure that you have the opportunity to work on a wide range of projects during your course. Some of these may have themes running through them, but all of them will give you the chance to generate ideas and think through production and business aspects in creative contexts.

Get the basics right

In the Creative and Media industries, basic skills in English, Maths and ICT are just as important as specialist or technical knowledge. Each unit of this book will give you opportunities to use and develop each of these three functional skills. You will need to reach the required standard in all three to pass the Diploma successfully.

Activity

Think about English first. Identify situations in which you will need to use both written and spoken English during your Diploma and in your chosen career. Do the same for Maths and for ICT.

How confident are you in each of the three areas?

Strengths and weaknesses

Think about each of the three functional skills (English, Maths and ICT). What do you think your skill level is in each of these subjects? Which one is your strongest? Which one is your weakest? Will you need any extra help and support in any of the three areas?

These are all important questions that you will need to ask yourself and talk over with your teacher.

Case Studies

Sarah

Sarah feels confident in her use of both written and spoken English and is also able to use a number of different software programmes on her PC. She is looking forward to using her existing English and ICT skills in the work she will be doing on the diploma and learning some new skills as she goes along.

However, she has always struggled with Maths and is worried that she won't be able to cope with this part of the course. She is surprised and worried that Maths is an important part of the Diploma, and hadn't realised how often she would need to draw on her Maths skills in any creative and media career.

Sarah's teacher has explained that she will need to use her Maths skills when she has to:

* put together budgets for the productions she may decide to do
* plan out, sequence and edit video or DVD material
* carry out surveys and analyse the results for performances.

Her teacher has arranged for Sarah to attend an extra Maths workshop to get some help with the sums and calculations that she will need to do. He has reassured Sarah that the calculations she'll work on will all be set within the context of the creative industries and will link in with her project work.

Nathaniel

Nathaniel loves drama and performance and has chosen the Creative and Media diploma because he hopes to be involved in a lot of drama work and theatrical projects. He is confident about presenting himself in front of an audience and contributing to discussions. However, he also realises that he will be using his reading and writing skills throughout his course when he needs to:

* research areas that are new to him, such as the development of art forms
* learn how to use new equipment
* write accurate production minutes and plans.

Evan

Evan has basic ICT skills, but has always preferred to handwrite his work and use the library instead of the internet for researching. However, he knows that the Diploma might require him to use and develop his ICT skills further, to:

* broaden his range of knowledge and research possibilities for his projects on the internet
* manage his work and store his data electronically throughout the course
* format and create materials using applications such as Photoshop.

Get ahead in Creative and Media

To get ahead in the Creative and Media industries, you will need to develop skills to help you work effectively, both alone and in a team. These skills are Personal, Learning and Thinking Skills, or PLTS. You will be able to use them in each stage of this qualification and take them with you when you progress to the next level or get a job. They are important in life, and important in passing this qualification and getting the best out of your studies.

Types of role

The PLTS have been broken down into the skills used by six main roles that people need to undertake in the world of work. However, it is important to remember that, for any role in the Creative and Media industries, you will need strong skills in all six areas. Your teacher will be able to give you feedback on the progress you are making on your PLTS and highlight the areas that you need to develop further. Examples of the six main roles are listed in the Case Study on page 8.

It takes people with many different skills to create a theatre production like this!

Team Worker

Backstage crew member

Sarah is a strong team worker who works in a collaborative way as a backstage crew member for a touring theatre company. She feels confident working with other people and is able to take responsibility for her own role in a team. She is a good listener and is able to understand and relate to other people's views. These qualities allow Sarah to form good working relationships with other people and to resolve issues so that the team can meet their goals.

Independent Enquirer

Account manager

Anna works as an account manager for a national radio station. She is able to plan and undertake her own investigations and then process and evaluate the information. This allows her to take informed and well-thought out decisions that also recognise that other people may well have different views and beliefs to her own.

Self Manager

Location manager

Bilal was a very organised and committed student who displayed good levels of initiative, responsibility and perseverance at college. He now works as a location manager and is responsible for organising shoots for a local television company. He has to respond positively to frequent changes to his schedule and organise his own time and resources effectively. He can prioritise and is able to balance many competing pressures and demands.

Reflective Learner

Visual artist

Stefan has always been a strong reflective learner, as he is able to evaluate his own strengths and limitations and then set himself realistic targets for further improvement. He is happy to receive feedback from other people and is able to respond to this feedback in a positive way. He works very effectively on his own and is now self-employed as a visual artist, creating pieces for art galleries and exhibitions.

Effective Participant

Stage manager

At college, Mai Lu could always be relied upon to engage with a range of different issues and play a full and leading role in getting things done. She has used that skill in her role as Stage manager for a local theatre company. She is a good communicator, is able to negotiate with others, and she acts as a representative for other members of her team.

Creative Thinker

Set designer

Blandina isn't afraid to ask questions in her role as a stage designer. She often comes up with imaginative set designs for popular plays, and has to solve problems such as conveying outdoor locations within a small indoor set. She is always keen to try out new and original ways of doing things. She is also able to adapt her ideas as each production changes and develops.

Activity

Think back to the practical projects you have worked on. Write down the words that best describe you and the way in which you like to work. Do you prefer to work alone or in a team? What motivates you? Are you a natural leader or do you prefer to let someone else take the lead?

Do you think that this description of yourself and the way you work will change as you progress through the course?

Get out to work!

Work experience is an important part of the Creative and Media Diploma and offers you the opportunity to apply and add to your knowledge, understanding, skills and experience of the world of work. Your school or college is likely to help you to organise your work experience, but if you've got firm ideas of what you want to do or have any contacts in the industry, here's some advice to get you started.

Getting quality work experience may not be easy; there is often a high demand for placements and the creative and media industries are busy and competitive environments. Don't let this put you off though; you will learn a lot through trying and even more when you succeed. So, go on, give it a go!

What's out there?

Although you don't **have** to do your work placement within a creative or media organisation, the sector is one of the fastest growing, and there's a shortage of skills in some areas. So, by making sure you get the right experience and develop the right skills for the future, there's a huge range of jobs that you could do.

You can gain a lot of knowledge and experience by finding a placement in a real-life working environment.

Compared with 1991, there are:

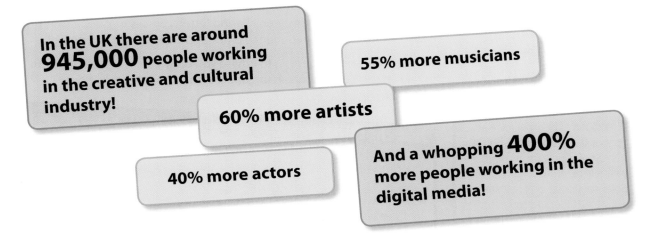

In the UK there are around **945,000** people working in the creative and cultural industry!

55% more musicians

60% more artists

40% more actors

And a whopping **400%** more people working in the digital media!

Creative and Cultural Skills Council, www.ccskills.org.uk

It doesn't really matter what form your work experience takes; what's more important is the knowledge and skills that you get out of it and the insight that you gain into the world of work. There is a wide range of jobs that you could investigate, so start thinking creatively!

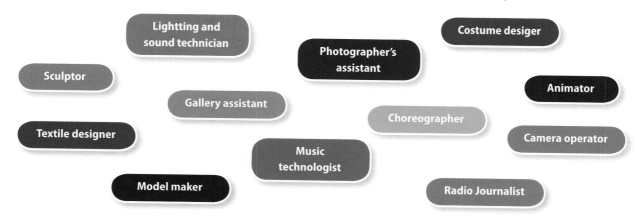

Work experience can come in lots of different shapes and sizes. Sometimes it is organised as a single two-week placement, but more often it can take the form of shorter, more regular activities that are linked in with the project work that you are undertaking.

Making contact

Even if your school or college is helping you to organise your work placement, you may still need to make contact with the individual, firm or company yourself. Sometimes the personal approach will be the best option; either talk to somebody that you already know face to face or telephone them.

An email or a more formal letter might also be appropriate for some organisations, but you need to remember that some companies will receive hundreds of requests for work experience and you must be prepared to receive a letter or email back saying that they have no time available for you. You might not even get a reply at all!

Don't let this put you off and don't take it personally. Working in the creative and media industries can be very stressful and people often have to work to very tight deadlines. This means that they have to prioritise their workloads; sometimes answering letters, emails or phone calls from people wanting work experience is not at the top of their to-do list!

Your teacher should be able to advise you on the best course of action to take in your particular circumstances, so it is best to talk it over with them first.

How to use this book

This book matches Edexcel's Level 2 Higher Diploma in Creative and Media. Each chapter follows the qualification's learning outcomes, with examples from a wide range of creative and media activities. There is a dedicated chapter on monitoring and reviewing your work and progress, which will help you throughout your course. There is also a special section to support the Level 2 Project Qualification.

Features of the book

Throughout the book you will find the following features:

Over to you!
A discussion point or short activity that will introduce the key concepts of the double-page spread.

Key words
Key concepts and new words are explained clearly and simply to make sure you don't miss anything important.

Case study
Case studies show the concepts covered in this book applied to the real world through real-life scenarios. Questions and activities will encourage you to push your understanding further.

Personal, Learning and Thinking Skills
Elements of the generic learning are embedded in the principal learning. These features highlight opportunities to develop and demonstrate your personal learning and thinking skills.

Functional skills
Functional skills have been built into many of the activities in this book. These features highlight opportunities to develop and practise your functional skills in English, IT or maths. Remember, you will need a Pass in all three functional skills to achieve the full Diploma.

For your project
These are useful things to consider when working on your project.

Just checking
The most important points to understand, summarised so you can quickly refresh your knowledge.

Activity
Each double-page spread contains an activity or a short sequence of questions to test your understanding and give you opportunities to apply your knowledge and skills.

Want to achieve more?

Each unit ends with advice on getting the best from the assessment. This tells you how you will be assessed and how your work will be marked and gives you useful reminders for key unit themes. Hints and tips give you guidance on how to aim for the higher mark band so you use your new skills and knowledge to best effect.

Introduction

A creative **scene** is the name for all the creative and media activities that go on in an area. From art exhibitions to music gigs, pantomimes to community radio, your local scene is what's happening now. You are going to investigate your local scene, including the kinds of jobs available in the creative and media industries. You will get to be a critic and comment on a local event or activity, then finally produce a guide to what's going on in your area.

Personal, learning and thinking skills

Investigating a creative and media scene and its career opportunities will give you the opportunity to demonstrate your skills as an Independent Enquirer.

Your learning

In this unit, you should work across at least two of the disciplines on page 4 to cover the four main topics.

Understanding creative and media activity

You have to produce a report that builds a picture of the creative and media scene in your area. To do this you need to understand how the public can access creative and media activities where you live: where are the exhibitions, performances and media facilities? You should also explore the organisations that help promote creative and media activity, and investigate the production activities themselves.

Understanding creative and media employment roles

Deciding what career path you want to follow is a major decision. The more research you do, the surer you can be that you're making a good choice. This topic will help you to investigate the types of jobs that exist within the creative and media industries and what kind of qualifications and experiences such jobs require.

By finding out more about the ways people are employed in this field, you will be able to develop your ideas about what roles you may like to take on and focus on what you will need to do to get there.

Developing a personal critical response to a creative or media activity or event

Imagine you want to go to the cinema; how will you decide what to see? Maybe you've got a favourite actor, or like a particular genre of film, but it's quite possible you'll choose a film because someone recommended it – or discount a film because it's had a bad **review**.

People can experience creative and media activities in a wide range of scenarios.

Reviews and **critiques** play an important part in the creative and media scene. You will develop your ability to form opinions about the work of other people as you build up to writing a critical response. Expressing opinions, or **criticism**, of other people's work requires you to understand what you do or don't like about their work, as well as to identify how they have handled things.

Analysing what others have done can show you new ways of working and increase your knowledge about what is good or bad practice. By expressing your thoughts and opinions appropriately, you will develop your ability to communicate effectively.

Creating a guide to the creative and media scene

Your final task in this unit is to produce a guide to the creative and media activities and events in your area. This guide should demonstrate the range of activities and events available, and communicate the information to your chosen audience.

With your teacher's guidance, you will select an appropriate medium and form for your guide, bearing in mind your audience, then present your information in an engaging and informative way. You must work to a production schedule, either on your own or in a group. Within all **sectors** of the creative and media industries, people rely on such guides to find out what is happening locally.

Process portfolio

In your process portfolio for this unit you should record and carefully store evidence from all stages of your work.

You will need to make sure your portfolio includes:

* Your research – include notes on different organisations that help promote creative and media activities, any recordings of interviews with practitioners/people involved in production activities, leaflets and **publicity** materials you collect, plus all your information on job roles and career opportunities within the creative and media arts.

* Your investigative reports – include final copies of your reports or presentations on your local scene and the creative and media arts job opportunities in your area.

* Your critical response – present your review of a local creative or media activity or event in your chosen format.

* Your finished guide – include your guide to what's going on in your local creative and media scene in your chosen format.

Activity

Get a copy of a local newspaper from within the last week. Use it to find out how you would access the following activities in your area:

* the screening of a film
* an art exhibition
* a play or theatrical performance
* a live music performance.

Mind-map – A diagram used to display potential ideas.

Scene – All of the creative and media activities in an area, e.g. 'Edinburgh has a busy arts scene'.

Review – An expression of views or opinions on the work of others usually including a rating in comparison to similar products.

Critique – A critical (analytical) essay or talk.

Criticism – Analysing what someone else has done whilst referring to your own opinions (being critical does not necessarily mean you are being negative).

Sector – A section or area of industry as a whole. The media sector, for example, includes all business related to television, film, print and radio.

Publicity – Advertising materials you distribute to make people aware of your activity.

Remember!

* Understanding your creative and media scene will help you become a part of it.
* Investigating creative and media roles could inform your career decisions.
* Critical response is a vital part of the creative and media scene.
* Your guide is a chance to showcase your knowledge of your creative and media scene.

1.1 Your local scene

OVER TO YOU!

Think of a creative or media activity that you have experienced recently. This could be a gig, the performance of a dance piece, an exhibition of art or craftwork or the screening of a film.

Discuss with a partner where you went to do this and what special features that place needed in order for that event to take place there, e.g. a gig would require space for an audience, a stage and some lighting.

To understand how creative and media practitioners present their work, you need to look at what's on offer to audiences in your area. This will also tell you how you can access creative and media products in your local area, which will be helpful as you develop your own creative skills.

There are so many different creative and media forms that your investigative options might seem a bit overwhelming at first – where to start? Investigate something you enjoy first, then move on to something you know less about. It is important to find information across a range of activities because this will give you a deeper understanding of how creative activities can be arranged and promoted, which will then improve your own work.

Creative and media productions

Creative and media practitioners need to get their work seen by the public. After all, most creators work with a purpose and audience in mind. It is sensible to go one step further and consider *how* and *where* your audience will get to see your work. People need to be able to find out about things easily and this is where **marketing** and publicity come in. All creative and media activities are promoted in some way, whether by simple flyers or a full-scale TV and radio campaign. Different types of activities happen in different types of locations and this will influence the type of promotion that takes place.

For artists or craftspeople, the activity they may use to let an audience see their work could be an exhibition. Performers of music, theatre or dance may put on a performance or show of their work. Media producers may use activities such as film screenings or television and radio broadcasts to present their work to an audience.

Organisations that promote creative and media activity

There are many national and local organisations whose purpose is to help those people who make creative and media products reach an audience. Some national organisations promote particular kinds of cultural activities such as dance or photography, whilst others focus on helping particular kinds of regions such as rural areas.

Local bodies concentrate on their own local area. Sometimes these are run by everyday people who are enthusiastic about a particular art form or cultural activity, e.g. the Women's Institute. Other local organisations are funded by government or charitable groups, such as The Milton Keynes Community Foundation who provide the money needed to produce promotional materials or publications to raise awareness of local activities. Most local councils also make money available to local arts projects and provide funding for them to promote their work.

Artists and craftspeople may present their work through exhibitions in galleries.

14

Case Study

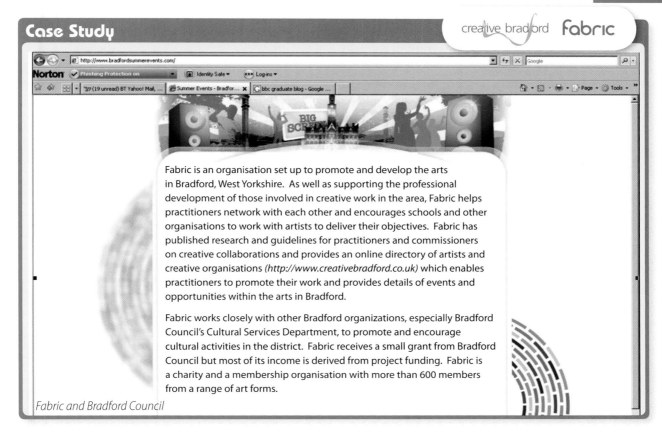

Fabric is an organisation set up to promote and develop the arts in Bradford, West Yorkshire. As well as supporting the professional development of those involved in creative work in the area, Fabric helps practitioners network with each other and encourages schools and other organisations to work with artists to deliver their objectives. Fabric has published research and guidelines for practitioners and commissioners on creative collaborations and provides an online directory of artists and creative organisations *(http://www.creativebradford.co.uk)* which enables practitioners to promote their work and provides details of events and opportunities within the arts in Bradford.

Fabric works closely with other Bradford organizations, especially Bradford Council's Cultural Services Department, to promote and encourage cultural activities in the district. Fabric receives a small grant from Bradford Council but most of its income is derived from project funding. Fabric is a charity and a membership organisation with more than 600 members from a range of art forms.

Fabric and Bradford Council

Carrying out your investigations

Before you can begin your investigations, you need to consider where you can find out information about cultural activities in your area.

Investigation methods

Your teacher may suggest different methods for investigating activities in your local area. You could:

* Study the 'What's on?' section of local newspapers and magazines.
* Look on the internet for local arts organisations that may promote activities.
* Make a list of the major venues in your chosen area and visit them, asking for information about upcoming shows, exhibitions, performances or presentations.
* Go to places where public information is available such as on public notice boards and at public libraries or tourist information centres. Make enquiries there and collect leaflets and flyers.

  Talk to local creative and media practitioners about where they present their work.
* Don't forget your own school or college. What is going on there? Consult your drama, art and music departments.

Marketing – Advertising materials that you have to buy space for, e.g. time on air, newspaper pages.

Local bodies – Local groups, organisations or council departments.

Network – Opportunities for people to meet up, discuss things and work together.

Activity

What organisations like Fabric are there in your local area? Visit the websites of your local council and the Arts Councils to find out more about culture and the arts in your area.

Activity

Construct a questionnaire to ask a range of people how they would find out where they might see the latest films, what art exhibitions are currently open or what is on at the local theatre.

Ask questions such as 'If you wanted to see a film tonight, how would you find out what was being shown and where?'

Note down their comments as this will give you a great starting point for your own investigations. You can find more information in Unit 7.

Conducting your investigation

You will need to plan how you will go about finding this information. Consider carefully what kind of resources you need and how you will record what you find. For example:

What I would like to find out	Method chosen	How I will store the information I find
What theatrical productions are on in the local area at the moment	Visit the Tourist Information office	Keep leaflets and flyers in my folder and make written notes of what the assistant at the Tourist Office tells me
Whether there are any exhibitions of textile work on in the local area	Go online to visit the local arts organisation in my area	I will print off my findings from the internet, highlight the sections that are useful and store these sheets in my folder.

Making contacts

Resources such as the Yellow Pages or online directories may be useful in identifying what kinds of creative and media companies or practitioners are active in your local area. You may find useful links to their websites or contact information that would allow you to communicate with them directly to find out more. Remember, when you are communicating with industry professionals or practitioners, you should always be polite and clear. Explain that you are a student and briefly outline what you are hoping to find out. Give clear details about how you can be contacted, should they have time to reply to you. Demanding information or failing to do things such as spell-check your messages will give the impression that you are rude and will make people less willing to help you.

Venues and locations

When the creators of products or artefacts are considering where to hold creative and media activities, different activities will often have very different needs. The requirements for staging a dance production, for example, would be very different to those needed to exhibit photographic work. Venues have to suit not only the work being presented but also how big the audience might be and where they will be within the venue.

There will be a variety of venues within a local area, e.g. theatres, public halls, bars, pubs, galleries, craft centres and public spaces such as town squares or village greens. Identifying the main venues is a good start to locating where activities may be happening.

Visiting local venues is one of the best ways to find information. The staff at galleries, theatres and arts centres will give you details of the organisation and the work on display there. By politely asking questions and paying careful attention to what is said, you can learn a great deal.

Creative and media activities can be presented to audiences in a range of different venues.

Storing your findings

Remember to store the information you find safely. You will need it for reference when you summarise your findings at the end of this topic, but also for the final task of this unit. During the final stage of this unit you will use your findings to produce a guide to your local scene and you will need to make careful reference to the details discovered at this stage.

Keeping paper-based resources in one folder or file would be wise; electronic information from internet or computer-based research should be stored on a data stick or in a folder on a computer.

Make careful notes about what each item you collect tells you. This will help you understand what you have collected and use it effectively when it comes to working on your guide.

Presenting your research findings

Your teacher will discuss with you the best way to present what you have found out at the end of this topic. It is most important that you demonstrate what you have found out in an effective way, either through a written or oral report.

Whatever form it takes, you should include clear explanations of what you have discovered and explain what your findings have taught you.

It is important to understand that this part of the unit is about collecting information and understanding *how* it is useful to you. Simply gathering a large folder of leaflets and print-outs without knowing why they are useful does not fulfil the topic requirements.

Personal, learning and thinking skills

When you present your research findings you will have to summarise your information on a creative and media activity and include a few carefully analysed examples to make your point, to demonstrate you are a good Independent Enquirer.

Functional skills

Using ICT...

You can use your ICT skills in many ways when you are researching your local creative and media scene, for example, to:

* show that you can use a variety of ICT systems on your own, evaluating their effectiveness to make sure you use the right system for the right job, e.g. an online encyclopaedia to check facts, a spreadsheet programme such as Excel to record data

* manage the information you find so it can easily be found, e.g. create separate folders for different information types

* select a variety of sources of information, e.g. 'what's on' websites, media review websites, newspaper websites.

For your project

You will need to record all of your findings when investigating the creative and media scene in your local area. Your work should show you have:

* looked at organisations that have been set up to promote and support cultural activities in your local area

* researched activities from across the creative and media industries – not just one chosen specialism or field

* used a variety of investigation methods – one method is not enough.

Choose a suitable format to present your findings – your teacher may suggest a written report, an illustrated poster or flyer. You may prefer to use PowerPoint or another interactive presentation tool.

Just checking

* Have you found organisations in your area that promote creative and media activity?
* Does your research plan cover all the necessary elements?
* Have you contacted and visited local media practitioners?
* Have you considered the best way to present your findings?

What kinds of arts venues are there?

OVER TO YOU!

Thought shower – think about any performance events you have seen recently in your local area. You might have been to the theatre lately or to see a concert. You may have watched a piece of street theatre or passed a busker in the street. Make a list of these performance activities or events.

Whether you live in a big city or a small village there will be performance arts activities happening near where you live. You may live near a theatre or concert hall. Perhaps your local community centre or library hosts music, dance or drama events. Your school or college may even act as a venue for performance arts.

Performance arts venues

Performance arts venues come in many shapes and sizes in terms of their facilities and the kinds of performances they stage or host. They fall into a smaller number of types however, in terms of the way they are run and funded.

Type of venue	Description	Examples
Producing Theatre	This is a theatre that has a company of performers and a production team who produce a number of shows each year. Many producing theatres are **subsidised**.	Northern Stage, Newcastle-upon-Tyne. The Stephen Joseph Theatre, Scarborough.
Receiving Theatre	A receiving theatre '**buys in**' productions from production companies and/or touring theatre companies rather than producing its own shows. Most of the theatres in London's West End are receiving theatres. Most receiving theatres operate in the **commercial** sector.	The Theatre Royal Drury Lane, London. The Sunderland Empire, Sunderland.
Arts Centre	An arts centre will host a larger variety of performance events than a theatre. It may buy in theatre, dance productions, gigs and concerts. Many hold events that involve public participation, e.g. drama workshops or dance classes. An arts centre may also screen films and have a gallery for exhibiting the visual arts. Most arts centres are subsidised.	Warwick Arts Centre. Pocklington Arts Centre, East Yorkshire.
Concert Hall	Concert halls generally host music events such as rock/pop gigs and classical concerts. Some concert halls are subsidised but some operate in the commercial sector.	The Royal Albert Hall, London. St George's, Bristol.
Other venues	Some performances take place in multi-purpose venues from small spaces such as community centres to huge sports arenas. Some performance events may even be staged out of doors.	The NEC, Birmingham The Odyssey Arena, Belfast.

Activity

* What kinds of performance venues can be found in your local area?
* Which categories from those listed on the table above do they fall into?

The Sunderland Empire is a typical example of a receiving theatre

The NEC in Birmingham is used for performances and other events.

Subsidised – Subsidised venues, companies and performers are given money from the government in the form of grants. The money is distributed by Arts Councils, regional arts boards and local councils.

Buy-in – A show that has been produced by a training company and is bought in by a receiving theatre.

Commercial – Venues, companies and performers who are not given money from the government are said to be commercial. This means they must ensure they make enough money from tickets sales, etc. to cover their costs.

Contemporary – Things that are happening now or have happened recently.

Production and touring companies

Whilst some of the performance arts productions and events happening in your area may be staged by local companies and performers, many are likely to be produced by touring performers or companies visiting a venue for a number of performances.

Case Study: The Henri Oguike Dance Company

The Henri Oguike Dance Company produce and tour **contemporary** dance both nationally and internationally. The company is based in London but tours the UK for five months of every year performing in a range of venues. Their 2007 tour included performances in The Lowry, Salford; Gardner Arts Centre, Brighton; Nottingham Playhouse; and the Peepul Centre, Leicester. During 2007 the company also performed in China, Portugal and Austria.

The company is headed by Artistic Director/Choreographer Henri Oguike and comprises an artistic team of two costume designers, a lighting designer, a rehearsal director and a production manager. Other members of the company include dancers and musicians, and a management team made up of a general manager, tour manager and media consultant.

Touring companies are important to the performance arts scene of any local area. Why do you think this is?

Functional skills

Using Maths…

You can use ICT to record, analyse and represent statistical information such as the percentage of performance arts events in your area are being staged by local performers, the proportion of art shops to galleries in a town, or cinema to theatre auditorium capacities.

Just checking

* Have you investigated the range of performance arts venues in your area?

* What's happening in your local area in terms of performance arts events?

* Does your research cover a wide range of performance activities and groups?

Activity

Find out what percentage of performance arts events in your area are staged by local performers and what percentage by those on tour.

Collect brochures/flyers, look in your local press or listings magazines and check out the websites of local venues to discover the types of performance arts events they are producing or hosting.

Where is the media?

The media arts scene is all around you. When you travel on a bus there will be posters advertising anything from special offers to medicines, and billboards on the road side advertising products and services. You will also see posters advertising local gigs, exhibitions and plays.

Media arts activity

You are going to investigate the media arts activity in your area.

Newspapers – Is there a local newspaper produced in your local area?

Radio – Do you have a local commercial, BBC or community radio station?

Television – Who is your local provider of TV programmes?

Video or audio – Are there any video or audio producers in your local area?

Photographers – Do you have a high-street photographer or specialist practitioner in your local area?

Media production

Who makes media products in your local area? For example, your local radio station broadcasts live shows, but it may also buy in special reports and performances, and it will definitely play jingles or advertisements that other media production companies have made.

Case Study: PMH Productions

PMH Productions is based in North Yorkshire. It is a media production company that specialises in producing video programmes on DVD format. It has a wide range of clients, the majority of whom are not based in North Yorkshire, so the company shoots much of its material on location across the UK and beyond.

What media might want to commission video programmes on DVD?

Why employ a specialist media production company to make your video?

Case Study: Talking Voices

Talking Voices is an international **podcast** production agency. They create podcasts for clients, and work on location and in-house. They employ professional presenters, voice-over artists, writers, editors and music composers to develop the content of the podcasts, as well as providing the technological know-how for internet, broadcast and digital on-demand media. They also run seminars and offer training to companies who want to develop their own online facilities. *http://talkingvoices.com/*

Where have you seen or used podcasts?

What benefits do podcasts have for:
a) the companies or organisations who use them,
b) the audience who download them?

OVER TO YOU!

Find examples of a range of companies in your area that are involved in the media. These could be from:

television   radio
cinema   newspapers
internet   advertising

Activity

Find out about other media exhibitions taking place in your local area. Find out when the exhibition is running, what the exhibition will be showing and who to contact for more details about the exhibition. Visit the exhibition centres and collect any brochures, flyers or reports that each one produces for your project portfolio. You could also download any online material on a hard drive, CD/DVD or datastick.

Podcast – A digital media text file downloadable from the internet for personal media players such as MP3 players or iPods.

Community Radio Licence – A licence to allow a community radio station to legally broadcast. They can last for up to five years.

Media organisations

As well as organisations that promote the media in your area, you may find national organisations such as Arts Council England and the Community Media Association.

Case Study: Community Media Association

community media association

The Community Media Association is the UK representative body for the community media sector. Its goal is to help people to establish and develop community-based communications media for empowerment, cultural expression, information and entertainment. The CMA provides a range of advice, information and consultancy, offering support to anyone with an interest in the sector.

It was founded in 1983 and is a non-profit making organisation. The CMA supports a number of projects, including community radio and television and community-based internet projects; it also speaks on behalf of community media groups to the Government, industry and regulatory bodies. Over 600 organisations, groups and individuals within the community media sector belong to the CMA.

One of the CMA's longest running campaigns was for **Community Radio Licences**, which were finally granted in 2004. Community radio stations are run by local people, mostly volunteers, and they enable communities throughout the UK to use the medium of radio to create new opportunities for regeneration, employment, learning and social inclusion, as well as cultural and creative expression. *http://www.commedia.org.uk*

What are the benefits of belonging to an organisation like the CMA if you are a small company or an individual media practitioner?

Why would the Government listen to an organisation like the CMA?

Community radio is growing in popularity since Community Radio Licence became available.

Media distribution and exhibition facilities

Think about how an audience gets to see media products. How are these products distributed or exhibited to their audience?

Local news

Local news is distributed through newspapers, television and radio, for example, the *Yorkshire Post* and the *Coventry Telegraph* are two regional newspapers that carry local and national news. The BBC offers local and national news through its regional radio and television stations, such as BBC Leeds and BBC Cornwall.

Exhibition facilities

The National Media Museum in Bradford is a museum and exhibition centre for many media areas. It has resources for television, radio, print and an archive of media material. You can find out what's happening in your area by reading the local papers, checking listings in magazines and publications, doing internet research and collecting brochures. It would also be a good idea to talk to your media arts teachers.

Just checking

* Have you considered the full range of media arts in your area?
* Do you understand the role media production plays in the media arts scene?
* How do media organisations work and promote the arts in your area?

Where can you see visual arts?

Gaining a better understanding of what activities visual artists and designers are already engaging in within your local area will give you insights into how you might work within the industry yourself.

Visual arts venues

Galleries, museums and exhibition spaces can be a mine of information about your local arts scene. Staff are likely to know a lot about different artists, not just the ones with current showcases. Your teacher is sure to be able to suggest some venues you could visit.

The places where you can see art and design activity and presentation depends on artists' specialisms. Some art pieces are designed to be experienced by an audience within a gallery or a specific setting. Other activities, such as jewellery design and creation have a functional purpose so they can be witnessed in everyday items or objects.

Visual arts production

Knowing where people who work in the visual arts are employed and how they produce their work will give you an insight into the industry around you. Use the table on the right to see if you can identify if any of the examples of visual art and design is happening in your local area. Remember, these are only examples – there are many more types of visual art and design activities that you could investigate

Try searching with some of the key words from the table on an internet search engine to find out what is near to where you live. Typing something like 'graphic design' and your local town into a search system such as www.yell.com will very often give you some immediate results that you can go on to investigate further.

Visual arts and design work can appear in a variety of places from exhibitions in shops, restaurants and bars to the graphic design work seen advertising materials.

Type of art or design activity	Where these people might work or operate
Photography	✱ Local newspaper ✱ Town-centre photographic studios ✱ Their own photographic business
Graphic designer	✱ Local graphic design agency ✱ Sign-writing/sign production company ✱ Local media businesses such as web design companies
Visual artist (such as a painter or a sculptor)	✱ From their own studio ✱ For a community art project ✱ As an **artist-in-residence** at a local gallery or museum
Fashion or textile designer	✱ Garment manufacture business ✱ In the costume department of a local theatre or media company ✱ Producing their own work from a studio or shop
A digital illustrator	✱ A local publishing firm ✱ A web design or graphic design company ✱ An advertising agency

Activity

Using a variety of investigative methods, look at the range of art and design activities listed below and see if you can find an individual or a company working in this field in your local area. When you have completed the task, share your findings with others so that you can benefit from each other's research.

Find examples of:

✱ a photographer

✱ a web design company

✱ a textile designer (may be listed as a dressmaker or tailor)

✱ a graphic design company

✱ an interior design company.

Artist-in-residence – An artist who is working with or in a company or organisation and is provided with a place to work.

Case Study: Out of the Box Design

Out of the Box Design is a design company who aim to provide a complete package of promotional resources for businesses. The team consists of a trained photographer, two graphic designers, a web designer, a part-time illustrator and an office manager. Between them the team can create a company's logo, a website, a full range of personalised stationery, shop signage, promotional leaflets and flyers and even the layouts for advertisements to be placed in print media like magazines and newspapers. The team all have very different skills and abilities, all of which contribute to the package of products that the company provides to customers.

Tim, the photographer, grew up in the area and returned home when he graduated from university with a degree in graphic design and communication. He says 'It is useful to have grown up in the area and have a good knowledge of the industries that surround us, as I can relate to the clients I work with and know immediately where they are based.'

Whilst Out of the Box is a small company, it is engaged in producing visual art and design products and is therefore part of the local design industry.

What are the advantages of working for a company like Out of the Box Design who produce a lot of different media products?

What might be the disadvantages?

Just checking

✱ What's special about the visual arts venues in your local area?

✱ How could you get involved in visual arts production in your area?

✱ Have you shared your research with your class?

Personal attributes – Qualities or personal skills, such as being organised or good-tempered.

CV – Curriculum Vitae – a document summarising your education, skills and employment history.

Freelance – Someone who takes on work for lots of different employers, rather than working for one person or company. Usually hired for a short period of time, from a single day to a few months.

Activity

In a small group, thought-shower how you could discover information on different creative and media career paths. Include any local careers advice service. Does your school or college have a careers advisor? Are there any local recruitment fairs or information days?

Functional skills

Using Maths…

If you are finding out numeric information regarding the budgets handled by professionals or the wages that they may earn, record this carefully to support your Maths portfolio.

Investigating what kinds of jobs are available in your local creative and media industry will give you the chance to think about your own future. You may have a firm idea of your ideal job, or you may have just vague ideas. In either situation, talking to people and researching organisations will help you to understand the reality of roles in the creative world, and which of these roles you could potentially fulfil when you finish your studies.

Making contact

In this topic the most important thing you will be doing is making contact with local people who work in the creative and media industries. Talking to people who have experience and first-hand knowledge of a role will give you the most valuable information you can find.

When arranging to meet with professional practitioners you may need to be flexible and meet when it is convenient to them. Before you meet, you will need to think carefully about the information you want to find out from them. You will probably find it useful to write a series of questions that will lead to the answers you need to find.

Your teacher may ask you to write a report at the end of this topic on what you find out. By broadening your knowledge of creative and media jobs now, you will be able to make an informed choice of career later on. For each job you investigate, it will help you to find out the following things:

* what the job involves
* the good and bad things about the job
* what qualifications or **personal attributes** you need to get the job
* what path people have taken to get to the position they currently hold
* what advice people have for anyone wanting a job similar to theirs.

Remember, try to be polite and patient at all times when dealing with professionals who have given up their time to help you. When working in creative and media jobs, time spent assisting you is often time that could have been spent earning money. Maintaining a good relationship with those in the industry is always a good idea as they may be able to offer you some work experience, which is extremely valuable when you are looking for work later in your career. Even a little bit of practical experience will help your **CV** stand out against others when you all have similar qualifications. Maintaining links with people in the same industry as you is called networking and it is important to do. People are more likely to help you when they remember you favourably. By staying in contact with people who are actually doing the job you're interested in, you will be aware of developments in your chosen role or field of work, and in your local area.

Job title	Positive points	Negative points
Freelance choreographer	Get to work with a variety of different people.	Not very financially secure as you rely on work coming in, rather than having a contract.
	Different projects will bring new challenges.	May be physically demanding and quite tiring.

Employers

You will also need to investigate what companies or organisations fall within the creative and media industries in your area. If you can find out who currently employs people in these creative sectors, you will improve your understanding of the opportunities that exist in your local area.

You can investigate which companies or organisations work in your area using a variety of different methods:

* Job vacancy searches available on newspaper websites, such as www. guardianunlimited.co.uk, will allow you to look at jobs from particular industries that are near to you. Not only will this give you vital information about the kinds of jobs available, it will also often provide you with details of the companies offering such work.

* Your careers advisor will know of local companies and organisations. They may also be able to advise on how these companies operate.

* Using internet search engines to search for the products made by companies you are interested in is always a good way to find information. For example, if you are interested in being a photographer, typing in 'wedding photographs' and then your local area may give you more useful links than just typing in 'photographer'.

* Some journals that relate to particular industries will feature a directory of local companies and services at the back of the publication and these are often split into regions.

* Many national organisations have regional branches or offices. The BBC for example, has regional offices around the country that employ people in a range of media and performance arts roles.

Activity

All jobs have positive and negative aspects. Make a list of three possible career paths you would be keen to take, then draw up a table like the one on the left. Do some research and use your own knowledge to find three positive and three negative things for each job. Understanding that there may be some negative points to a job should not put you off following that career path, but instead give you a realistic expectation of what working in that role might be like.

Functional skills

Using English...

The skills you have learnt in speaking and listening will be helpful when you are discussing career opportunities with creative and media professionals. It is important to be able to contribute effectively and thoughtfully to discussions so you find out all the information you require, as well as presenting yourself in a favourable light as a potential future employee!

Talking to professionals about their roles and experience will give you invaluable information.

Case Study: Cadbury Schweppes

Organisations often give lots of useful information on their websites about the kinds of skills or attributes they look for in potential employees. Larger organisations may also run a graduate or entry-level scheme – an opportunity for newly qualified individuals with little or no work experience to start at the bottom and learn their job under supervision and guidance. They often have opportunities within departments such as Marketing and Commercial Communications that may suit those with creative media skills.

Cadbury Schweppes has a whole mini-site dedicated to their UK graduate recruitment, which includes blogs from their current graduate intake, so you can see what life is really like as an employee. They also have 'top tips' for their selection process and a 'do we match?' link so you can assess how your own personal attributes may compare to their ideals.

Investigate the kind of information local creative and media companies give on their recruitment criteria on their websites. Do any of them feature real-life examples of people who work for them already?

However, it is often the case within the creative and media sectors that people are not employed by a company or organisation, but are self-employed freelance workers. This means that they work on a short-term or project basis for whoever needs their skills or abilities at any one time. Freelance workers have a lot of freedom to choose their projects and often face new challenges within their work, but they do not have the financial security of those with a salaried position and permanent contract.

Qualifications and requirements

It's crucial to know what qualifications you will need to get the jobs you are interested in. When investigating the kinds of qualifications that are required for roles in the creative and media industries, there are several different routes to information that you could follow:

* You could talk to people already working in the industry and find out what qualifications they obtained in order to gain work.
* You could look at job advertisements in newspapers, magazines, journals and on the internet. See what they require people to have in order to apply for posts and roles.
* You could look at university and further education college websites and prospectuses for information about their previous students, the qualifications they gained and the careers they have gone into.

It's always worth remembering that jobs do not always require qualifications such as diplomas and degrees. Some roles, such as those in journalism, may require skills like the ability to use shorthand or touch-type. Others, such as a location manager for a media company may require a driving licence. Those who work in musical professions may be expected to have recognised music performance and theory – **ABRSM** – qualifications. Make sure you investigate these specialist requirements of your chosen roles.

Case Study: professional bodies, societies and groups

Professional bodies and groups such as ABRSM or the Royal Television Society are great places to find out about the qualifications you can acquire, but they also offer huge amounts of information on what's going on in those creative or media fields, offer of scholarships and conferences and provide the opportunity to join discussion forums.

Research the different bodies, societies and groups that exist in the following creative and media fields:

Journalism   Photography   Art   Theatre

Visit their websites. What useful information can you find?

Often experience of working in a particular situation or scenario is also required. This is why it is so important to take every opportunity to gain work experience and spend time in a work-based environment. It's a crucial part of gaining and demonstrating the personal attributes that employers will look for when they are recruiting staff.

Developing a career

One of the best ways to discuss your future career is to talk to a careers advisory service such as your local **Connexions** office (www. connexions-direct.com). The advisors there are trained to give advice on the different ways into particular careers. The jobs4u search that is also available on the Connexions direct website can also guide you to information about the different kinds of career paths available in the creative and media industries.

You can also use library and online resources to discover this information. Always be aware that you need to record the information you find for your portfolio, so it is essential to take careful notes and store them safely, along with any information you have printed out.

It may be useful to gather your research into a table to help you focus on how you might aim towards gaining the qualifications you need to do your chosen jobs, for example:

Qualification needed	How I would get this qualification?	When might this happen?
HND / BA (Hons) Media	At college or university after I complete some Level 3 Diploma courses	When I complete my Level 2, then Level 3 Diploma courses
Driving licence	Take driving lessons and pass my driving theory and practical tests	When I am 17 or 18

For your project

You will need to record your findings on creative and media employment roles and responsibilities. Your work should show you have looked at individuals, organisations and companies, and used a range of different research methods.

You will need to show you have investigated jobs from different areas of the creative and media sectors, but when investigating how to gain employment you should focus on particular sectors.

You should show that you have investigated the qualifications needed to gain employment in roles within the creative and media sectors. You may choose to focus on several roles to do this, but you should be able to show evidence of how you have discovered these facts.

Your teacher may suggest a suitable format to present your findings – this could be an illustrated written report, or you could use interactive presentation methods in order to share your findings with others.

Just checking

* Do you feel confident in approaching creative and media professionals?
* Have you decided which roles you want to investigate?
* Do you have a plan for how you will find out about the opportunities available in your area?

Jobs in the performing arts

The performing arts industry is a complex business that employs people with a wide range of different skills. Within your local area there will be some people, who are freelance or self-employed and others who work in larger organisations and companies.

OVER TO YOU!

Discuss – How many people does it take to put on a show?

Imagine you are sitting in a theatre or concert hall watching a production or gig. How many people do you think are involved in the production of the show you are watching? What jobs might they carry out?

CAD – Computer Aided Design – electronic design software.

Get-in – The process of delivering and taking scenery and props into the theatre.

Fit-up – Setting up the whole theatre for a show.

Case Study: Kym

I am a freelance musician working in the Newcastle area. I play saxophone and clarinet and since finishing music college four years ago, I have worked in a number of different venues in the north-east.

The best thing is the variety. It's about as far away from a nine-to-five job as you can get! One week I might be playing in the horn section of a jazz band and the next I could be part of the orchestra for a musical. I've been pretty lucky so far in that I've managed to get plenty of bookings, but like a lot of musicians I also teach part-time in local schools.

The worst thing, I guess, is the hours. I have to work evenings, including most Fridays and Saturdays. When my friends are out partying I'm normally playing at a gig or in the orchestra pit of a theatre. Christmas is also a busy time. Last year I got a five-week contract playing in the pit for the pantomime at one of the big theatres. The money was good but I had to work right through the holidays as we only got Christmas day and New Year's day off.

What do you think the advantages are of working freelance?

What might the disadvantages be?

Many visiting music teachers who work in schools are also freelance musicians. Find out if any visit your school. If any do, talk to them about what their jobs entail.

The Royal Shakespeare Company

The Royal Shakespeare Company employs over 700 people, either directly involved in their stage productions or in supporting work. With so many employees, the RSC needs a strong organisational structure and the ability to work as a team. Each department takes its responsibilities very seriously.

The Artistic Director chooses the productions, then the casting team works closely with the production Director to ensure that the right actors get the right parts. The Director and Designer plan the production, including the style and the period in which the production is set. Once decisions have been made, the Production Manager and the various workshop and wardrobe departments take control of the detail. The set is the responsibility of the Technical Director and the Stage Department, and every item of scenery has detailed construction drawings produced on **CAD**. The plans are then handed to the Scenic Paint Shop and Props team. The specialists in the Lighting and Sound Departments work closely with the Director and Designer to build up an atmosphere with the lighting and sound for a production. In collaboration with the Costume Department, the Costume Supervisor and Designer decide on the best way to create the costumes. Hairdressing, wigs and make-up complete the final look.

The RSC spends approximately six weeks rehearsing a production with the Director, Voice Coach, Fight Directors, Musical Directors and Stage Management team. While all this is going on, a dedicated array of non-production departments, including Marketing, Education, Press and Public Affairs and Development are busy promoting and supporting the work of the RSC.

For more informatio visit www.rsc.org.uk

Case Study: Marcus

I always wanted to work in the theatre, ever since I went to see *The Wizard of Oz* as a child. Whereas a lot of people you meet are keen to be in the spotlight onstage, I was always more interested in what happens backstage and how a show is put together. When I was young I got involved in amateur dramatics, helping out with the sets and lighting, and from there I went to college to do a course in stage management.

I now work for a producing theatre in the midlands as Assistant Stage Manager (ASM). It's a hectic life but I love it. My job is helping the Stage Manager and Deputy Stage Manager. During the rehearsals of a show this entails setting up the rehearsal space for the performers, buying and/or making props, drawing up scene, change plans, assisting with the **get-in** and **fit-up** and helping in the technical and dress rehearsals. When we have a show in production I run scene changes with the stage crew and keep the backstage areas organised. Many of the stage crew work as casuals. This means they are taken on to work on large productions only.

Within a few years I hope to become a deputy stage manager. Some day I may even get to be in charge myself. I'd also like to do some work for a touring company as it would be nice to travel and work in lots of different venues.

What might be the rewards of working backstage in a theatre?

What pressures do you think the role of ASM has?

Find out if there are any venues in your local area that employ casual workers when undertaking large productions.

Activity

Divide into groups/pairs. Choose a job role from the list below. Undertake some research into the job including duties and qualifications required:

Lighting Technician, Set Designer, Dance Captain, Musical Director, Deputy Stage Manager, Wardrobe Assistant, Sound Designer, Flyman, Front of House Manager, Box Office Manager, Choreographer.

Draft a job specification for the chosen role.

Activity

You will need to find out about employment possibilities in the performance arts in your local area. Here are some starting points:

* Arts Councils websites have information about performers, companies and venues in your local area who receive funding.

* Many websites of local venues/companies include details about the people who work for them and their duties.

* Talk to people who work in the performance arts, e.g. by arranging a backstage visit to a local theatre or concert hall or inviting a professional performer into school/college. Find out about their training and how they got started in their chosen professions.

Many people are involved in the fit-up of a show.

Just checking

* Have you investigated a range of roles within different performance arts?
* Have you found out what some of these jobs entail and the qualification/training requirements?
* Do you know how people get started in your chosen roles?

Jobs in the media

The media industry employs many people in a range of different jobs, from the **runner** on a television or film production to the editor of a local or national newspaper. Media roles often cross over into the performance and visual arts arenas, which can be part of their popular appeal.

Roles in the media industries

There are many roles in the media industries that you might want to consider as a potential career, but in order to progress in them, you must think carefully about the kind of courses you undertake and the experience you try to gain.

Many people think that getting a job in the media industries is simple. As cameras and video camera become increasingly easy to use, it's natural to think that working as a photographer or filmmaker is easy too. However, the reality of working in the media industries is that you need a mixture of creativity, commitment to hard work and a willingness to work long hours for small reward. Some jobs in the media industries pay well and are glamorous, but it usually takes a while to get to that point, so it would be wise to aspire to this later in your career. Working in the media industry is like any other job: whatever you put in, you get out and you will get satisfaction from your work when you do it well, regardless of whether you are lucky enough to see the results of your work on the big screen or in print.

OVER TO YOU!

Watch the final credits of a feature film of your choice. Make a note of all the job roles that appear in the credits. If there are any titles you don't recognise, find out what they mean, then write a brief summary of each role.

Runner – The most junior role in the production department of a broadcast, film or video company.

Activity

What tasks and responsibilities do you think you would have in the following roles? Work with a partner to list them all, then work individually to categorise them into good and bad points. Did you differ on anything? Would any of the roles suit either of you?

* Nature photographer
* TV breakfast show reporter
* Theatre promoter
* Media animator

Personal, learning and thinking skills

Being able to demonstrate knowledge of the qualifications needed for the media jobs available in your area means you have worked successfully as an Independent Enquirer.

Case Study: Stuart

Stuart was a student on a National Diploma in Media course at a college in the East Midlands. On this course he learnt the skills of photography, video production and sound recording. He enjoyed his photography work and decided that he would like to take this further with a Higher National Diploma in Photography.

Whilst studying for his HND, Stuart met a local photographer who was producing portraits of celebrities for magazines such as the *Radio Times*. Stuart was able to complete some work experience as his assistant and gained valuable experience of the world of professional photography whilst studying. After completing his HND, Stuart started his career as a professional photographer.

Stuart has his own studio in the East Midlands and takes on a wide range of work for a variety of clients. He has further developed his skills in portrait photography, as well as magazine work, packaging shots, architectural photography and fashion photographs.

Because Stuart used his time on the NDM and HND courses constructively, he was able to try out a range of media and photography work, and to find out what he really wanted to do.

What are the benefits of working for a variety of clients?

What challenges might Stuart face when offering services in different areas?

The balancing act

No job is fun all the time. Meetings, paperwork, telephone calls… some people find these tasks tedious. Some people shy away from promotional work, others hate having to work outside in bad weather. Every job in the creative and media arts will have some bad points – and these will also vary from person to person. The important thing is to know the potential difficulties a role might present so that you can evaluate whether it's enough to put you off the job entirely, or whether you can be flexible and take it in your stride.

How to get a job

The two things that are most important for getting the job you want are studying hard and hands-on experience in that area.

Activity

Employers want to see that you have the right qualifications and some work experience in your chosen field, but they will also be looking at your practical skills and personal attributes.

* What skills and attributes do you think are important in all media professions?
* What particular skills or attributes do you think would be helpful in your chosen media field?

A job in radio

The Managing Director of a local commercial radio station was asked how he chose people to work at his station. He said that he received lots of letters from would-be radio presenters and DJs asking for jobs. He would read through the letters and reject anyone who had no experience of media or working in radio. He particularly wanted people with an education, but who also knew what a microphone was and how to use a mixing desk. These people would have been working part-time, maybe voluntarily, at a radio studio, or in hospital radio or perhaps as part of a group operating a community radio station.

Work experience is a great way to find out if you would be suited to a media role.

You could arrange to go in and interview a few staff to discover how they found work in the industry. You could prepare a questionnaire to take with you so that if time is short, you could always leave a few behind for people to complete and return to you.

Try and arrange to undertake work experience at a local media company. You could see first-hand how the company operates and how you might fit in, as well as picking up some useful practical skills along the way.

Role requirements

When you are beginning to research the media industry that you would like to work in there are a number of sources of information you can turn to. Skillset.org.uk is a specialist online media career service, offering advice and guidance for broadcast, film, video, interactive media and photo imaging. There are media trade publications that you can read, for example the Monday Media section in the *Guardian* and *Broadcast*.

Just checking

* Have you investigated how realistic it might be for you to get your dream media job?
* Have you taken a balanced view of the media roles you have investigated?
* Do you feel confident about how you could try to develop your skills to achieve a media role?

Jobs in the visual arts

Knowing how visual artists and designers in your local area work and how they came to work in their field will help you hone your plans for developing a career.

OVER TO YOU!

Think about which area of the visual arts you might like to work in. Then see if you can find out what kind of work is available in that field. Do those jobs pay as much money as you would expect? Which areas of the world are those jobs mostly available in?

Visual arts variety

The visual arts is a large field to choose a career from. People often think of the more practical, creative jobs like painter or sculptor when they think of visual arts, but there are many more varied roles available, for example:

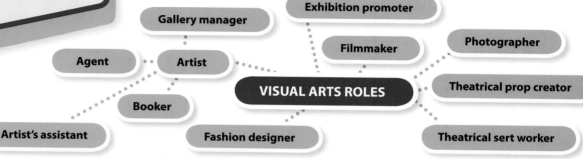

Making contact with practitioners

It is important that you meet with and talk to people who work in the visual arts industries. They will be able to give you the best information about what it is like to work in their field and what the industry demands of people working in jobs like theirs.

When you meet with practitioners, make sure that you take careful note of what they say. You could record your interviews and transcribe them later so you can pay full attention to what is said (but check with the person first!). You might want to ask them particularly about the creative nature of their job.

Working in the visual arts

Kate and Simon were both on the same art course at college, but have taken very different paths since leaving university.

Activity

During your work in this topic you will need to make contact with people who work in the creative and media industries. Before meeting them, take some time to draw up a list of things that you think would be positive aspects of the job they do, and what may be negative aspects.

Think carefully about what the job might entail and how you might feel if you had to complete these tasks.

Keep your notes safe, but when talking to the practitioner ask them what they see as the positive and negative points of their work. When you are reflecting on your meeting with them, get out the list you made and compare it to what they said. What things are similar on the two lists? Did anything they said surprise you?

Case Study: Kate

Kate is a graphic designer for a local newspaper. Her role includes creating graphics for advertisements, using digital image manipulation packages to process images, creating special page layouts for features in the paper, and designing the company's personalised stationery.

Kate works within a busy office and since she has been in the role she has already been promoted from Design Junior to Designer, and seen an increase in her pay. Kate says: 'The work I do needs me to be creative and work well with other people. Sometimes it is hard work and I occasionally need to do ten-hour days. I was very pleased to be promoted recently and eventually I see myself moving on to a bigger newspaper, possibly a big national publication, and working my way to Lead Designer.'

Case Study: Simon

Simon is a freelance graphic designer who works within the community on projects which encourage local people to take an active part in art and design activities. He organises activities with local groups such as youth clubs and in particular settings, like old people's homes.

Simon sets a particular task or purpose for his activities and works with the participants to create artworks that are then displayed in the local community. He uses his own creative knowledge and abilities to encourage others to demonstrate theirs. He says: 'I feel that the role I play in the development of other people's artistic skills is very important. This job is one of the most rewarding experiences I have ever had.'

Compare the two case studies: Kate and Simon. Write out a list of the skills that each of their jobs would require. What are the sacrifices each has made to do their chosen job?

Some areas of visual art work can lead to work in a wide variety of settings.

Qualifications and gaining experience

Certain roles within the visual arts industries often require certain qualifications – either minimum academic standards and/or experience of working in particular environments.

Case Study: Sharon

Sharon owns her own interior design consultancy business. She meets with and advises clients on suitable décor and schemes within projects, such as major renovations of older buildings and new builds of shopping centres. Her company also takes on individual clients who employ Sharon and her employees to design and furnish the interiors of their homes.

Sharon left school and began by taking a vocational course in art and design, specialising in 3D design. She found architecture and interior design of particular interest and whilst on her course secured some unpaid work experience in a local interior decoration business. Sharon built up contacts during her time there and gained a great deal of very valuable experience about how the business worked and effective ways to deal with clients. On completing her Level 3 course, Sharon moved on to study for a degree in interior architecture and design, graduating three years later. This not only gave Sharon the qualification required for many positions within large interior design firms, but also meant that she could become an Associate Member of the British Interior Design Association, which is the professional body for interior designers and would be a name that employers in that field would recognise.

Sharon got her first job in the industry as a Design Assistant in a large interior design firm in Manchester. Whilst working in this role, Sharon built up further contacts and gained some useful advice from others in that area of work. After three years, and a promotion to Design Associate, Sharon began to consider starting up her own small company. She then did this and opened her first office in her home town. She soon learned she would need to learn to drive in order to meet with her clients.

Over the past five years, Sharon's business has continued to grow, and now she employs other people to work for her. She says: 'When I am employing someone I now look for the things I was once asked for. I need people who are enthusiastic and dedicated, who have taken the right qualifications and shown how much they want to work in this very competitive field'.

Pick out the key moments, actions or decisions in Sharon's career that have helped her get where she is.

What can you learn from her career path?

Just checking

* Have you met with visual artists in your local area?
* Have you considered the different visual arts paths the same training can offer you?
* Have you investigated what part formal qualifications play in visual arts roles?

1.3 Developing a critical response

Being able to express your opinions and thoughts about a creative or media activity that you have experienced is an important skill. This topic will help you to develop the skills and attributes you need to do this well.

Investigating other responses

Before you begin to form your own response, it is a good idea to see how other people have presented their opinions and thoughts about creative and media activities that they have experienced. By reading, listening to and watching other people expressing their responses, you will learn good and bad ways to go about this task.

Your opinion counts!

What you think and feel about a creative and media activity that you have experienced is important, not only because your views will matter to those around you, but also because by evaluating what others have done and creating a focused response to it, you will learn about good and bad practices to incorporate or avoid when you are working on projects yourself.

Preparing to respond

When you know you're going to review a media activity you're watching, looking at or listening to, you need to make some preparations before you start. Have you thought about how you will record your thoughts? How does the location restrict the activity? For example, if it is a recorded form of activity such as a DVD of a film or television show, or a CD of music, then you should prepare by:

* ensuring that you can watch/listen to the DVD/CD undisturbed
* allowing time to watch/listen to the DVD/CD more than once, if necessary
* having materials to record your responses during and after the activity – this could be a notebook and pencil, a voice recorder or even a video camera.

If you choose to respond to a piece of theatre, dance, live music or a film at the cinema, then you will only have a certain amount of time in which to experience that activity and you need to prepare in a slightly different way:

* Arrive at the activity venue in plenty of time to ensure you get a good view of the action and can hear what is happening clearly.
* Make sure you have materials with you to record your initial thoughts and reactions. This is likely to be a notebook, as it will not disturb those around you, whereas talking into a voice recorder would.

Film 2008 with Jonathan Ross: Reviews of creative and media activities are often featured on TV programmes. They help an audience evaluate whether they might like to experience that activity.

If you choose to respond to an art exhibition or display then you will need to ensure that you:

* arrive with plenty of time to view the works you want to before the gallery closes
* take materials to note your reaction and responses with – most galleries will discourage you from making much noise, so a voice recorder may not be appropriate and it is unlikely that you will be able to film within galleries.

Recording your response

Although the methods you use to record your response will depend on the situation you are working in, the process should be fairly similar. For example, it's always important to record your immediate or initial response to something – this ensures that you capture a true picture of your personal feeling about the experience. If you wait for a week before recording your thoughts on an activity, they will not be very accurate or clearly reflect your thoughts and feelings, as you will forget certain aspects of the experience over time. You will also find that it is easy to be influenced by the thoughts of others if you discuss your opinions with other people before recording your own reaction.

Remember, your opinions are just that. Whether you do or don't like something, an opinion is never wrong. In order to gain respect for the points that you make, you must always be able to justify or back-up the opinions you express.

Structuring your response

When you looked at how others presented their responses to creative and media activities, did you notice a particular style to the reviews? Audiences have come to expect a certain style and structure in the presentation of critical responses. A written review that starts 'Well, I thought this play was dead rubbish' looks unprofessional, and does not introduce a reader to your theme.

When you read reviews written by professionals or watch a reviewer on television, you will see that they follow a very particular structure as they deliver their response. They often introduce their audience to the activity that they are discussing, before giving an overview of what happens within the activity and then moving on to explain their opinions, backing up the points they make with examples. You should aim to do the same in your work. The structure for your response might look something like the example on the next page.

Taking careful notes of your opinions and the reasons for them will ensure that you remember all you want to say when formulating your response later.

Webcast – A media file distributed over the internet.

Video-streaming – Film sent over the internet in a continuous stream and played as it arrives, rather than a downloaded file.

Activity

Find one review from a printed medium like a newspaper or a magazine, one televised review from a TV programme or via a **webcast** or **video-streaming** site and one radio review, either on broadcast or via a repeat listening service on the internet.

For each of them note down the following:

* which creative and media activity the reviewer or critic is discussing
* what their overall opinion about the activity is
* how they justify their opinion – i.e. if they say it was bad, what do they give as an example of what made it bad?

Observe carefully the way that they structure the information and opinions they are giving to their audience. What do you notice about the kind of words they use in their responses? Note down words which might be useful for when you evaluate an activity.

Harry Potter and the Order of the Phoenix

DVD release November 2007

So Daniel Radcliffe is back on the small screen after record box-office takings in his latest jaunt as Harry Potter. He's joined by the usual suspects: Ron (Rupert Grint), Hermione (Emma Watson), Dumbledore (Michael Gambon) and arch nemesis Lord Voldemort (Ralph Fiennes).

As a keen fan of the books, I wondered how Director David Yates would approach this one. Order of the Phoenix is perhaps the most pivotal book of the septuplet series with Harry beginning to confront his darkest fears about his connection with Voldemort, and the twists of fate that led to Harry as The Boy Who Lived. Throw in the usual twisted new teacher at Hogwarts, public backlash against Harry and reinforcement of the mantra that friends are forever not just for Christmas, and you have a film as good as the previous four, and probably better.

The key to Phoenix success is in the characterisation. Luna Lovegood is kookily endearing, when it would have been so easy to go overboard on the nuttiness. There are moments of genius in the humour Alan Rickman manages to bring to the character of Severus Snape (look out for his interview by Dolores Umbridge).

As always the set design is spot on – the Department of Mysteries is superb: eerie and dungeonesque, with a respectful nod to The Matrix. Nothing on screen strikes you as out of place, which is a quiet testament to excellent prop design. My only criticism was with the special effects: Fred and George's dramatic firework-filled exit had so much promise but was more damp squib than catherine wheel.

Yes, there are a few clichés in the Harry Potter saga, but it does not necessarily follow that they detract from the film (except the closing scene – pass me a bucket, please). Overall, David Yates has created a pretty dark and questioning film, but he manages to haul it into light entertainment through clever moments of humour and the wonderfully awkward romance of Harry and Cho Chang. I thoroughly enjoyed this adaptation and, as long as you have long-shelved the hopes that a HP book will make it uncut into film form, I think you will too.

THE REBELLION BEGINS

Introduction

Tell the audience what you are reviewing, who the main people are that were involved in it and where and when you witnessed it.

Referring to people the audience might already know at this stage is useful. Plays, films and TV programmes may feature famous actors; art exhibitions often feature the work of well-known artists and those giving music or dance performances may be well known.

Overview or Synopsis

Tell your audience what you have witnessed. You may have already told them what the activity was called, but you now need to set the scene for what happens in the activity you are reviewing.

Summarise the story or action in a few sentences. This might be a summary of the story from a film or play, an overview of the set-list from a gig or the scenario behind a computer game.

Remember not to give away the whole plot and spoil the end of the story for narrative-based activities like plays, films and TV programmes.

Opinion

Now move on to expressing your own opinion about what you have experienced. Deal with your thoughts or comments (good or bad) one at a time. For each point you make, give an example of why you feel this way, for example a reviewer who says 'I thought that the sound on stage during the play hadn't been thought through very well' may go on to explain that 'At times when special effects were being put in place, it became very difficult to hear the actors speak.'

You need to justify the points you make, as this will add weight to your comments and show the audience for your review that you have thought about your opinions and can explain them.

Relevant points to include

When expressing your opinions, consider what is relevant to your written response. Your review should give useful feedback to others who may be thinking of experiencing that activity themselves.

Make sure that the opinions you express relate directly to things that happened within the creative and media activity you witnessed. Things that affect you personally are not relevant to your review.

Presenting your response

How you decide to present your response to an audience depends on your strengths and the formats available to you. You may choose to write up your review as it would appear in a newspaper or magazine or on the internet. Alternatively, you could make a video of yourself presenting your response verbally using a script or **cue-cards**. You might choose to record a verbal response using sound recording techniques.

Whichever methods you choose, ensure that you impose a structure and that the information you wish to cover is delivered to the audience.

For your project

You will need to record all of the work you do towards the development and creation of your personal response in your project portfolio.

* You will need to collect together the examples of reviews you gathered and your notes or observations about the ways the reviewers expressed their opinions.

* You should save the evidence of the creative and media activity that you have chosen to look at, e.g. the program for a play or a cutting from a listing for a TV programme.

* Keep all of the notes you make about your own response to the activity and any drafting of your personal response, whatever form it is in.

* Remember to include your finished personal response, or review. It should be presented in the form you have chosen and agreed with your teacher.

Cue-cards – Brief notes to help prompt you when making an oral presentation.

Activity

Read the extracts from the reviews below and write a short description of what is wrong with them:

* The play wasn't exactly exciting, but there were moments which were OK. I thought the music wasn't as good as it could have been. I think it was from the 1960s, but possibly the 1970s. I don't know if I would really want to recommend it, or not.

* It was such a wicked film! The first thing was the bank robbery, the camera shots were amazing. Then Sienna Miller, the woman who helped the robbers, well, she was on the run from some mobsters, so of course you knew there was major blood-spill coming her way, and the director pulled it out until you were on tenterhooks, but in the end they managed to get out of the hotel and get away – the girlfriend got her happy ending!

* I thought the exhibition was a hedonistic fusion of pre-Raphaelite theatre and post-modern concept. The artists are unknown yet their work seemed familiar. I think this speaks for itself and is a reflection of the paradoxes we find in life everywhere, from politics to love.

Just checking

* Do you understand the techniques used in forming and expressing opinions?

* Have you chosen an activity from an area of the creative and media arts that interests you?

* Have you considered how to present your critical response in an appropriate way?

Responding to a performance

Whenever we watch a performance, whether it's the latest episode of our favourite soap or a band playing at a local community centre, we will form a critical response to what we see or hear. In the simplest terms this involves the question 'Did we enjoy the performance or not?'

The intention of the creators

Performance arts productions can entertain, educate, inform or even shock. Those creating pieces of drama, dance or music will often have specific intentions in terms of the form and content and how the audience may respond to it. Make sure you discuss these intentions and evaluate whether or not they were carried through to the performance.

Case Study: The Woman in Black

Functional skills

Using English…

You can use your reading skills to help you choose an event or activity to respond to critically, or to research other people's opinions and ideas on it after the event, or even any critical arguments that have taken place!

Students on a Creative and Media course at St Anne's Community School are going to see a touring production of *The Woman in Black* at their local theatre.

Before going to see the production they undertake some research into the piece. They discover the play is based on a novel by Susan Hill. Hill was keen to write a traditional Victorian ghost story. Before beginning work on the book she researched classic ghost stories to discover the essential components of the form.

In preparation for seeing the production, the students read a range of traditional ghost stories and go on to list and discuss their essential elements.

After seeing the production they discuss which of these elements were present in *The Woman in Black* and how they were used.

If you were going to write a critical response to a ghost story, what elements would you expect to feature in the story? What kinds of characters would be involved? What visual and sound effects might be used?

What kind of feelings and emotions would you hope a ghost story would evoke in you as the audience?

Case Study: Response The Woman in Black

Extract from a critical response to *The Woman in Black*.

'When I found out that there were only two actors in the play I wondered how that would work, as I knew the story of *The Woman in Black* has several characters. The way it is done is really effective. The main character wants to tell his family the story of something that happened to him years ago and is getting advice from an actor who is helping him to act it out. This means the story actually takes place in the very theatre in which you are sitting. I think this was one of the things that made it so real and helped pull you in.

What struck me most about the show was how scary it was. I never imagined that a play could be so frightening. It was much creepier than any horror film I have ever watched. I think this was because of the atmosphere. At times it was really dark and sometimes there were noises that seemed to come from behind which made me feel really on edge. There were also a few real shocks when the whole audience jumped out of their seats.

The Woman in Black has all the things you would expect from a traditional ghost story. There is an old deserted house, a locked room, a haunted graveyard and a terrible secret that the locals refuse to talk about. Because these things are familiar you get involved in the story immediately. When the young solicitor decides to stay alone in the house overnight you just know something awful will happen. I felt myself wanting to shout 'no don't, get away while you still can!'.

How does this critical response succeed?

What elements would you change or improve. Explain your reasoning?

Would you like to see the show based on this critical response?

Responding to media

When you experience a media product, you form thoughts and opinions about whether you have enjoyed the experience or not. Learning how to express these thoughts effectively is a key part of learning to analyse products and communicate with an audience.

Choosing what to review

When working on this unit, it is probably best to avoid choosing something that you have had a lot of experience of or you know to be your favourite or least favourite thing. It is sometimes harder to formulate a clear argument for why you like something if you already have feelings about it.

Justifying your personal response

When compiling your response it is important that you justify the observations you make. You will need to present your response with a balance of opinion and evidence.

Presenting your response

Traditionally, reviews are delivered in a written medium and published in newspapers and event guides and on the internet. However, you are free to choose any medium you wish for your response. You could consider using dramatic techniques yourself in an audio or filmed recording as long as they help you convey your opinions appropriately. Don't get too carried away with comic impressions of *Macbeth* witches!

OVER TO YOU!

Make a list of media products that you like. You could include your favourite advert, favourite radio programme or station and the websites you visit most often.

Next to each product, list what it is that you like so much. Try to give good clear examples to illustrate your opinions; this is a key part of writing effective reviews.

Case Study: Get unhooked campaign

The recent 'Get unhooked' national anti-smoking campaign consists of four posters and four television adverts. People had described the campaign as 'thought-provoking' and 'grotesquely realistic', so I was keen to see it for myself.

The campaign poster I saw portrays a young guy whose top lip has been pierced with a huge silver fish hook. 'Addiction' has captured him and is tugging him like a fish caught on a line. The caption says 'The average smoker needs over 5000 cigarettes a year. Get unhooked. 'It then gives a helpline number and website details.

The hard-hitting campaign has clearly been designed to shock the public, and highlight 'the controlling nature of tobacco. 'In my opinion, this is a fantastic visual representation of addiction. The caption really does make you think about how much you smoke, even if like me, you think you're just a light smoker. I think the poster is just the right balance of graphics and text, and the campaign has struck the perfect combination of shock tactics and helpful information. The poster never loses its impact, no matter how many times you see it. All in all, a very effective national campaign.

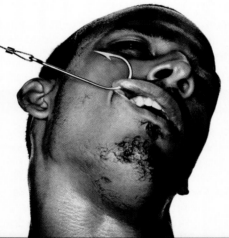

The average smoker needs over five thousand cigarettes a year.

Get unhooked. Call 0800 169 0 169 or visit getunhooked.co.uk

NHS

SMOKEFREE

The Get unhooked campaign.

Activity

Read Craig's review in this case study and answer the following questions:

* Do you think Craig did a good job of reviewing this campaign poster?

* What do you think was good or bad about it?

* Did Craig give any examples to back up his opinions?

* How could Craig have improved this review?

Just checking

* Make sure that your review is suitable for the audience, so it is fit for purpose.

* Ask other people to read your reviews and give you feedback on their thoughts. This will help you improve your work.

* Record how you do this, and the responses people give, as it will help the process of reviewing and monitoring your work in this unit.

Responding to a visual art form

Visual art and design is a very **subjective** thing, and often people's opinions of particular works vary wildly. Thinking carefully about your own opinions on artistic activities will help you develop an understanding of how you want your own work to be.

Investigating other responses to art

Just like reviews of films, TV programmes, computer games or books, the published opinions of art critics are used by those interested in art as they choose what they might wish to experience for themselves, and assess other people's responses to activities and artefacts.

Sometimes contemporary works of art are seen as **controversial**, which means that many people outside the art world, as well as those within it, might debate the artists or pieces.

OVER TO YOU!

Look through a local or national guide to what's happening in the media and creative world. Pick four or five events at random. What's your initial reaction to them? Interest? Boredom? Intrigue? Explain your reaction and the reasons for your opinion.

Personal, learning and thinking skills

Exploring issues, events or problems from different perspectives in critical reviews allows you to develop your critical Independent Enquiry skills.

Activity

In a library or from a newsagent, get hold of a copy of a recent newspaper that reviews art works and activities. Choose a particular piece and read it carefully. Decide whether you think that the reviewer liked or disliked the piece they are discussing.

Now do some further research, either using the internet or other newspapers, magazines and journals, and see if you can find an opinion that differs from that which you have discovered.

Make a careful record of how the critics in both cases argue their point. Do they use similar techniques? Do they use examples to justify what they have said?

Case Study: Damien Hirst

Damien Hirst is one of the most controversial artists of recent times. Many people have expressed opinions about his art work, both within the art world and in the wider media. He is known for creating pieces that often involve controversial subjects such as death, sex and religion. Many have criticised him for creating work where he has developed the ideas for but not actually physically created himself, such as the 2005 collection he produced called 'The Elusive Truth'. Hirst came up with the idea for the collection of work and directed others on how it should look, but a team of assistants actually painted the works that were put on display. People's opinions on the collection varied, but when it was shown in New York, the critics were particularly negative about the work.

Damien Hirst has defended his role in the creation of his art work: 'Art goes on in your head. If you said something interesting, that might be a title for a work of art and I'd write it down. Art comes from everywhere. It's your response to your surroundings.'

What makes an artist? Their ideas or the execution of their work?

Research some of the reviews of 'The Elusive Truth' and the images from the 2005 collection. Do you agree or disagree with the reviews?

Conflicting critical responses

Sometimes, the same work can generate very different responses in their critical reviews.

Case Study: Suriah

When conducting some research into critical reviews of an exhibition of work at her local gallery, Suriah finds two reviews of interest. The first was from an art journal dedicated to work in her local area:

'When asked to review local art group DIODE's current exhibition "Serendipity" I arrived at the North Park Gallery in full anticipation that I would see work such as the inspired, and often moving, pieces I had seen them exhibit before. On arrival, it was clear that a more minimalist approach to the display of work had been taken for this particular show. The gallery space was sparsely dotted with **installation work** which, to me, did not appear to be on any particular theme. Pieces such as 'Convergence Alpha' by Mark Hillier for example, consisted of a photographic enlargement of a map of the North Yorkshire town of Whitby, accompanied by an audio loop playing the sounds of heavy machinery. Whilst the artist's statement described the 'loneliness of living in a seaside town out of season' the piece itself failed to move me and appeared to be having a similar effect on the other visitors to the gallery who moved swiftly past the piece. The other pieces in the show left a similarly underwhelming impression on me and generally echoed the seeming lack of depth that I saw in the Hillier piece. Overall, a disappointing show from this most promising group.'

The second review Suriah found was from a national newspaper that had a feature about arts in the region in a recent issue:

'The DIODE exhibition 'Serendipity' is a good example of the high quality of experimental installation work available in local galleries today. Hosting a range of installation pieces which invite visitors to experience the sights, sounds and even smells intended by the artists is both inspiring and brave. Of particular note was the work of local video artist, Sharon Fortune, whose imaginative use of time-lapse photography created a piece which captivated my attention for the majority of my time in the gallery. A highly imaginative exhibition that demonstrates the wide range of talent active in this region.'

Did the first critic from the local art journal like the exhibition or not?

What evidence did they give to back up their opinions?

Did the second critic from the national newspaper like the exhibition or not?

What evidence did they give to justify their statements?

Are there any ways that these critics could have improved their reviews?

Were there any words in the reviews that you didn't know or understand? Note them down and then use a dictionary to find out what they mean. They may be useful in your own work. You should do the same when reading other reviews that you find.

Another controversial piece of work by Damien Hirst is this piece, which is entitled 'The Physical Impossibility of Death in the Mind of Someone Living'. It was nicknamed 'The Pickled Shark' by critics who had a negative opinion of the work.

Subjective – Something which is based on feelings, opinions and ideas rather than facts.

Controversial – Something that raises debate or discussion. Usually controversial subjects involve people's beliefs or ethics.

Installation work – Installation art uses sculptural materials and other media to modify the way you experience a particular space.

Just checking

* Have you practised responding critically to visual art pieces or shows?
* Have you investigated other people's critical responses to the same piece?

1.4 Creating a creative and media guide

For this part of the unit you will be creating a guide for others to use, which will inform them of the creative and media activities and events available to them in your local area. Without an audience, many creative and media activities have a limited purpose. Ensuring you can communicate with potential audience members is crucial.

Target audience

Knowing who your product is aimed at is key to understanding how you can make a successful guide. You could choose to aim your guide at any audience you wish – but remember there are some groups who are already quite aware of the creative and media activities in your local area. Selecting a group who need further information will help you come up with more original and effective ideas.

Finding out how your target audience get information already can help you in many ways:

* Writing style – read the way things are written to appeal to this audience and try to copy it in the information you present to them in the guide.

* Imagery – look carefully at the way photographs have been taken or video has been shot and see if this gives you any clue as to how to shoot your own images. Look at how graphics and illustrations have been used to capture audience attention.

* Tone of delivery – what kind of tone or feeling is created by the guide. Do things look bright, fun and active or are they more muted, relaxing and calming?

* Content – what kind of things are covered within the guide. Are issues or subjects dealt with? If things are reviewed, how is this done?

Many young people get information about cultural activities from magazines. What can looking at popular youth magazines tell you about effective ways to communicate with this audience?

Planning and developing ideas

Think back to your work about your target audience to help you decide *how* to communicate with them. Ask yourself what kind of products your audience seem to prefer or access most often.

Choosing a medium

With your teacher's input you could use a wide variety of formats for your guide. Media and creative arts scene guides come in a variety of formats:

* Print-based formats – this includes leaflets, posters, flyers, magazines and newspaper articles. These formats are often used as people can take the information away and refer to it at their leisure. To produce a print product you may need access to print production technologies like desktop-publishing and word-processing packages, the internet, digital cameras, photo-manipulation software and colour printers. Choosing the right kind of print product for your purposes will be important. Can a poster say everything you want to? Have you got enough information to fill a ten-page booklet?

* Electronic formats – this includes websites, interactive DVDs, emails and mobile phone-based communications. These formats have the advantage that the creator can update and publish information and make it accessible to an audience very quickly. They are also popular with audiences who can access the information when they want and often find it more up-to-date and relevant. To produce electronic products you may need access to computers, the internet, web design packages, digital cameras and photo manipulation software. Ask yourself what kind of product you should use. Would an email be able to include elements to attract your target audience? How would you make people aware of a website?

* Spoken-word and moving-image formats – this includes radio and TV programmes, podcasts and **vidcasts**. Audio and video formats can be very useful as they can contain a lot of visual or aural information in a format proven to gain attention and be easily understood by audiences. There are already a lot of established ways of broadcasting these products to an audience. To produce audio products you may need sound-recording and sound-editing equipment or software on a computer. To produce moving-image products you may need a camera, a tripod, sound-recording equipment and video-editing facilities. You need to decide whether you have the ability to broadcast these products effectively to your target audience. Have you got enough material to fill a short bulletin in audio or visual form?

When choosing your format you need to decide:

* What are the advantages and disadvantages of the formats available to you?
* Do you have the resources you would need to produce a guide in the format you have chosen?
* Do you have the skills to create a guide in this way?
* How will you present the final guide to an audience?

Personal, learning and thinking skills

Creating a guide to the creative and media scene in your area offers you lots of opportunity to show your creative thinking skills. Make sure you address your target audience in an appropriate, informative and interesting way. Use imaginative design to help make it as appealing as possible. If your circumstances should change, try to adapt your existing ideas where you can otherwise try out alternatives or new solutions.

Vidcast – A digital media video file downloadable from the internet for PCs, TVs or mobile multimedia devices like a BlackBerry or iPhone.

Making sure you have the skills and resources to create a guide using your chosen format is key to working successfully

It may be that you initially decide to use a method for which you don't have the materials or equipment. The ideas you have for this will not be wasted, but you may have to adapt to using different media and methods.

Managing your time

To achieve a higher grade in this unit you will need to show that you not only know how to manage your time well but that you can work well to these plans.

Producing a work schedule during the planning stages and setting realistic goals for when you will complete your work helps you to be more efficient and effective in your work throughout the project. Without these plans you run the risk of spending too long on one particular part of the project and not leaving yourself enough time.

If you do not manage to stick to your schedule for some reason, showing how you have adapted your plans over time is also evidence that you have managed your time well and have kept track of your progress.

You could develop a plan that looks like this:

Activity	Start Date	Completion Date	Complete on time?	Reason for delay
Researching target audience	Sept 23rd	Sept 27th	No	Lost research file
Initial ideas planning	~~Sept 27th~~ Sept 28th	~~Sept 28th~~ Sept 29th		

Producing your guide

How you go about actually producing your guide depends on the format you have chosen to use to communicate this information to an audience. Checking that you have the skills to use the equipment needed to create a guide in this format will have been an important part of your planning.

Whilst working on actually making your guide you will need to ensure that you stick to the plans you have made, bear in mind the needs and tastes of your target audience and stick to the schedules you have drawn up for managing your time.

Broadcasting or distribution

Whilst this unit doesn't require you to mass produce and distribute or broadcast the guide you have made, you should think carefully about how it would be delivered to an audience. Mind-mapping some ideas, based on the information you gathered earlier about your target audience, would help with this. Consider where they might be most easily reached and how you could position your guide near to or alongside other products in order to gain attention or increase its appeal.

Personal, learning and thinking skills

As a Self Manager you will be able to manage a schedule and any time constraints your project may have. You should also be able to show you can balance personal and work-related demands as you work towards your goals. Initiative, commitment and perseverance are the personal skills that make a great Self Manager stand out from an average one.

For your project

You will need to include the following in your project portfolio for this part of the unit:

* Your research into targeting your audience for the guide. This could include any information you find out about your target audiences tastes or preferences.
* Your planning and development work for the guide. This will vary depending on the format you choose to use to present your guide. If you are producing a print product or a website this would include screen shots of your work in progress on the computer. For a piece for television this would include storyboards and scripts.
* Evidence of how you managed your time whilst working on this project – time schedules or diaries that note down what you aimed to complete and when, accompanied by notes of whether you managed to stick to this would see you gain higher marks.
* Your completed guide in the format you have chosen to use. Make sure this is ready for the person marking your work to view or access.
* Some notes on how you would broadcast or distribute this material.

Activity

Imagine you have completed your project and have now been given an unlimited budget to distribute, exhibit or broadcast your guide.

Decide how you would like to see your guide used. If it is a print product where would it gain the most attention or reach your target audience most effectively? If it is a broadcast product, what time and station would your product be shown on – what media products would it be near to in the schedules?

Just checking

* Have you identified and investigated your target audience?
* Is the form you have selected the most appropriate for reaching your target audience?
* Have you considered how to work as a team to create your guide?

Preparation for assessment

In this unit you have been finding out about your local creative and media scene. This has involved looking at venues and investigating the types of jobs available within the creative and media industries. Your work should cover at least two of the disciplines listed in the Introduction to this book. For example, you might combine your local radio and visual arts scenes and look at jobs that are different or similar in each area.

Your portfolio

Your process portfolio will be expected to contain evidence of your involvement in your assignments. Your teacher may tell you what form your portfolio should take and how to present your work.

You will be assessed on…	This will be evidenced in your portfolio by…
…your understanding of the range and types of arts and media activity in your area. …your understanding of creative and media employment roles and requirements in your area.	Your research notes. These may be notes taken in class as well as information found on the internet and in magazine articles. You may also gather information when visiting venues in your area or speaking to local people working in the creative and media industries. Your presentation of your findings. This could be in written form or a talk, perhaps using PowerPoint slides. If you give a talk, remember to include the notes you use in your portfolio. **Tips for success:** • Prepare a list of relevant questions to use when talking to people who work in the creative and media industries. • Use local press and listings magazines to find out about events, activities and job opportunities in your area.
…your ability to develop a critical response to a creative or media artefact, activity or event.	All notes and drafts produced when planning your work. The presentation of your review/critical response. Your teacher may ask for a written article, an audio or video recording, or an illustrated talk. **Tips for success**: • Choose an artefact, activity or event that particularly interests you. • Read a range of critical reviews in newspapers and magazines to see how they are presented.
…your ability to create a guide to the creative and media scene in your area.	All notes, drafts and preparatory work you produce when planning your guide. The completed guide could be a booklet, a set of posters, a website or radio programme. **Tips for success**: • When designing your guide, consider the target audience you are producing the guide for. Will it appeal to those who will read it? Will the type of language used be appropriate?

The assessment of the unit

This unit is assessed by your teachers.

You must show that you…	Guidance	To gain higher marks:
…can undertake an investigation into the creative and media scene of your area. …can summarise your findings with reference to examples. …can understand creative and media employment roles and requirements in your area.	You should use a range of resources when carrying out your investigations (not just the internet). Visit as many venues as you can and speak to people who work in your area. You should investigate a range of job roles from across a number of different areas within the creative and media industries. You should find out about qualifications and training requirements.	Your research should be wide-ranging and well focused. You must summarise your findings making reference to examples that might be expected as well as arts and media activities and job roles that are more unusual. Your summary should be well organised and thorough. You must show that you have substantial knowledge of the qualifications needed for jobs available.
…can explore an event, artefact or activity you have experienced. …can explain what was effective, enjoyable or striking about the event, artefact or activity.	When explaining what was effective, enjoyable or striking about the event, artefact or activity, refer to examples to illustrate your opinions. Always proofread your written work carefully to check for errors such as incorrect spellings.	Your investigations should be wide-ranging and well focused. You must present your response in a clear and confident manner. You should explain in detail the qualities of the work that were effective, enjoyable or striking.
…can create a guide to the creative and media scene of your area.	Plan the creation of your guide carefully. Draw up a schedule of tasks to ensure you finish your work on time. Consider the way you organise the presentation of your guide, e.g. you could have a section on music, another on visual arts, etc.	Your guide must be attractive and comprehensive. Your work should show a disciplined approach to the planning of the guide. You should show that you have considered your target audience. You should produce your guide to given deadlines.

2 PERFORMANCE

Introduction

Performance can involve a wide variety of **genres** and forms. Circus, musical theatre, stand-up comedy, radio drama and music gigs are all forms of performance. In this unit you will study a form of performance, looking at the origins of the form and how it has developed over time. You will then help to plan and present a performance. This may mean you are involved as a performer, writer, designer or member of the technical crew.

OVER TO YOU!

Thought shower – how many performance genres and forms can you think of? Make a list beginning with the examples on the left, then group them into categories that are similar, e.g. a pantomime and a musical both involve drama, music and dance.

Activity

When deciding on a performance project to undertake, you should begin by considering the skills you have within your group/class.

Begin by carrying out an individual skills audit in which you list your existing skills, e.g. in music, dance, drama, art and design and/or technical theatre.

Include skills you already have but would like to improve, as well as new areas of skill you would like to develop.

Personal, learning and thinking skills

To gain the skills of a Reflective Learner, you must monitor your progress as you plan and produce your performance. This will enable you to refine your ideas and improve your performance, as well as understand your own strengths and weaknesses for future self-improvement.

Your learning

In this unit, you should work across at least two of the disciplines on page 4 to cover the four main topics.

Understanding the origins and development of a form of performance

Some forms of performance have been around for a very long time. The 'play' for example, has its roots in ancient Greece. Some forms, such as the rock concert, are relatively recent creations.

In this unit you will study how a particular form of performance arose and how it has developed over time. You will need to investigate the history of a particular form of performance. This will include studying how the form originated and the ways in which it has changed over time. Your research will look at the impact that developing technologies have had on the form as well as the ways in which **social conditions** have influenced its development.

Contributing to the planning of a performance

Planning is vital to the success of any performance **production** whether it is a musical, play, concert or dance piece. Think of the organisation involved in the staging of a West End musical. Without meticulous planning the process would be chaotic!

You will need to take on a role in the planning of a performance. You must ensure that you understand your allocated role and what is required of you. You must consider the resources, materials and time you have available. You will need to work cooperatively as part of a team. It will also be important to ensure that safe working practices are observed at all times.

Contributing to the production of a performance

Once the preparations are complete and the rehearsals undertaken, the production will open. This is an exciting time for all concerned as their plans are put into action.

You may be a performer or a technician, or you may be contributing to the production by designing and/or making a costume, prop or piece of scenery. Whatever your role, the production will be the culmination of your efforts where hard work and planning pay off.

Knowing how to monitor and evaluate your contribution

Imagine going to see a play set in the Victorian era, only to find one of the actors performing in modern dress because the wardrobe team had forgotten to make his costume.

You will need to monitor your work at all stages of the project to ensure that all tasks are completed on time. If you find you are not achieving your aims, you must be prepared to make adjustments to your plans. This topic is covered in the Monitoring and Reviewing unit.

Process portfolio

In your process portfolio for this unit you will need to make sure that you have recorded evidence from all stages of your work.

You will need to make sure your portfolio includes:

* Your research and investigations – document what you find out about the form of performance you have studied. Include information about how it originated, how it has changed over the years and how technology and changing social conditions have affected the form.

* Your planning – you must keep a record of all activities undertaken during the planning phase of the project. This may include ideas for costumes, **props** and **sets**, rehearsal notes and minutes of production meetings. A personal log detailing your own contribution should also be included in your portfolio.

* A record of the production itself – if you are an actor, musician or dancer your performance will need to be recorded. If you have produced costumes, props and/or items of scenery, what you have designed and/or made will need to be photographed. If you are part of the production team (e.g. stage manager or lighting technician) you will need to document your activities during the run of the production by completing a **production diary** or logbook.

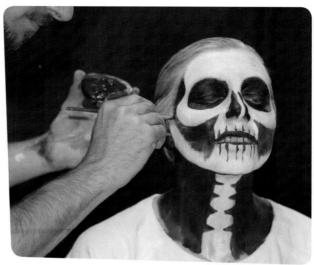

Every detail counts: a production without costumes or make-up would lose much of its dramatic atmosphere.

Genres – Different types or themes of performance, e.g. romance, mystery and soap opera.

Social conditions – The way in which people live at a particular time in history.

Production – A term that refers to the presentation of any performance such as a play, musical, dance piece or concert.

Props – Short for property. Items that the actors use on stage, e.g. a walking stick or a cup.

Sets – Also known as the scenery. Items that provide the setting in which the action takes place.

Production diary – A document to record all the things that you do and how you do them during the production of your performance.

Just checking

* It is important to understand the development of a performance form.
* Careful planning is vital to a successful performance.
* Monitoring must take place on a regular basis to ensure tasks are completed and you are working safely, ethically and legally.

2.1 Understanding the development of a form of performance

OVER TO YOU!

List and describe your favourite TV programmes. Ask your teacher to list and describe the programmes they used to watch in their teens. Compare and discuss the differences in your lists.

A performance is the presentation of an artistic work to an audience. Performances come in all shapes and sizes, from stadium rock concerts to stand-up comedy in the back room of a pub. They can involve large numbers of people or a single performer. They can take place at specially-designed theatrical or music venues or on a street corner.

In this topic you will investigate a single type of performance to find out how the form originated and how and why it has developed over time.

Choosing a form of performance

Your teacher may decide on the form of performance you will investigate, or they may leave the choice to you. In either case, you should consider this unit as a whole. Ideally the form of performance you investigate in this topic should relate to the eventual production you will plan and take part in. For example, if your class are keen to produce a piece of television drama you may decide to focus your research on British television soap operas. If you are planning to perform an extract from a musical you may study American musicals of the 1960s and 1970s.

Remember to focus your research on the origins of the form and its development over a specific period of time. This will be particularly important if you select a form of performance that has been around for hundreds of years! Focusing on a particular period of time in its development will allow you to undertake detailed research.

By conducting research and investigating the type of performance you are involved in, you will gain a greater understanding of how practitioners before you have tackled the same tasks that you are about to face. Learning more about how things have changed over time will help you appreciate the tools and processes you have available to you as you work.

A study of British 'soaps' will provide a good insight into the development of television drama.

At this stage you should also begin to think about the role you will eventually take on in your production. Think carefully about the kind of information you will need to discover whilst researching and what will be of use to you in your role. For example, if you are planning to take on a marketing role and produce publicity material, perhaps you should be focusing on how such performances have been marketed by others. Contacting a local theatre may help you source some examples of posters or programmes used to promote past performances. If you are planning to act in the production you may include details on acting styles in your research.

Beginning your research

Once your choice is made you should begin collecting materials that are relevant to your chosen form of performance.

You could begin by:

* searching books, newspapers and magazines for information about your chosen form of performance and its history

* using the internet as a starting point to find past examples of that performance form

* watching and/or listening to recorded performances of the type you are working on

* going to see an example of the work live (if possible)

* talking to practitioners about their experiences of working on this type of performance.

The origins of performance

Many forms of performance were conceived for very particular reasons. In Victorian Britain the **Industrial Revolution** had led to large numbers of working people moving from the country into cities and towns. A new form of popular theatre, **melodrama,** was devised to provide entertainment for the factory workers. Melodrama made use of advances in theatre technology to include special effects to support their extravagant plots. Trapdoors and **cannonball runs** (used to produce the sound of thunder) were regularly used. The music video emerged in the late 1970s when video recording and editing processes were developed. They became a cheap and easy way of promoting the work of pop and rock musicians. MTV, an American cable television channel, was then developed to screen the videos.

How and why performance changes

Nothing ever exists in a vacuum. Like most things, performance is affected by the world in which it exists.

The impact of changing social conditions

Changes in social conditions, customs and attitudes are reflected in all types of performance. Understanding what life was like and how people lived will help to place a performance in **context**. Geography, culture and belief also have an impact.

Since its beginnings the early twentieth century, film drama has developed and changed in line with the issues and morals of the times. The 1945 British film *Brief Encounter*, for example, reflects the morals of middle-class life in the mid-twentieth century. It tells the story of a bored housewife who embarks on a relationship with a married man she meets in the waiting room of a railway station. They meet secretly in cafés and cinemas but despite temptation are never actually unfaithful to their respective partners. At the time the film was made infidelity was very much a taboo, particularly amongst the middle-classes. The two therefore do 'the decent thing' and end the 'affair'. How

Music video took advantage of developments in recording and editing processes.

For your project

You will need to investigate how your chosen form of performance began.

* What external factors led to its origin?

* How did the needs of a potential audience or market play a part?

Industrial Revolution – The period when factories and machine production first came to Britain in the late 1800s.

Melodrama – A theatrical genre often including musical items, with simple characters, sensational events and usually a happy ending.

Cannonball run – A wooden structure where cannonballs could be safely and noisily rolled for a sound effect.

Context – The wider circumstances in which an event takes place.

does this compare with the way in which the subject is treated in film and TV drama today?

In the late 1950s and early 1960s a movement known as 'kitchen sink realism' was seen in performance and art. Writers and directors began to aim for a more realistic portrayal of social life in their work; they tried to reflect the real lives of their audience. Dramas were often set in northern towns rather than London. Regional accents were used and characters were often working class. *Billy Liar,* Keith Waterhouse's novel, which was adapted into a play, film and TV series, is typical of the form. Billy is a clerk for an undertaker and lives with his parents in a town in Yorkshire. He spends his time fantasising about a life as a famous writer whilst trying to keep three girlfriends on the go.

Films often reflect the morals and issues of the times in which they were made.

The impact of developing technologies

The 2007 production of *The Lord of the Rings* performed at the Theatre Royal Drury Lane in London hit the headlines for its use of cutting-edge stage technology. The production cost an estimated £14 million with much of the cash spent on technical wizardry, including a stage in numerous sections that revolved and moved up and down to create the many settings required to tell the story.

In recorded forms of performance the impact of technology is immense. Until the 1980s for example, recording studios used magnetic tape rather than digital recording methods. As tape was expensive many small errors by performers were overlooked and appeared on the final recording. Digital technology not only allows performers endless opportunities to get it right but it can also fix inaccuracies in pitch and timing.

The Lord of the Rings *used cutting-edge theatre technology.*

Your process portfolio

You should put copies of all research materials in a file and annotate them with your own notes and comments on:

* why they are relevant
* what they tell you about the origins and development of your chosen form of performance.

You should also present your conclusions in written form or in the form of a verbal presentation.

Functional Skills

Using ICT...

* Use the internet as a research tool and keep a record of websites you have found useful.
* Your research could be presented using presentation software such as PowerPoint.

Activity

* Use the skills audit completed in the introduction to this unit to compile a profile of your group showing your strengths.
* Use the profile to discuss possible forms of performance your group could produce.
* Come up with a shortlist of three ideas for a performance project in consultation with your teacher.

Just checking

* Have you chosen a form of performance on which to base your research?
* Have you investigated the origins of your chosen form of performance?
* Have you considered the ways in which changing social conditions and developing technology have affected the development of your chosen form of performance?

Development in musical theatre

One of the most popular forms of theatre is the musical. Combining drama, dance and music, the musical has been around for over a century, and in that time has kept pace with changing tastes and social conditions, as well as advances in theatre technology. Many modern musicals are known for their spectacular sets, lighting and other effects.

From music hall to the jukebox musical

The musical has its roots in **music hall**, **vaudeville** and **operetta**: popular forms of entertainment which emerged in the late nineteenth century for people living and working in towns after the Industrial Revolution. The form as we know it today developed in the mid-twentieth century in America when shows such as *Oklahoma*, *South Pacific* and *Guys and Dolls* were produced. Shows often used the same formula: boy gets girl, boy loses girl, boy gets girl back; as well as the same mixture of solo songs, duets and big chorus song and dance pieces. These 'classic musicals' are still performed regularly today by professional companies as well as amateur performers.

OVER TO YOU!

The musical is the most popular form of theatre in Britain. Why do you think it is loved by so many people?

Activity

Many musicals have been adapted into film versions over the years.

Watch an extract from a 'classic' American musical produced in the 1950s or 1960s (e.g. *South Pacific*), as well as an extract from a more recently filmed musical (e.g. *Phantom of the Opera* or *Chicago*).

* Discuss their similarities and differences.

* How far does each example reflect the times in which it was made in terms of the style of the music and the style of the film itself?

Guys and Dolls *was revived in London's West End in 2006.*

The musical has always moved with the times to take into account changing musical tastes and to keep audiences coming to the theatre, despite competition from TV and video. From the 1960s onwards the popularity of pop and rock music was exploited by composers of musicals, creating shows like *Jesus Christ Super Star* and *Tommy* and causing the term 'Rock Opera' to be used for the first time. Advances in theatre technology led to spectacular lighting and stage effects being used on a regular basis.

A more recent development has been the songbook or jukebox musical; one of the earliest examples is Bob Carlton's *Return to the Forbidden Planet*. Using pop and rock songs from the 1950s and 1960s instead of a specially written score, it opened the way for such modern productions as *We Will Rock You*, a musical based on the music of Queen, and *Mama Mia* which uses music by ABBA.

Music hall – A popular form of British variety entertainment that included a mixture of popular songs, comedy and 'speciality acts'.

Vaudeville – The American equivalent of music hall entertainment.

Operetta – This is a form of musical theatre that is a 'lighter' form of opera in terms of music and subject matter. Most are comedies.

For your project

Once you have decided what form of performance project you are going to undertake, you will need to research its history and development. Your research should focus on a specific period of time.

For example, if you are planning to stage a pop/rock gig you could investigate popular music styles from the 1970s to the present day, looking at major developments and changes in styles during that time. Your research could include how:

* pop/rock has been influenced by historical and political events
* pop/rock music is connected with youth culture and fashion
* advances in technology have affected developments in pop/rock music.

Where possible you should refer to specific examples, for example how the invention of the synthesiser affected music performance and recording in the 1970s and 1980s. Remember to keep a copy of your research in your project portfolio.

Just checking

* How and why did the musical originate?
* How have changing musical tastes and changes in social conditions affected the development of the musical?
* How have advances in theatre technology affected the development of the form?

How developments in visual arts affect performance

The visual arts play a big role in the preparation and staging of performances. Many of the items in a performance are produced or provided by visual arts practitioners. All of these transform a performance into a living, breathing reality.

Communicating a message

A performance often relies heavily on communicating a message, be that a story or factual information, to an audience. The audience's visual experience is key to this communication being successful. Visual arts practitioners play a vital part in this by creating sets, props, costumes and other materials which support those involved in the performance.

The development of props and scenery

Nowadays if you attend a London show you expect an extravaganza of lights and music, innovative scenery and technical wizardry, but in the late sixteenth century theatre goers were just looking for entertainment and escapism – that is until a new theatre came along.

Heavens – The top level of the theatre.

Multimedia elements – The parts of a performance that use different types of media, such as video, interactive media products and advanced sound effects.

Live performances of dance, theatre or music require costumes, props and scenery within the performance.

The Globe Theatre

Purpose-built theatres offered new and exciting opportunities for the use of props and scenery. Travelling acting groups had always been physically limited in the things they could carry with them. When the Globe Theatre was built, a range of large and small props were collected to add interest and realism to the performances.

Small props were nothing unusual and would have included swords, daggers, blood-soaked handkerchiefs, crowns, flags and banners. Larger props ranged from beds and tables to wells, caves and even cannons. Very large or heavy props might remain on stage throughout the show, and the actors would simply work around them.

The Globe Theatre then went one step further. Competition for audiences was fierce and they began to use dramatic special effects: flying entrances, real animal blood (and body parts for extra gruesomeness in fight scenes!), fireworks, music and even live animals. The cannons located in the **heavens** were loaded with real gunpowder to mimic the sounds of the battlefield, and it was this that actually caused the destruction of the Globe by fire in 1613. Drama at any cost!

www.globe-theatre.org.uk/globe-theatre-props.htm

Case Study: Sam

Sam is part of a group working on a production of Shakespeare's *Hamlet*. She has been given the task of designing a flyer to promote the play and a programme to distribute to those attending the performance. Sam realises that the flyer will need to tell the potential audience what is special about the play and to encourage them to attend.

Sam begins her investigations by looking at some of the more famous productions of *Hamlet* and researching other visual arts pieces related to the play. She discovers that the play is one of Shakespeare's most famous works, and that since its first performance in the early 1600's many artists have created artworks based on the story. Sam finds that the image most commonly associated with the play is from Act Five, when Hamlet is at a graveside holding a skull. She decides to use an image of a skull within her artwork for the flyer, using digital image manipulation to incorporate photographs of the cast into the image.

What technology do you have available to you to use for designing things like publicity, scenery or props?

What methods of research could you employ to come up with your ideas?

What resources are available to you? Remember, a skilled practitioner can be a resource – don't overlook your teachers!

Activity

As you can see from the information on the Globe Theatre, innovative props and special effects aren't just modern creations. Compare and contrast the props and effects that were used in the Globe's performances with their modern equivalent. How much has changed? Does this surprise you?

The impact of developing technologies

Over time the changes in the technology available to production teams has affected the work they produce. Before the invention of electric light, all live performances had to be staged by candlelight or gaslight. This meant that those making sets and props had to consider carefully how they would emphasise the features of objects and props to make sure they were visible in the light available.

In more recent times, designers have worked with technical teams in more depth to incorporate special effects and **multimedia elements** such as video projection and lighting effects to adjust or alter the appearance of sets.

Multimedia elements have recently become more commonly used in performances like touring live comedy shows, such as Little Britain.

Just checking

* How will researching the history of a performance form help you when you come to take part in a similar performance?
* What factors can influence the way in which forms of performance develop over time?

2.2 Planning a performance

Once the form of your performance has been decided, the planning phase of the project can begin. In many ways this is the most crucial time of the project. Failing to ensure that careful and detailed plans are made will jeopardise the success of the performance. Teamwork and good organisational skills will be vital.

Your role in the planning phase

You will need to be sure of your role in the performance you are involved in. Depending on the type of performance being planned there may be many roles to fill.

* Performer: you may be involved as an actor, dancer and/or musician.
  Writer/Composer: you may be producing a script for a play or composing a song.
* Director/Choreographer: you may be directing actors or creating dance routines.
* Designer: your role may be to create designs for and/or make costumes, props and/or items of scenery.
* Technician/Member of Crew: you may be working with lighting and/or sound, or stage-managing the performance.
* Marketing: you may be creating materials that will publicise the performance.

Whatever your job title, it is important that you find out what responsibilities you have and what is expected of you. This can be done by undertaking some research. You could use the internet to discover the roles and responsibilities of, for example, a lighting technician in a professional theatre. Think about recording your research in a different way to just taking notes. You could record a video diary or update a blog. That way you can instantly record the information, plus any thoughts you have on how that information is useful to your project.

Researching, generating and choosing ideas

Remember to keep copies of your research and notes on your ideas/design processes for your process portfolio.

Research activities

The early planning stages of a performance involve research activities that will generate ideas for the production. For example, if you are planning to put on a pantomime and you have a role within the design team, you might begin by searching in books and on the internet for images of traditional pantomime costumes. These images can then be used to inspire ideas for costumes for your own cast.

You may also be required to come up with ideas for the content of the performance itself. If you are planning an end-of-year concert, for example, you may need to generate ideas for a **theme** as well as coming up with ideas for songs, dance pieces and sketches for the show.

Care must be taken when choosing materials for scenery, props and costumes.

OVER TO YOU!

Thought shower – what are the main ingredients needed for successful teamwork? What kind of behaviour is required of good team players? Collate your ideas into a list.

Personal, learning and thinking skills

When you take on a defined role and do things that contribute to the planning of a performance, you are demonstrating the skills of a Creative Thinker.

Selecting and developing ideas

When you are searching for ideas it is always sensible to collect more than you will actually need. This will allow you to select the most feasible suggestions for your performance. You may find it useful to mind-map as many ideas as possible. Once you have collected a good number of suggestions, you will need to have a group meeting to discuss each idea in turn and to select those that are practical and can be developed.

When selecting ideas remember to consider any limitations you are working to, for example:

Finance: even the large professional theatre companies have to work to a **budget**. Consider the amount of money you have available to spend on materials. For example, you might want to make elaborate costumes for twenty-five performers, but this may not be feasible on your budget. Adapting costumes you already have may be more appropriate.

Time: consider the amount of time you have to prepare for the performance. You may want to stage a full-length musical, but if time is limited then a showcase of shorter extracts may be more appropriate.

Skills: select ideas that will make the most of the strengths within your group. Staging a rock concert may seem an exciting idea, but if the musicians in the group play classical orchestral instruments then a more traditional recital will be more appropriate.

Equipment and facilities: the space where the performance is to take place and the technical equipment you have available must be considered in any decision-making. For example, will your ideas for choreographing a dance be appropriate for the shape and size of the performance space?

Developing performance work

Performers and directors often use the early rehearsals to experiment with ideas. This may be done through drama games and improvisation. If the piece you are planning is to be devised rather than scripted, the rehearsal process may begin with a number of sessions where you work with various stimuli to produce ideas for a piece of theatre.

Selecting appropriate materials

If you are involved in the design elements of the performance you will need to select appropriate materials for what needs to be made. Again, cost may play a part in the selection process but other factors may also influence choices. For example, items of scenery that must be moved on and off stage may need to be constructed from lightweight materials. Fabric for costumes might be chosen for ease of washing or because it will move well when worn by a dancer.

It is important that you understand what is required of the role you undertake.

Personal, learning and thinking skills

It is important to **collaborate** with others. Listen to the contributions that others in your group make when you are exploring ideas. It shows consideration as a Team Worker, but also provides the opportunity for you, as a Creative Thinker, to improve or expand your own ideas in the light of someone else's experiences. Creative thinking also requires you to be prepared to adapt your ideas to take into account changes in circumstances, for example a change in the venue or difficulties in getting hold of a particular material.

Working as a team

Teamwork is vital to successful planning. There will be lots of different jobs to be done with various deadlines for completion. Good organisation within your group will therefore be very important.

Planning a schedule

A good way of making sure that everything that needs to be done is completed on time is to draw up a production **schedule**. It should include all the **milestone** points in the planning and preparation phases of your project.

Cinderella: Foxwood Community College Production Schedule

5th February	Initial 'ideas' meeting. **Roles and responsibilities finalised.**
12th February	Presentations of marketing design ideas. **Images for posters and flyers finalised.**
13th February	**Rehearsals begin.**
14th February	Presentation of set/props design ideas. **Designs finalised and materials ordered.**
15th February	Presentation of costume design ideas. **Designs finalised and materials ordered.**
16th February	**Deadline for publicity materials.**
19th February	Performers measured for costumes.
22nd February	Set/props/costumes making begins.
13th March	Production meeting: review progress on set, props and costumes. **Costume fittings.**
16th March	Presentation of lighting design ideas. **Lighting designs finalised.**
23rd March	Production meeting: review progress on set, props and costumes.
29th March	**Costume fittings.**
30th March	Production meeting: arrangements for production week. Final deadline for costumes, props and set.

A separate rehearsal schedule must also be drawn up. An example of a rehearsal schedule is given on page 65.

Production meetings

Regular production meetings will also be vital to the smooth running of your project. Draw up an **agenda** for each meeting, showing what is going to be covered and any preparations members of the group will need to make.

Memo

To: Production Team and Cast 'Cinderella'

From: Production Manager

Subject: Production meeting 13th March

Regular production meetings are vital to the smooth running of the schedule.

Legal and ethical requirements

The copyright law protects those who create music and lyrics, and dramatic works such as plays and musicals. If you intend to use a copyright piece during a public performance you must seek permission before using it. Permission is normally applied for through the Rights department of the publisher of the work.

Planning a theatrical production

The planning of a theatrical production is a complex business involving many people. Performers must undertake a great deal of preparation before they take to the stage. Actors will have dialogue and moves to rehearse, and character research to undertake to ensure that the role being played is believable. Dancers will have choreography to rehearse; musicians will have songs or a score to practise. The process, however, will also include people who are not performers, such as the director, designers and technicians.

Preparation

It is important to prepare for a performance as a group, but you must also take responsibility for your own personal preparation. You owe it to the group to make your contribution as good as it can be.

Schedules and rehearsals

Jobbing actor – An actor who is not necessarily paid for their work – the companies they work for often offer a share of the profits instead.

Warm-up – Performers normally undertake physical and vocal exercises and games at the beginning of each rehearsal to prepare their bodies, voices and minds for work.

Off-text exercises – Actors may explore themes from the play through improvisation, e.g. two characters who do not like each other may explore how they fell out.

Case Study: Karen

I've been working as a **jobbing actor** since leaving college three years ago. My most recent job was in a touring production of *Pygmalion* by George Bernard Shaw. The rehearsal and planning process began with the 'meet and greet'. This is when all the people involved in the production get together for the first time. It was good to meet the other actors, as well as the production team and the director who talked us through his ideas for the play. Next was the read-through. As you might expect, this is where the actors and director sit in a circle and read through the play together for the first time. I was quite nervous even though I had already read through my part several times at home, as well as doing some research into the play, my character and the era in which it was set.

The rehearsal process was really hard work. The director draws up a rehearsal schedule and the deputy stage-manager puts up a list each day showing the scenes that were being rehearsed and who was needed. Each rehearsal would begin with a **warm-up**, then we worked on the script or did **off-text exercises** to help us explore our characters. There were also costume fittings to attend and lines to be learnt.

Note down everything Karen has done which could be classified as planning for her acting role.

Now use this as a starting point for your own plan.

What things can you apply from Karen's list to your own role in your production; what extra things might you need to do?

Case Study: Gary

I work for a small touring theatre company that specialises in productions for children. Our shows combine music, dance and drama and are devised by the company. This means the planning and rehearsal process are very different to that undertaken by a company working on a scripted play. A devised piece has no script to begin with. It is created from scratch by the company and our director.

We generally begin with a starting point. It could be an idea for a story, a picture, a piece of music or a costume. It could be anything – as long as it is interesting or intriguing – as we use it as a stimulus to generate ideas. The next stage is to select, develop and shape the most useable ideas into a story that will work as a piece of theatre. If we are devising a show for a particular age group that will have a bearing on what will work and what will not. We will also consider how music and dance can be used to tell the story.

How could you use Gary's style of creating ideas in your group's planning?

Activity

As a group draw up a 'contract of employment' for members of your performance company, stating what is required of them. You could consult the list you complied in the teamwork exercise on page 60.

When you have drawn up a contract, type it out and give everyone a copy to sign. Post a copy on the wall of your rehearsal room to remind members of the company of required standards of behaviour. Keep one for your process portfolio as well.

Your planning activities should include drawing up schedules to ensure deadlines are met. It is vital that the group keeps to these deadlines to ensure the production is ready in time for the first performance. It is also important to set a detailed rehearsal schedule, like the one for 'Christmas Revue' below.

Hillside Community School – 'Christmas Revue' Rehearsal schedule: Week beginning 18th November			
Date/Time	Company	Call	**Location**
Mon 9.15 a.m.	Full Company	Sleigh Bells Medley	Main Hall
Mon 12.00 p.m.	Ellen, Omar, Kerry and Linda	Twas the Night before Christmas	Drama Studio
Tues 1.15 p.m.	Musicians	Deck the Halls	Music Room
Wed 2.30 p.m.	Full Company	Jingle All the Way	Drama Studio
Thurs 3.15 p.m.	Kerry, James, Faye, Micia and Omar	Santa Claus Routine	Drama Studio
Fri midday	Dancers and Musicians	Sugar Plum Fairies	Main Hall

Within rehearsals it is important that good discipline is maintained at all times. Producing a show requires a lot of hard work from all involved, so time is precious and must not be wasted.

Just checking

* Have you considered what impact the style of performance may have on your preparations?
* Does your project have a clear aim or goal?
* Have you researched your role in the project thoroughly?
* Have you set aside time to create schedules to ensure deadlines are met?

Planning props for a performance

Visual artists play a key role in the development of ideas, planning and production of props for performance. It is important that everyone is involved in the planning stages to ensure that they are meeting the needs of the rest of the group and working safely.

OVER TO YOU!

A group who are planning a piece of street theatre have asked a designer to produce some props for use in their play. After the designer is given a written list of items he does not communicate with the group again until he presents them with the props on the day of the performance.

Mind-map what problems this might cause for the performers, the designer and the audience.

Working with a group

It is always important that everyone involved in a production communicates with the others involved on a regular basis. Visual arts practitioners involved in productions will often spend some of their time working with equipment in specialist environments, such as studios or workshops. However, they must make sure that they meet with or talk to other group members on a regular basis.

As you will see from the structure of preparing for a performance on page 60, there are several important stages in the process of planning and production. Depending on what role you take in the production, the stages at which you will be involved may vary. For example, if you are designing props and scenery, you will need to understand not only what items are required but also what **visual message** the items are intended to communicate. A play may demand a scene set in a wood, but the difference between the images used to depict a creepy wood at night and a sun-drenched forest glade would be very different. Knowing the **mood** and intention of a scene will inform the ideas you begin to develop.

Researching and generating ideas

Visual artists record the progress of their ideas carefully, recording things that have inspired or interested them. Usually this will be done in the form of a sketchbook or working book where everything can be stored safely and securely. You can see an example of pages from a sketchbook on page 218-219.

Producing visual representations of your ideas for the items you are working on at an early stage is essential. You will need to show those who are planning the performance what you intend to do, and to use the feedback they give you to develop your ideas. You may also need to give constructive feedback to other group members on what they are planning. If you are planning to produce items that are to be on stage or on a set, you will need to talk carefully with the technical crew who will be coordinating lighting and sound. You'll need to make sure your plans work well together. If you are producing promotional material you will need to make regular checks with the Producer or Director to make sure the details you include are correct.

Regular meetings can help to ensure that everyone involved has an overview of progress.

Selecting materials

Making sure you have selected and sourced the right materials for your work is an important part of preparing to begin practical activity. When communicating with the group you will need to find out exactly what the items you produce are going to be used for, so that you can make sure the materials you choose are appropriate. Checking what purpose the items will be used for is important. A prop to be used during a play may be handled by actors and required on many nights of a performance, so it would need to be hardwearing and solidly constructed. However, items for use on the set of a television show could only be used once, but may need to be lightweight to allow the set dressers to put them in place easily. Communication with other members of the production team early on will allow you to find this information out and use it in your planning.

> **Visual message** – A visual message tells the audience something without words, e.g. a beautiful dress might tell the audience that a character is rich, or dim lights that it is dusk or night time.
>
> **Mood** – The feeling a scene is trying to generate in an audience.
>
> **Commission** – To ask someone to create or do something.

Case Study: Ben

Ben is a freelance designer. A local club that is planning to stage a series of gigs has contacted him. They are aiming to hold Rock, Electro and Folk nights and have **commissioned** Ben to design a graphic reflecting those genres. Ben is also to have the graphics printed onto cloth backdrops to hang on stage behind the bands as they perform. Ben meets with the Club Manager first to discuss her needs, and then has a separate meeting with the technical crew at the club to find out where the banners will go and what practical considerations he needs to make. The Technical Manager highlights the need for the cloth to be fire resistant so that it will not be an added danger in the event of a fire. Ben also discovers that his plans to print onto a silk-like fabric are not ideal as the air conditioning in the room may make such a light fabric billow and flap. Whilst producing his designs, Ben regularly sends his work over to the club via email and asks for their feedback. He then adjusts his designs according to the Club Manager's comments.

Safety is a very important consideration. To make sure your group has thought of everything, you could pair up then swap roles.

Write out as many health and safety issues as you can think of that are relevant to your partner's role in the production, then swap notes. Did your partner think of anything that you hadn't considered? What will your next actions be?

Health and safety

Ensuring that you work safely when producing artefacts for use in a performance is of great importance. You should make sure that you have carefully planned your activities and considered the possible risks and dangers of using the tools and equipment you need in the production process. The table on page 73 details what you should consider.

Just checking

* Are you communicating well with other members of your group?
* Are you keeping a careful record of all your ideas for your process portfolio?
* Have you sourced the best materials for your work?
* Have you considered the health and safety requirements of your work?

2.3 Producing a performance

Along with the rest of your group you will now need to put the plans you have made in to action. If you are involved as a performer you will take part in final rehearsals of the performance itself. If you are involved in the design of the set, costumes or props, you will need to gather your resources and produce what you have planned to make. If you are a member of the technical team you may be involved in technical rehearsals. It will be vital that everyone works as a team to meet the deadlines you have set.

Your role and responsibilities

Your role in the production of a performance will determine how involved you are within the performance itself. For the performers in the group the production will be the culmination of their work on the project. For some, such as those responsible for producing marketing materials, involvement will be more intense during the planning and pre-performance stages of production. Others, such as costume designers, may be involved during the planning stages as well as at the time of performance, making final alterations and helping performers dress. Whatever your role it is essential that you understand what is required of you.

Gathering your resources

In the planning stage of the project you will have identified the resources needed to carry out your particular role in the production. As the deadline for the performance approaches it is important that checks are made to ensure you have everything you need in terms of materials and equipment.

Performers often act as their own resource in a production. If you are a performer you will need to prepare yourself both physically and mentally for your performance. If you are an actor this will involve making sure lines are learnt by required deadlines. Musicians will need to undertake practice to ensure parts can be played fluently. Dancers may need to work on skills such as strength, balance and stamina. Having developed these resources in rehearsals you will now need to use them to ensure you perform to your best ability.

Deadlines

The final deadline you will work to is the opening of the show itself. Depending on the type of performance being staged you may have other deadlines to which you must work:

* The Get-in: all the equipment and materials for the performance are moved into the performance space.

Performers will need to gather their physical and mental resources.

* The Fit-up: lighting and sound equipment is installed. Scenery is set on the 'stage'.
* The Technical Rehearsal: the performance is run to allow the technical and backstage teams to practise their cues and to allow the performers to get used to working with the set and any lighting effects.
* The Dress Rehearsal: The performance is run with the performers in full costume. This rehearsal should be treated like a performance.
* The Photo Call: The performers have publicity photos taken in costume on the 'stage'.

In the theatre these deadlines all happen in an intense period of working known as 'production week'. In school or college projects the deadlines may be spread over a number of weeks. Either way, clear deadlines must be set in the run-up to your performance.

Working safely

When working on any performing arts production it is crucial to take the safety of the performers and crew into account at all times. Theatres and other performing arts venues can be dangerous places with many hazards.

These may include:

* working at height, e.g. when **rigging** lights, sound equipment or scenery
* lifting and carrying heavy or bulky objects, e.g. scenery and furniture
* holes in the floor, e.g. **traps**
* working with hand and power tools, e.g. when constructing scenery and props
* objects overhead, e.g. lights, speakers and other equipment.

Before any work begins on a production a risk assessment should be carried out to identify any potential hazards and steps should be taken to minimise the risk.

An example of a risk assessment report can be found on page 85.

Curtain up!

During the performance itself it will be important to stay focused. In live performance work things can go wrong, even when detailed plans have been made. Errors however can be 'invisible' to the audience if those involved in the performance stay calm, react quickly and don't make it obvious that something has gone wrong!

An example of a risk assessment report can be found on page 85.

Functional skills

Using ICT...
* When organising 'production week' activities use ICT to communicate and exchange information.

Activity

Carry out your final pre-production checks:

* Produce a checklist of all the materials, equipment and resources you have planned to use in your performance.
* Make sure that everything is available and that any technical equipment is in good working order.
* Make sure everyone in the group understands their responsibilities.
* Remember to think about how you will make a record of the performance itself for your process portfolio.

Rigging – The process of hanging lights, sound equipment and sometimes items of scenery from a grid above the performance area.

Traps – Also known as trapdoors. Many theatres have 'doors' in the floor of the stage to allow access to the under-stage area, or to allow actors to enter or exit 'as if by magic'.

Just checking

* Do you have all the resources you need for the performance?
* Do you fully understand your own role and responsibilities?
* Have you identified the deadlines you are working to?
* Have you made sure that you are working safely?

Getting ready for opening night

The first night of a show can be an anxious time for all involved. A successful performance involves the successful collaboration of many people – from the performers to the stage crew, from the lighting technicians to the front-of-house staff. To achieve this, everyone involved needs to understand what is required of them and concentrate at all times.

Front-of-house responsibilities

The front-of-house (FOH) team swing into action on opening night. They are responsible for the comfort and safety of the audience. It is essential that roles are assigned within the FOH team to ensure that everyone knows what they are meant to be doing.

Case Study: Christmas revue

Hillside Community School have been planning their Christmas Revue for six weeks. With the opening night only a week away they are keen to make sure everything runs smoothly front-of-house. A FOH team has been assembled, made up of members of the class who are not performing in the show: James and Fiona, who worked on the designs for the publicity materials and Gina, who designed and made props for the show.

The three will work with a small team of Year 9 volunteers. They decide to allocate roles as follows:

Gina and Fiona will be in charge of refreshments before the show and during the interval with three Y9 helpers.

James will manage the collection of tickets and the sale of programmes with four Y9 helpers before the show. During the interval his team will check the auditorium, removing litter, etc.

They also draw up a pre-show checklist to ensure that everything is ready.

What are the health and safety implications of using volunteers?

Think about the different considerations that might apply if those volunteers are younger students, or disabled.

The front of house team are vital to the smooth running of a performance.

Hillside Community School – Christmas Revue
Pre-show FOH checklist

Health and Safety

Emergency exits clear	Fiona
Emergency lights working	Fiona
Auditorium set out as per plan	Fiona

Sales

Floats available for ticket, refreshment and programme sellers	Gina
Refreshments table stocked	Gina
Programmes ready	James

General

All public areas free of litter	James
'No Flash Photography' signage in place	James
'Ladies/Gents' signage in place	Gina

Activity

Draw up a chart showing everybody's responsibilities during the performance of your show. Include brief job descriptions.

Go on to draw up a series of checklists similar to the 'Christmas Revue' one above for your front-of-house team, backstage crew, technicians and performers.

Performance deadlines

During performances actors, musicians and/or dancers will need to work together, responding to each other and to the audience. Final rehearsals, particularly technical and dress rehearsals, may involve final changes or adjustments. It is also not unusual for extra rehearsals to be called because of approaching deadlines. All members of the group must pull together at this time.

Personal, learning and thinking skills

When taking rehearsal notes you need to be able to deal with praise and criticism in a positive way. As a Team Worker it is also important to provide support and feedback to others.

Case Study: Jodie

I am playing Maisie in our production of 'The Boyfriend', which we have been rehearsing for three months. Today was the dress rehearsal. We were all very excited to finally get to wear our costumes.

It started well and we got through Acts One and Two without any real hitches. However, Act Three was less successful. First, there was a problem with the lights and we had to wait while that was sorted. Then one of the dance routines went very badly.

We had to stay behind after the rehearsal to go through the routine again. Mrs Davies made us go through it three times until it was perfect! Some people were moaning because they wanted to get away but it couldn't be helped. I'm sure this happens in the professional theatre when things go wrong. The fact is that tomorrow we have to do the show in front of an audience, so it was really important that we got it right!

What adjustments to your personal schedule might you have to be prepared to make to ensure the production goes as smoothly as possible?

Just checking

* Have you created a pre-show checklist for your production?
* Have you allowed extra time in your personal schedule in case any last-minute problems arise with the production?
* Have you taken on board any criticism to improve what you are doing?

Producing props and scenery

The involvement of visual arts practitioners within a performance is vital at all stages to ensure that all the props and scenery meet the brief and are ready for opening night. You will need to put all the careful plans you have made into practice to contribute to the performance and fulfil the requirements of your role.

Preparing to work

Following the plans you have drawn up, and based on the agreements you have made with your teacher and the rest of your group, you will need to produce the items you are responsible for. This will involve:

* gathering together the resources you have decided to use and making sure they are easily accessible as you work
* making sure you have access to the tools and facilities you will need to use, which may involve booking to use particular studios, computers or machinery
* making sure you are aware of where others are working and that you have taken note of the safety issues that are involved with working with your chosen materials.

Maintaining contact

Working safely and methodically is an important part of succeeding in your task.

It is crucial that you keep communicating with the others working on the production throughout this stage. If you find that you need to make changes to your plans as you work, make a careful note of what changes you have made and why. You can then inform the rest of the group and they can alert you to any problems that the changes might bring. For example, if you cannot get a particular kind of material and choose to use another, this may affect how much it weighs, what it will look like or its durability, and this could affect how it is going to be used.

Remembering what your item will eventually be used for is key, as to succeed your final piece should be useful for the purposes of the production.

Working safely

Making sure that you have carefully considered the risks and dangers of working with your chosen medium in the specialist studios and workshops you will use is important for all creative and media practitioners.

Visual artists need to consider all of the dangers of working in a particular area. You should carry out research into the safety requirements of your chosen activities thoroughly. Consider the following factors when carrying out your checks and make sure you have clearly recorded information about how you have planned to work safely. (Keep your record close at hand as you work, to remind you of what you should be aware of as you work.)

OVER TO YOU!

Draw a table with two columns, headed 'Pre-performance' and 'Performance'. For each of the visual arts roles listed here, write down what activity they might be involved in at these two stages:

Costume designer
Set designer
Programme designer
Make-up artist

Personal, learning and thinking skills

Whatever medium you work in, following safe working practices is an essential skill to demonstrate.

The materials you plan to use	Do you need to be aware of any particular risks involved with your chosen materials? For example, if you are using dyes or chemicals, do they have hazard warnings on the bottles?
	Do you need to be in a well-ventilated area when using materials? This is particularly important when using adhesives and some inks.
	Is your material light-sensitive? If so, as in the case of photography, have you planned to use specialist resources such as a darkroom in order to work effectively?
The rooms you will be working in	Do the studios or workshops you will be working in have any particular rules or regulations? For example, many workshops will need you to keep floor-spaces clear of bags and personal belongings, due to people carrying delicate or dangerous materials around.
	Is the room you are working in suitable for the purpose you have planned? For example, if you are planning to work at a computer, have you chosen a supportive chair for sitting on for a long period of time?
The machinery or equipment you plan to use	What dangers are associated with using the equipment or machinery you will need to operate to work on your project? Ceramics, for example, may be fired in a kiln, which will heat your work to extremely high temperatures and may need a technician or skilled person to operate it.
	What kind of protective equipment might you need to wear when operating the machinery? Depending on the nature of the machine you use, you might need to protect your eyes from fast-moving fragments of materials by wearing goggles, or your lungs from dust or fumes by wearing a mask over your nose and mouth.
	Any machinery or equipment with moving parts carries with it the danger of trapping or catching things other than the items you are working on. Loose long hair, dangling jewellery, scarves and loose clothing can all become trapped in machines, causing risk to you and those around you.
Your behaviour	What considerations must you make about your behaviour in this environment? Loud noise, fast movement and activity not focused on your work will not only be distracting to others around you, but could also be dangerous. Even when you are not operating machinery or equipment, others may be and inappropriate behaviour could distract them and cause them to injure themselves.

Case Study: Alex

Alex is a set designer who has recently been commissioned to work on a fantasy-horror film being shot in England. He has been asked to help create the set for a scene in a dragon's lair. The script calls for rock formations encrusted with jewels. The film's budget is fairly limited and Alex has been told by the Director of Photography, who has planned all the lighting on set, that the rock formations will be in low light. Alex therefore realises that he needs to make the formations look fairly realistic but that they will not be involved in any close-up shots, so he can be less worried about the detail on his props.

After experimenting with different materials and talking to other designers who have worked on similar projects, Alex discovers that the most effective way to create the rocks is to build a wire frame shape which he will then coat in plaster-soaked fabric strips. This will be ideal as the wire frame will ensure the rocks stay hollow, making them lighter to move around the set. He will also be able to mould and shape the plaster while it is wet and then sand, chip and paint it when it dries. Alex sources some resin shapes in jewel colours that have a highly polished surface which will reflect the light on set and pushes these into the plaster while it is wet to fix them to the surface of the 'rocks' he is creating.

What might have happened if Alex hadn't bothered to talk to the Director of Photography or other designers? What effect would these things have had on the other members of the production team?

Just checking

* Have you gathered together all your resources?
* Have you booked any specialist tools/facilities required to create your artefacts?
* Are you confident you can work safely?

Preparation for assessment

In this unit you have taken part in the planning and staging of a performance. You may have been involved as a musician, actor or dancer and may have used design or technical skills to produce sets, costumes, lighting or sound effects – in this way, you should have been able to show how you have combined at least two disciplines. Your teacher may set one or two assignments, one of which will be a live performance. If you were performing, your performance will be assessed; if you produced costumes, props or effects, your final products will be assessed.

Your portfolio

Your process portfolio will be expected to contain evidence of your involvement in the performance and any other assignments. Your teacher may tell you what form your portfolio should take and how to present your work.

You will be assessed on…	This will be evidenced in your portfolio by…
…your understanding of the origins of a chosen form of performance and the ways in which it has developed over time.	Your research notes. These may be notes taken in class as well as articles found on the internet, in books and magazines. Your presentation of your findings. This could be in written form or a talk, perhaps using PowerPoint slides. If you give a talk, remember to include the notes you use in your portfolio. **Tips for success:** • Keep your computer files in order, using sensible names. • Always back up important documents.
…your contribution to the planning of a performance.	A log or diary giving details of the work you undertook when planning the performance. You should include documents such as schedules and notes taken at meetings. Remember to annotate these, for example by writing comments in the margins to show your own contribution. If you are a performer you should include notes made during rehearsals and practice sessions. If you are contributing as a designer, you should include drawings and sketches. Your teachers will also produce observation reports on how well you carry out practical tasks. **Tips for success:** • Manage your time wisely. Using a short time at the end of each session to write up work completed and decisions made will ensure your log is always up to date. • Make sure you have blank copies of documents you may need, e.g. rehearsal schedules, production meeting records.
…your contribution to the production of a performance.	You will need to keep a log or diary during the production stage of the performance. This might involve writing up how successful the performance was in terms of your work as a performer, or how the costumes you designed contributed to the overall effect of the piece on stage. You may wish to include photographs of products made. Your teachers will also make a recording of the performance. **Tips for success:** • Write up your feelings about the performance while the experience is fresh in your mind.
…your ability to monitor your contribution to the project.	The documents in your portfolio. As well as providing evidence of your contribution to the planning and production of the performance, your log will be used to assess your ability to monitor your progress and contribution to the project. You may also be asked to take part in a de-brief meeting (which may be recorded) and/or complete a written evaluation of the project. **Tips for success:** • Remember to personalise all documents that go into your portfolio. You may spend a good deal of time working as part of a group, so it is important that your portfolio shows your contribution.

The assessment of the unit

This unit is assessed by your teachers. Whatever your role is in the performance, you must be clear about your responsibilities, as you will be assessed not only **what** you do, but also your teacher's observations of **how** you have worked throughout the unit.

You must show that you:	Guidance	To gain higher marks:
…can undertake an investigation into the origins and development of a form of performance	Think carefully when choosing topic (your teacher will help). A topic that is too narrow may mean you struggle to find enough information. Too broad a topic may prevent you from including enough detail. You should use a range of resources when carrying out your investigations (not just the internet).	Your research must be well-focused and your findings must be relevant. Your presentation must include a detailed description of how your chosen performance form developed over time. You should explain how and why any major changes have occurred.
…can take on a role in the planning of a performance, coming up with and exploring ideas.	It is vital that you fully understand the role you are taking on in the planning of the performance. Explore ideas put forward carefully to make sure they will work. Don't be afraid to change or even get rid of ideas that are not practical, as this is an important part of the planning process. Teamwork is vital to the success of the planning process. Remember to listen to others and respect their views.	You must come up with a number of imaginative ideas for the performance project. You must be able to explain the strengths and weaknesses of your ideas. You must work confidently and make a positive contribution in group work. You must be able to carry out planning tasks with only occasional help from your teachers.
…can carry out the tasks required for your role during the production of a performance.	You must make sure you understand exactly what your role requires you to do. Make a checklist of all your duties and refer to it regularly. If you have a number of tasks to complete, prioritise them according to deadlines, i.e. start with the one that has to be completed first. Always work safely. Check any health and safety guidance you have been given before beginning a task.	You must carry out your role in the production team with skill and confidence. You must manage your time to make sure you meet deadlines and everything happens when it should. Follow safe working practices at all times. You must be able to carry out your role with only occasional help from your teachers.
…can monitor your progress during the planning and production stages of the project.	Review your progress regularly, not just at the end of the project. When describing the strengths and weaknesses of your work, give examples to illustrate your comments. If you find something isn't working, make changes as you go along.	You must show that you have used monitoring to improve the work you have done throughout the project. You must describe your contribution to the project showing that you have a thorough understanding of the strengths and weaknesses of your work.

Introduction

In this unit you will be making an **artefact**: a physical object that exists in both space and time. You will be learning how to carefully plan the creation of your artefact, gathering the **resources** you need to work on your plans and developing the skills you need to work successfully.

In all creative and media activities, people make artefacts. Often they are created for a specific purpose or use. Some artefacts are made simply because they are beautiful or because their creator wants to express a thought or a feeling.

OVER TO YOU!

Place three man-made objects from a pocket or bag on the table in front of you. See if you can identify what materials they are made from. Try to identify what processes could have been used to make these items – were they made by hand or using machinery?

Artefact – An object or item that is created either by hand or using machinery.

Resources – Things that are needed to create a particular project or task, like objects, equipment or labour.

Monitor – Keeping a record of your progress and using this information to help you in your work.

Your learning

In this unit, you should work across at least two of the disciplines on page 4 to cover the four main topics.

Understanding the process of creating an artefact

Artistic processes are always changing, but tradition plays an important part in the creation of artefacts. New technologies can improve existing processes or create brand new ones, but they all began with ancient handcrafts. You need to research this to understand the way in which existing artefacts have been created. You will also need to know how the circumstances surrounding the creation of an artefact can influence it.

Investigating the thoughts and processes behind the creation of other artefacts will help and inspire you as you plan and create your own.

Planning the creation of an artefact

Producing an artefact is a very imaginative and creative process, but that does not mean planning is not important. On the contrary, professionals in this area would not begin to create an artefact without carefully thinking through their intentions. Imagine the preparations Michelangelo would have made to carve his statue of David; he wouldn't have just jumped in with a chisel: the block of marble would have been extremely expensive (he eventually took three years to finish the work).

Planning is key. You must first generate ideas for your product and investigate how these ideas could be produced. You will then need to carefully plan how you intend to create your artefact and make sure you are prepared for the activities involved, including how long they will take you and how to work safely.

Artefacts can be produced by hand or using machinery.

Creating an artefact

Once you have clear and thorough plans, then you can create your planned artefact using materials and methods suitable to your discipline. You will need to make sure you are aware of the safety issues surrounding your practical work, taking advice from technicians and your teachers.

Whilst the creation of an artefact might be the most active part of the process, it is also often the most time-consuming, so monitoring and reviewing the plans you have made for your time is important.

Knowing how to monitor your own creative activity

You need to **monitor** how you are progressing in your work constantly. By keeping a record of the decisions made, activities completed and experiences you have during each stage of the process, you will naturally ensure that you are staying on track or quickly realise when something is going wrong and decide what to do about it.

Professionals always keep notes on what they have achieved and how they have worked. They can then use these to improve on their performance or to give them ideas for future projects.

Reviewing your comments on your achievement, mistakes made, new things discovered or decisions taken will help you understand how things may be improved as you work. This topic is covered in the Monitoring and Reviewing unit.

Process portfolio

In your process portfolio for this unit you will need to make sure that you have recorded and carefully stored evidence from all stages of your work.

You will need to make sure your portfolio includes:

* Your research and investigations – document what you find out about how other artefacts were created and how the circumstances surrounding an artefact's creation can influence it.
* Your planning – you must record all of the ideas you have for your artefact and keep all of the plans you produce safe and easily accessible.
* Your final artefact – your artefact must be finished and ready to submit for assessment. See Unit 4 for advice on submitting a record of artefacts that cannot be physically handed over to a teacher.

Personal, learning and thinking skills

By regularly reviewing and monitoring your work and recording this in your process portfolio, you can show that you are a Reflective Learner. You can also demonstrate this skill by actively seeking feedback on your work, then considering any criticism and applying the advice to your work.

Activity

Below is a list of creative and media companies who require some artefacts to be created. Make a list of the materials you would consider using if you were planning to create these artefacts.

* A children's theatre company needs some masks and animal costumes.
* An animation company needs some puppets.
* A local art gallery would like some sculptural work to display.
* An advertising company would like some promotional photographs.

Just checking

* It is important to understand the process of creating artefacts.
* Careful planning is vital to the successful creation of a piece.
* Monitoring must take place on a regular basis to ensure tasks are completed and you are working safely, ethically and legally.

3.1 Understanding the process of creating artefacts

By investigating how other creative **practitioners** work we can understand more about the reasons behind the decisions they make during the planning and production of their artefacts. You can then use this information to develop your own ideas and learn more about materials and their uses.

There are often materials and media that we would expect to be used for particular kinds of artefacts. For example, when you think of a painting, the media you may first think of is paint. However, some artists choose to use more unusual materials, for example the artist Chris Ofili uses elephant dung within his paintings.

Investigating artefacts

Your teacher may select the artefacts you are going to investigate or they may leave you to choose by deciding what will help you in your own work. If you have been asked to make some props for the set of a television quiz show for example, you would start your investigations by looking at examples of television quiz shows that have been made before and concentrating on the props used in them. Ensuring that you are looking at the right kinds of product is essential to getting useful information from your investigations.

You then need to examine those products in detail and work out how they were created. There are a variety of methods you can use to do this.

Using your senses

Simple observation: touching, squeezing, smelling and looking at an artefact may give us some clues as to what it is made from and how it was produced.

Research

Research is another reliable way of finding out about an artefact. For more famous works you may find information in books or on the internet. Images of artefacts are often accompanied by text that tells you what the creator used to make the artefact. Investigating the creator of an artefact and their other works can also help you work out more about their preferred practices. If you are able to, it is useful to talk to practitioners themselves. Talking to artefact creators about their own work, and why they choose to work the way they do, will provide lots of very useful information that will help you develop your own ideas.

Making a research plan will help you to keep your ideas and findings in order. Your research plan may look like the one at the top of the page facing.

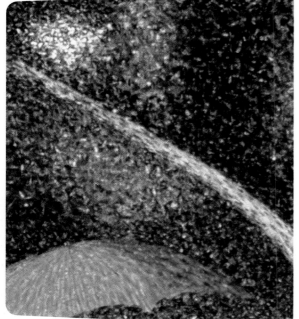

The thumbprints left on the surface of this clay sculpture indicate that it was produced by hand.

What I need to find out	How I will find this out	How I will record my findings
What materials Antony Gormley used to make the Angel of the North.	By looking in the library for books and journals.	By writing down what I find in my **sketchbook** and photocopying the pages from the book that are useful.
What processes Gormley used to make the sculpture.	By searching the internet using a search engine.	I will print out useful pages and highlight sections that are helpful to me.

Analysing the work of others

When you investigate examples of artefacts it is important that you think carefully about what you are trying to discover and what your findings tell you. Analysing artefacts means considering all the information you can gather about the artefact and its creator, and recording what this tells you.

* When you look at artefacts created by someone else, ask yourself:
* What materials is the artefact made from?
* What processes would have been used to design and make this artefact?
* How does the finished artefact look?

For all of the answers you find to these questions you should then ask yourself:

* Why might the creator of this artefact have chosen to use those materials and processes?
* What might have influenced the creator to make the creative decisions they did about that artefact? (This could include looking at the colours they have used or the way that an artefact has been finished.)
* How might the **context** that the artefact has been produced in influence its design?

> ### Personal, learning and thinking skills
>
> It is important to understand the way different factors have influenced the production of particular artefacts, for example how the war affected Otto Dix's work. However, you must be able to *show* your understanding when your work as an Independent Enquirer is being assessed, and this is why you should support the conclusions you make with evidence, and make your arguments clear and sensible.

Otto Dix often used images of war in his work.

> **Practitioner** – A person who practices a particular skill, craft or profession.
>
> **Sketchbook** – Also sometimes called a Visual Diary. A book that contains all of an artist's work towards a particular project or activity.
>
> **Context** – The social and physical environments that an artefact was created in.

Context

When we look into the background of an artefact and think about the time it was produced, we are investigating the context in which the artefact was created. Understanding what was happening in the world when an artefact was made can give us vital clues as to why it might look the way it does. It can also help us understand why the creator made the decisions they did when creating the artefact.

Major world events, like wars, have a big influence on the work that an artist or designer can or will produce. Otto Dix, who lived through two World Wars, often featured images of violence and death in his work (see example on page 79). Likewise, clothing designers who were working in wartime, like Claire McCardell, were limited in the kinds of materials they used because the war made many fabrics difficult to obtain. In knowing that a war was happening, we can therefore understand more about the choices such creators made in their subject matter and working practices.

To investigate the context that your chosen artefacts were created in you should determine the following:

* What time period were they made in?
* What country were they made in?
* What kind of life did the artefact's creator lead? What were his/her experiences?

Developing technologies

The technology available to artists and designers will have a big impact on what materials they choose and the processes they use in their work. Looking at when an artefact was created can tell us a lot about it too. Some key events in the development of technology and industry can be seen as very important in the ways that artefact creation evolved.

Developments in technology mean that modern video cameras are much more portable and lightweight than older versions.

The Industrial Revolution was the period when factories and machine production first came to Britain in the late 1800s. Before this, nearly all products were made by hand, using crafts such as wood-carving, pottery, embroidery, typography and glass-blowing. The Industrial Revolution saw a move from hand-crafted products produced by a skilled individual, to items constructed from **components** in a factory.

In media and live arts, the development of technology influences not only how things are produced, but also how they are presented to an audience. There have been great shifts in the technology available to design, create and present or broadcast things. For example, the shift from the original heavy and expensive video cameras to the portable, lightweight and affordable ones available now has had a big impact on how moving image footage is shot and how multimedia elements are used in stage productions.

Activity

Digital cameras, high-definition recording techniques, DVDs and the move to digital television broadcasting have all meant that there has been an increase in the quality of images that we see on television and cinema screens, as well as on the internet and in print media.

Make a list of how the increase in image quality might affect those who make artefacts for use in products like films and TV programmes that are recorded using these new technologies.

Components – Parts or elements of an artefact.

For your project

You will need to record everything you find out about the artefacts that you investigate:

* the materials and process used and the impact of developing technologies on them
* the purposes of their creators
* the context in which they were created and your thoughts on how this affected the creators' work.

You must also explain why you have chosen to look at the artefacts that you have, and why you think that investigating them will help you with your project.

It's a good idea to begin by making a plan for how you are going to investigate and research your chosen artefacts. This plan should be included in your process portfolio as evidence of your planning process.

Just checking

* Have you made sure that you are investigating artefacts in the past that will help you develop your own artefact ideas?
* Do you understand how researching the context that artefacts have been created in helps you understand the creative decisions others have made?
* Have you put a copy of all your research plans into your process portfolio?

3.2 Planning the creation of an artefact

Professional practitioners in the creative and media industries need to plan their practical activity well to ensure that they are successful and work safely. Generating ideas for your artefact is the first critical stage in the process of creating an artefact.

OVER TO YOU!

Think of an artefact you would love to make as a gift for someone else. Write a checklist of the materials and equipment you would need to do this, then consider how you would **source** these things. Do your ideas change when you consider the cost and availability of the resources you would need?

Generating ideas

Coming up with good ideas to work on is an important part of creating good work. If you came up with one idea and went straight to creating that piece, you may find that your finished work does not demonstrate the full range of your abilities. You may find that you have ideas that are more suitable or excite you more after you have begun work. Once you have started doing practical work on an artefact it can be expensive and time consuming to change your mind about how it will look or how you will work. When trying to generate ideas, or come up with solutions for the task that your brief has set you, ask yourself the following questions:

What skills do I have that might be useful in the creation of an artefact like this?

Have I seen artefacts similar to this before? If so, what were they like?

How will this artefact be used and how does this affect how it will look or operate?

Recording your ideas

It is important that you make sure you note down the ideas you have for your artefact in a safe place so that you can return to them later. You may have some good ideas that you choose not to use, but that may be of use in a later project. Noting down all of the details, including any sketches or plans you draw up will be helpful as you develop ideas now and in the future. You can keep them safe in your project portfolio as evidence of your first stage of planning.

Choosing an idea

When you have come up with several different ideas, you will need to decide which one is best. One of the best ways to do this is to ask yourself questions. You should always make notes about both the positive and negative decisions you make, as they are all part of your progress, which must be monitored throughout this unit.

Here is a mind-map of questions that you could ask yourself when choosing which idea to work on:

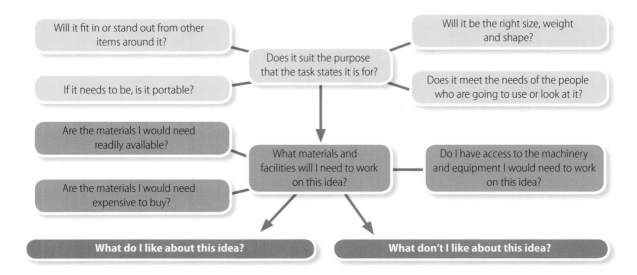

Selecting appropriate materials

When you come to plan how you will produce your item, careful thought needs to be given to the materials you choose to use in the creation of your artefact.

You can refer back to the notes you made when selecting your idea; this will remind you of your thoughts on the materials you originally planned to use, plus their cost and availability. Changing your mind about what materials you will eventually use often happens during the planning stage, and your thoughts on why these alterations have been made should be carefully recorded in your process portfolio.

You should always ask yourself the following questions when considering which materials will be appropriate:

* Can this material be formed, cut, shaped, moulded or altered in the way I need it to be?
* What skills will I need to work with this material?
* What equipment, machinery or environment will I need to have access to in order to work with this material?
* Does the finished artefact need to have any special features, such as being lightweight, flexible or waterproof?
* When the product is finished, will the material be durable enough to be used for the purpose it is intended for?
* How might this material age over time?

Once you have considered all of these questions, review the materials you have chosen to use. Investigate alternative materials where necessary and note down why you have made the decisions you have.

Choosing your methods and processes

Once you have selected what your artefact is to be made of, you need to consider what methods and processes you will actually use to construct, design or produce your artefact.

Source – To find, locate and get things.

Personal, learning and thinking skills

You must show a number of skills as a Creative Thinker. You must first generate a number of ideas for an artefact and then develop those ideas by asking sensible questions. You can then plan the creation of your chosen artefact, making sure you keep good records of the creative process.

One of the hardest things for a creative practitioner to do is to tone down their ambitious ideas. There is a fine line between an ambitious idea and an unrealistic one. You should always try to challenge yourself and learn new skills, but you must also be able to accept when your skills are not equal to a task, or the materials/equipment you need are unavailable or too expensive. One way to avoid disappointment is only to consider artefacts that can be made with the technology/equipment you have access to in your school or college.

Create a list of all the different resources that you have available to you. Group them under the disciplines of performance arts, media arts and visual arts.

Risk assessment – A pre-production assessment of potential risks associated with the production process and how these can be overcome.

Depending on the disciplines you choose to work in, this will vary, but there are some common factors you will always need to consider:

* Do I have access to the machinery or equipment I need?
* Will I have limited time to use this machinery or equipment, e.g. a glass workshop or IT suite may only be available for a short period of time.
* How much time does a method like this take and can I use it effectively within my schedule?
* Can I work safely using this method and what precautions must I take to be safe whilst I work in this way?
* Is there a quicker, more effective, more cost-efficient or safer method or process I could use and get the same effect?

Planning your time

Carefully planning the time you can allow yourself to complete an activity is a crucial part of your preparations. Whilst artists and designers often work at different paces, most professional practitioners have to produce work to deadlines, whether for an exhibition or to meet the needs of a client.

Whatever kind of creative and media discipline you choose to work in, you will need to schedule your activities before you enter the production stage of your project. How you choose to document your time planning will depend on the kind of artefact you are creating and the discipline you have chosen to work in. Whenever you are planning your time you should always ask yourself:

* When is the deadline for completion?
* How long will it take me to create the artefact I have chosen to work on?
* Do I need to book any special equipment of facilities, e.g. specialist workshops, computers?
* Where will I get my resources from and can I do this before I must start?
* Do I need any assistance from any other people and, if so, when are they available?

Contingency planning

When working on any creative project, it is always wise to be prepared for unforeseen events or circumstances. This is called contingency planning and it allows you to consider what problems you may face during the production stage and be ready to solve them with pre-prepared solutions or actions.

A contingency plan for the production of an on-screen graphic for a media arts product might look like this:

Potential problem	Contingency plan
The computer crashes.	I will backup all my work regularly onto my data stick as I work.
The logo I have made does not show up properly on screen.	I will produce an alternative colour scheme idea as a back-up.

Budgeting

All creative and media practitioners need to be aware of how much the production of an artefact costs. Although you may not be working with a real budget, you will be expected to know how to cost a project. Setting out clearly what you intend to use, how much of it you will use and where you will work will help you break down the overall cost of your project. You will need to consider the cost of the:

* materials – how much will you need and how much will it cost?
* equipment, machinery or facilities you will use – how much will it cost to hire or rent these things?
* assistance of other people – if you need people to help you practically in your work, how much will you need to pay for their time?

Legal and ethical considerations

Make sure that you are not planning to work in any way that would be considered illegal or unethical. One of the key things that you must be aware of is the need to observe copyright law; if you use something in your work that someone else has created, say a photographic image, then you must ask their permission. Often in professional work, people will grant their permission for you to use their work for a fee.

Ethical considerations mean thinking about things which may be considered unfair or unjust to other people. It would be unethical to copy someone else's design very closely without giving them any credit for their work. Other ethical considerations could include choosing to use environmentally-friendly materials or methods.

Working safely

Finding out the health and safety issues surrounding the materials and methods you have chosen is vital to ensure you can complete your work safely and successfully. You should undertake a **risk assessment** before you begin any work to identify any potential problems.

Risk Assessment
Project title: News Item – Logo design
Client: Mary Smith School
Designer: Roberta Carr
Woodwork technician: Mr Greig
Date: 18th November 2007

PRODUCING THE LOGO IN WOOD

Major Issues	Solutions
Using machinery to cut out the initial letter shapes	Make sure that the guards are on the machine and wear gloves and goggles
Bonding the wood together	Use glue in a well-ventilated area
Painting the logo	Wear old clothes and cover all areas with sheeting and use paint in well-ventilated area

Contacts
Woodwork office: 01220 313257

Emergency Services
Local police: 01220 286412
Local fire: 01220 293330
Local hospital: 01220 287700

3.3 Creating an artefact

Once you have chosen the artefact you are going to make and planned how you will make it, you need to start work on creating it. Whichever way you choose to work, the key to success at this stage is to work safely and methodically.

Collecting your materials

When planning your artefact you decided what resources you would need to create it. You must now ensure that the resources you need are available to you and, as far as possible, gather them together. When you are creating something, you will want your energy and concentration to be focused on making that artefact. If you are constantly stopping work to find materials or equipment, this will be difficult.

If you are working with **mark-making** or 3D materials, collect all the resources in one place. If you are working on a computer, store your resources in one folder or on a data stick so that you know where to find them when you need them.

OVER TO YOU!

Look at the list of resources and materials you made when planning your artefact. Look at each item and imagine what alternative materials or equipment you would use if any of those things were not available. Is there anything that you could not work without?

Having materials to hand will help you focus on your creative work.

Preparing your work area

You need to ensure that you have a suitable work area before you start creating your artefact. It is important that:

* you have space both for the piece you are working on and the materials you will be using
* your materials can be stored together and near where you are working
* any surfaces you intend to work on are clean and free from anything that might damage your work
* you have planned how and where you will use any material with special safety requirements.

Working safely

Through your planning you will have become aware of the possible risks involved in working with your chosen materials and the methods you have selected. Being aware of the dangers your activities could cause, both to you and others, is key to working effectively in this area.

Make sure that you have carried out a risk assessment on your materials and processes. Having carefully considered the precautions you need to take and how you may deal with problems or issues, you will be far safer as you work, particularly if you refer back to them regularly.

Of great importance when working in busy environments is your awareness of how your behaviour and actions might affect others around you. Take careful note of the guidance for working safely with other people on page 73 before starting work.

Wearing the correct protective equipment is always important.

Activity

What are the possible risks to others in each of these situations?

* Adnan is painting a large piece of scenery on stage while a group of actors are rehearsing a sword-fight.
* Claire is taking delivery of her hired media equipment. It has been stacked in the foyer of her school and the caretaker is going to help her carry it.
* Ruby is sorting the beads for her textured wall covering on the floor of the common room.

Mark-making – Materials such as pens, pencils and paints.

For your project

Your finished piece will form an important part of the project work that you submit at the end of this unit.

Make sure that you carry out the processes you have planned for and remember to document the production process as you work. If you reflect upon and monitor your own work carefully then you will be able to alter your plans more easily if something changes. Advice on how to do this can be found in Monitoring and Reviewing.

Personal, learning and thinking skills

Following your plans carefully and showing that you can solve problems when they arise by trying out alternatives or new solutions, will help demonstrate your skills as a Creative Thinker.

Just checking

* Have you organised a way to have your materials close at hand as you work?
* Remember to prepare yourself and your work area before you begin.
* Remember to use the plans you've made! Take care to stick to schedules and deadlines.
* Have you conducted a risk assessment?

Artefacts for the stage

In this topic, we will look at artefacts for the stage. Performers rely on artists with a wide range of skills to create the artefacts needed to put the finishing touches to a performance. Items of scenery, costumes and props are vital to the look of a play or musical. Pop and rock musicians are also increasingly using extravagant sets and costumes for their live shows, as well as for their music videos.

OVER TO YOU!

Think of a show you have been involved in or watched. What artefacts were used? How did they affect the look of the show?

Personal, learning and thinking skills

When you can describe the processes involved in the creation of a particular artefact, you are showing you have made investigations as an Independent Enquirer.

The role of costume

Kylie the Showgirl

In 2007 the Victoria and Albert Museum in London staged an exhibition of clothes worn by Kylie Minogue on stage and in her numerous pop videos. It included costumes created by many of the world's leading fashion designers. The clothing worn by artists is important in the music industry, as costumes and accessories are central to a performer's image. Think of the white hooded jumpsuit worn by Kylie in the video for 'Can't Get You Out Of My Head' or the corset and feathered headdress she wore on stage during her *Showgirl* tour.

What image do you think Kylie Minogue has tried to create through her clothing? Has she been successful?

Kylie Minogue's costumes are integral to her image.

Case Study: Creating clothes for the stage

The way in which a costume is created may be different from the way everyday clothes are manufactured. Costumes may need to withstand heavy use. The design of costumes has to take into account the way in which a performer will need to move. Period costumes need to be historically accurate and some clothes may need to be **broken down** to make them look realistic on stage.

Large professional theatres will have a costume (or wardrobe) department whose job it is to provide everything worn by the performers on stage. This will entail making costumes as well as adapting existing stock and hiring clothing, shoes and accessories.

The Costume Designer

A costume designer must understand how clothing is constructed, and must have a good knowledge of period fashion. In the early stages of the production process the Designers – costume, set, lighting and sound – will meet with the Director to discuss the look of the production. The Costume Designer will then produce drawings of the costumes. The designs will have to be agreed by the Director before the costumes are produced.

The Wardrobe Supervisor and Cutters

Under the management of the Wardrobe Supervisor a team of cutters will convert the designs into costumes. This may involve a number of processes:

Suitable fabric(s) will need to be chosen for each costume, and may need dyeing before use.

A pattern for each costume will need to be created.

The pattern will then be pinned to the fabric and the individual pieces cut out.

The pieces are stitched together by hand or machine.

The raw edges of the seams may need to be **overlocked**.

Each costume will need to be tried on by the performer.

Alterations may need to be made to ensure each costume fits.

Decorative work such as beading and/or embroidery will be completed by hand or machine.

The costumes may need to be broken down so they appear realistic on stage.

What skills do you think a wardrobe supervisor and his/her team need to be successful? List personal and team skills as well as technique-related ones.

Broken down – The process of distressing or ageing new clothes to make them look worn or old.

Overlocked – The process of finishing raw seam edges to help the seam stay strong and prevent raw edges fraying when worn or washed.

Just checking

* Have you considered the wide range of artefacts, including scenery, props and costumes, that performing arts events often use?
* Do you feel confident that you now understand the detail required to create a performing arts artefact?

Planning artefacts for the stage

Before making an artefact for the performing arts, whether it is a costume, item of scenery or a prop, it is important to identify and plan carefully the stages of the production process.

Props

Props (or properties) are artefacts that performers use on stage. As a theatrical production is rehearsed, a list of required props will be established. It is the job of the Assistant Stage Manager (ASM) to assemble the required props. The ASM may make some of the props; others might be taken from stock, hired or made by the company's construction department. It is important that the list accurately describes the required props. A prop list may look like this:

Props List: 'Merlin the Great' Act One

Prop	Details	Source
Antique-style hand-held lantern	Must light up	Hire
Goblet	Cup-shaped with stem. Gold coloured decorated with jewels. Does not have to hold liquid	Construction dept to make
Decorative chest	With hinged lid. Approx 40cm x 25cm. Silver coloured and highly decorated	Construction dept to make
Scroll	Aged looking with ragged edges. Tied with red ribbon	ASM to make
Paper money	20 notes, old looking.	ASM to make
Book of spells	Large, approx. A4. Aged looking and highly decorated	ASM to make
Cauldron	Black with handle	From stock
Pocket watch	Gold with chain	From stock
Hand-held mirror	Round with handle	From stock

Materials

The materials needed for individual props will of course vary, however, a stock of commonly-used materials is useful for any props department. Many props are made from materials that would otherwise be discarded.

A stock of commonly used materials might include:

* Cardboard: shoeboxes and larger boxes made of corrugated card are always useful, as are cardboard tubes.
* Newspaper is very versatile as it can be used to protect working areas as well as for papier-mâché.

OVER TO YOU!

How would you begin to identify the kinds of scenery, props and costumes needed for a theatrical production?

* Scraps of fabric, beads, buttons, etc. can be used for decoration.
* Wire and wire mesh for creating structures.
* Plastic bottles, tubes, etc. are useful for making 'antique' goblets, vases and jugs.
* Plaster of Paris bandage can be used like papier-mâché.

A props department should also have a stock of adhesives, various types of paints and varnishes, as well as items like paintbrushes and hand tools.

Planning to make a prop

An ASM will generally make 'paper props' such as money, letters and other documents. The spell book listed would be made by the ASM who may plan its production as follows:

Materials	Tools	Health and Safety
Old hard-backed book (approx. A4); source from second-hand shop Fabric: dark green, crimson and black felt 'Jewels' emerald and ruby coloured String (sprayed gold) Black permanent marker Multi-purpose adhesive Varnish	Craft knife and cutting mat Scissors Paintbrush	Be careful when working with the craft knife; ensure I have plenty of work space around me. When using adhesive, ensure my working area is well-ventilated.

Using an old second-hand book will ensure the pages (which will only be seen at a distance by the audience) will be suitably aged. The cover of the book can then be covered in fabric and decorated. A final coat of clear varnish will ensure a durable finish. Before beginning to work on the book, a design for the decoration should be drawn on a paper template.

The template for the front cover of the spell book.

Activity

* Create a plan for the construction of the 'decorative chest' from the props list.
* Undertake some research into 'decorative chests' from the Middle Ages.
* Produce a design for the chest.
* List the materials and tools required.
* Identify any health and safety issues to be considered.
* Indicate how you would organise your workspace.

Just checking

* Do you feel confident with the level of detail and accuracy required in a props list?
* Have you considered a wide range of materials in your artefact plans?
* Have you considered how using different materials and tools raise different health and safety issues?

Creating artefacts for the stage

Once designs have been agreed and the materials that are needed are assembled, it's time for the props, costumes and scenery required for a production to be made. This is a time-consuming business and it is vital that deadlines are met so everything is ready for the opening night of the show. It is also important that production teams keep in touch with the Director in case any decisions impact on what they are making.

OVER TO YOU!

What decisions made during the rehearsal of a show or concert might change the requirements for scenery, props and/or costumes?

Case Study: Sarah

I work in the construction department of the North West Repertory Theatre. We make sets and large pieces of furniture in our workshop. The set designer begins by producing a scale model of the set. Once it is agreed with the Director a series of scale drawings will be produced for us to work from.

Health and safety is a really important consideration whenever we are working. We often work with large and/or heavy pieces of timber or other materials, so safe lifting techniques are essential. Working with hand and power tools can also be hazardous so the correct safety equipment, for example gloves and/or goggles, must be used.

Once a piece of scenery, a **flat** for example, is finished we then need to pass it on to the paint shop where the scenic artist will apply paint or textured finishes. This means we need to stick to the given deadlines to ensure everything is ready on time.

What would happen if Sarah's team were late in handing over their piece of scenery? Who would it affect and how? Write out the chain of events that might follow on from this initial delay.

Costume designs sometimes have to be altered during the making process.

Case Study: Kareem

I work in the costume department of the North West Repertory Theatre. We provide costumes for the company's various productions, normally three per season. At the moment we are working on costumes for *A Midsummer Night's Dream*. The costumes for the mortal characters are being adapted from existing stock. This leaves us time to work on the costumes for the immortals. The designs are complicated and require a lot of hand embellishment. Several costumes are heavily decorated with stones and crystals. This has caused problems because it has made some of the costumes very heavy. The Designer has had to make several adjustments to the designs, particularly for the costume being made for Titania. The Director recently decided that she is to be **flown** so the costume has had to be altered to allow it to fit over the flying harness the actress will have to wear.

All the costumes have to be ready for the dress rehearsal so the Designer and the Director can see them on stage. After the dress rehearsal it is not uncommon for alterations to be made – and these have to be done very quickly before the opening of the show. During **the run** I will be responsible for maintenance of the costumes, undertaking any repairs as necessary.

List all the issues that Kareem has faced so far on *A Midsummer's Night's Dream*. Detail exactly how you would solve each one. Could any of these solutions be adapted for problems you may face in your own work?

Flat – A timber frame generally covered in plywood, then painted or given a textured finish as a piece of scenery.

Flying – Many theatres have the capability to fly performers or pieces of scenery. A wire is attached to a flying harness that allows the performer to be lifted off the ground and moved around the stage.

The run – The series of performances of a show are known as 'the run'. Shows in the West End can run for months or even years.

Activity

Health and safety issues can crop up in all sorts of ways. Sometimes the problems are simple and can easily be solved, like putting up a 'wet paint' sign by freshly painted seats. At other times you will need to make awkward decisions, like asking for help from a busy technician because you don't feel confident in your abilities. Making the right decision will not only ensure you stay safe, but it will often improve the quality of the artefacts that you are working on.

* Danny needs to strip the paint off a large wardrobe to make it look older. What are the health and safety risks in this activity? What precautions should Danny take? List any specialist items he will need.

* Grace is adjusting some costumes when the sewing machine breaks. The Wardrobe Supervisor tells her to use the new machine, but Grace has never used it before. Are there any health and safety issues here? What would you do in Grace's position?

* During the dress rehearsal, three spotlights malfunction. It is late in the evening and Sean is tired from a long day. There are no other lighting technicians left in the theatre and he is asked to go up to check out the lighting rig. What should Sean do?

Just checking

* Describe how teamwork is important in the creation of artefacts for the stage.
* Why is it important to stick to deadlines?
* Why is flexibility important when reviewing your plans?
* What benefits does good communication between the Director and the production team bring?

Artefacts for the media

In this topic, we will look at creating artefacts in a media context. A station **ident** or **logo** for a television company could be considered 'artefacts'.

Why use logos and idents?

A logo is a design used by a company or an individual to identify itself and be recognised by an audience. It reminds a viewer that they are watching a particular station and helps to ensure that programmes are not pirated. The advent of satellite and digital television meant that a programme could be transmitted worldwide. Television stations now need to ensure that their output is not stolen or copied, so they embed a logo in the corner of the screen.

Logos can be created in a range of forms. They can be produced as a design that is attached to a backdrop or curtain. This is then included in a studio scene where the news is being read or a link being made. A reporter on location may have a microphone with the logo displayed to identify the station. The logo could be generated electronically and then added to the station output in the gallery.

Logos are designed by a graphic designer who has the skills to create a logo that will easily be recognisable. They have to consider the name of the station and the typeface that could be used. They will need to consider the colour scheme and size of the logo and how it will appear on screen. Designing a logo is a specialist job and the designer needs to liaise with the client to make sure the logo they design meets all their requirements.

Logos allow global recognition of a programme.

Logos and idents allow a viewer to recognise instantly the channel or programme they are watching.

Case Study: Media Productions

Media Productions provide news footage for small television stations. They have spent a considerable amount of money on training and equipping their staff. They have reporters who go out on location to film news stories and a studio team where all the items are edited and packaged for broadcast.

They sell their news packages to a range of television stations around the world. In order to ensure that their news material is not stolen or **pirated** they have a station ident that they insert in all their material. This means that they can monitor where their material is being used and can charge clients a fee for using this material.

Should news reports belong to any one organisation? Write down as many arguments as you can for and against the ownership of news reports.

The Creative Director at Media Productions received a **commission** to produce a series of news programmes for a client who wanted the programmes to be instantly recognisable. The Creative Director asked their in-house graphic designer to think about suitable ideas. To do this they:

* undertook a mind-map exercise and chose one idea
* developed this idea into a working model of the logo
* experimented with the design using hard copy and electronic versions
* presented this to the client and received feedback
* made some alterations to the logo after the feedback
* agreed the final design with the client and used it in the commissioned programmes.

Designing a logo for a charitable organisation raises particular issues – what might these be? Think about the intended audience of the charity news programme, how would they differ to, say, the audience of a national news programme?

Personal, learning and thinking skills

By identifying questions to answer in your research into logos you will be demonstrating skills as an Independent Enquirer.

Activity

Imagine you want to create a logo using the name of your school or college. This logo will be used for a school television news programme. You need to persuade your teacher that a logo is needed by producing an illustrated report:

Companies have used logos for decades to encourage customers to recognise and buy their brand, but how have logos evolved over this time?

* Choose a retail area to focus on, e.g. fashion, food or sport and include examples of these logos in your report.
* For each logo identify the name of the company and explain where each logo is used.
* Explain the purpose and say how and why it is appropriate.
* Analyse how one logo uses **font**, colour and design particularly effectively.
* Suggest how you could use a logo as an ident for the news programme.

Ident – The logo when used as an identification of a company on screen.

Logo – A graphic design device used to identify a company or product.

Pirated – Used by someone other than the person that made it without their permission.

Font – The style of text used in the logo.

Commission – A request to create or do something.

Medium – In media, the presentation form in which something is created.

Just checking

Consider the:

* **medium** for which the logo is being created, e.g. for print, television, a website
* constraints that each of these media has on the design, e.g. size, shape, colour, font
* name to be used in the final design, e.g. length, spelling, capitalization
* purpose/aim the logo needs to fulfil, e.g. to create a certain image for a company.

Planning a logo

Careful planning helps to ensure a logo is fit for purpose. A designer must consider the size and shape of the logo and the materials needed to make it. The logo must also be clearly visible on screen and not clash with the set or the presenters' clothes.

Choosing an idea

You should begin by producing a range of ideas for your logo, then trim them down to one idea that is effective and fit for purpose. The purpose of a logo can vary tremendously, for example, a brand new company might want to make a bold design statement outside their premises, or an old company might want to freshen up their image in their new TV marketing campaign. Whatever it might be, you must always keep the purpose in mind as you are working.

OVER TO YOU!

Choose two news or radio station logos. What design decisions do you think were made to ensure they were fit for purpose?

DTP package – Desktop publishing software, e.g. QuarkXPress or Microsoft Publisher.

Case Study: *Guthrie College Today!*

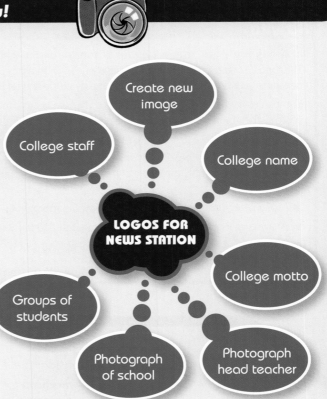

Yasmin has been asked to design and produce the logo for her college news programme, *Guthrie College Today!* She begins the planning process by meeting with the programme Director and the college Marketing Manager to find out the purpose of the logo and the different media it will be used in. They establish that the logo will be used as an ident in their news programme and on the newsroom backdrop, but also on posters which will go up around campus to advertise the launch of the news programme and on T-shirts that will be given away to viewers.

The Director does not have any firm ideas on the style of logo, but he suggests something bold and colourful to reflect the programme's cheerful and positive approach to news.

Can you clarify the purpose of the logo Yasmin must design in one sentence?

What points can you identify from the Director's brief which Yasmin will need to consider carefully in her design plans?

Yasmin now goes away to choose an idea and begin planning the logo design. She uses a mind-map to set out all her initial ideas.

She then begins to work through each idea to consider which are feasible and sensible and which are ineffective or cost too much. She narrows down her ideas to two: one using a black and white image of college students with the text 'GT Today!' in red, and one which just uses the name of the programme in a rainbow of colours 'Guthrie College Today!' Yasmin plans to use a **DTP package** to produce her designs, then to print them on to a selection of coloured papers to test how well the logos stand out. She is also considering having the logos printed onto coloured T-shirts before presenting the designs to the Director.

Do Yasmin's logo designs fulfil the purpose? How, or why not? Can you identify any problems in her plans?

Yasmin has realised she needs to make some careful plans before she starts work on her logo designs. She makes an audit document that lists the materials and resources she will need. This helps her to identify where materials are stored and highlights anything she needs to obtain:

Material required	Resources required	Where they can be found or do I need to buy them?
Coloured paper		Stored in the art department – see Ms Jones
	Computer with Photoshop	10 computers with Photoshop in IT lab – ask Ms Jones for a booking form
T-shirts		Need to buy – Ask Mr McRae about college suppliers

Yasmin then produces a production schedule that indicates when she will need to undertake tasks and any deadlines. She includes extra time early on to apply for permission to use photographs that are under copyright.

Finally she draws up a budget plan including the possible cost of materials and resources.

Budget		
Hiring a printer and equipment to print T-shirts	1/2 day @ £50 per day	£25
Cost of coloured T-shirts	5 at £4.99 each (white = £2.99)	£24.95
Cost of a memory card	1gig card @ £30 each	£30
Hire of computer	2 days @ £50 per day	£100
Copyright fee for photo	£100 for use in UK marketing material	£100
		TOTAL: £279.95

Yasmin's plans help her to realise she needs to reconsider her ambitious ideas to print her initial designs on T-shirts – it will be too time consuming. Her budget calculations also reveal she doesn't have enough money for T-shirts which might end up being wasted. Instead, she decides to present her logos on coloured paper which could also be used when considering T-shirt colours. The Director loves her rainbow-coloured design and they decide that a white background would be best to show off all the colours. It also reduces the cost of the T-shirts as white was the cheapest.

What would have been the result if Yasmin hadn't thought about costs or time constraints when designing her logo?

Functional skills

Using English...
* Use your speaking and listening skills in order to contribute successfully to group discussions when planning the production of a logo.

Using Maths...
* Use your skills to estimate the cost of your resources and materials and keep to budget.

Just checking

* Is the purpose of your logo clear and recorded for your process portfolio?
* Have you considered as many ideas as possible?
* Are your production schedule and budget plans thorough and precise?
* Have you listed all your materials and resources in an audit document?
* Remember to keep a copy of all plans and any revisions you make to them as you work for your process portfolio.

Creating a logo

Creating a logo is not as simple as merely creating a design. The many different ways a logo can be used means the production process is full of challenges. For example, you must consider how a television company logo will be seen on screen. Will the logo be fixed to a wall and therefore need to be made in card, foam or even plastic; will it be sewn into a backdrop and need to be created in fabric materials; or will it be electronically generated?

OVER TO YOU!

Find a range of logos from newspapers, magazines and other printed material. Mount them on a poster and by the side of each one put the name of the company that uses this logo. Identify why this logo has been used and see how it has been constructed. Is there a reason for the colours used, the font type and style or the way that letters and numbers have been intertwined? Discuss your findings with your classmates.

Creating your design

In order to create your logo you must first collect and check all the materials and resources you have planned to use. If you have problems getting hold of anything, make sure you refer to your contingency plans: what alternatives do you have? You may, however, make a conscious decision to change something. For example, suppose you had ruled out using 5cm deep foam because it was too expensive, but when you go to buy the 2cm foam, the deeper material is on offer. If it would make a big improvement to your finished piece, you have enough money and the time to alter your plans, then consider using it! Just make sure you keep a record of what you're changing and the reasons why in your production journal.

Testing your logo

It's essential to test your logo to make sure that it is fit for purpose – you would not want to have a logo on screen that did not work.

If your logo is printed on paper or fabric, try hanging it in a studio and setting up some lights to see how it works. It may be that the logo is too reflective and shines into a camera. The logo might not be colourful enough to be seen on camera, or it might be too big and overpower the scene, or too small and be lost in the background.

If the logo has been designed electronically you should try overlaying it on pre-recorded material to see how and where it should be positioned on the screen.

The design of logos is as diverse as the purposes for which they are created.

Activity

Test your logo in the ways suggested above. Do you need to make any changes, or could you make improvements? Consider:

* using a different grade of paper or card
* using stronger types of paint, ink or dye
* adding a flash of colour or a solid background behind your electronic logo to help it stand out.

Health and safety

Working safely at all times is a key consideration. This means that you must:

* use sharp tools carefully
* use glue and other bonding agents safely and only in well-ventilated areas
* use a computer with care – using a keyboard can cause repetitive strain injury and looking at a monitor for long periods can damage your eyes
* be careful when putting your logo on a backdrop or curtain
* get help if you are working with a ladder.

Remember that you carried out a risk assessment for a reason – put your safety first and make sure you follow your own plans and recommendations. It's easy to get caught up in the excitement and tension of the production process.

Personal, learning and thinking skills

In collecting resources and materials, then creating your artefact, you are showing yourself to be a Self Motivator. Completing a project is a big achievement, and if you can demonstrate other key skills along the way, such as being able to follow safe working practices and working to a schedule, then you should be pleased with your performance.

For your project

To create your logo successfully you will need to:

* create your logo using materials and resources imaginatively
* work to deadlines
* demonstrate that you can produce your logo confidently and with little assistance from your teacher
* pay close attention to detail making sure that your finished logo is fit for purpose
* reflect on your on-going work and make changes when you need to
* ask someone else to comment on your logo and then make changes, if necessary
* experiment with your logo to ensure that it is fit for purpose
* produce a final version.

Functional skills

Using English...

When you contribute to group discussions, use effective English to join in and contribute to the on-going review of the production process. You should be able to know and vocalise when changes need to be made.

You're more likely to take risks when you're under pressure to meet a deadline.

Just checking

* Are you working as creatively as possible?
* Have you planned to work safely?
* Have you allowed enough time to review your work and makes changes where needed?

Visual artefact

The ways in which other visual arts practitioners have created artefacts can tell you a great deal about successful methods to use when producing your own work.

Researching visual arts artefacts

There are lots of books, magazines and journals published about visual arts artefacts, as well as many exhibitions and collections of works available in museums and art galleries. You should use all of the information available and store what you discover carefully.

Practitioners in the visual arts always research carefully before generating ideas of their own.

Developing technologies

The materials and methods available to you today were not always available to artists and designers in the past. When we look at the work of **Impressionist** artists we can see that they painted many scenes outdoors. It was during the Impressionist period that paint-production technology advanced enough to allow the sale of ready-mixed, portable paints. Before this, artists had to blend their own paints in their studio using dangerous substances, like lead. This new development meant that they could work away from their studios for the first time. In this way we can see how the development of technology altered both how the Impressionist painters worked, and what they chose as their subjects.

OVER TO YOU!

The methods chosen by a practitioner to create an artefact are often heavily influenced by what is available to them at the time. What methods would you use today to create the artefacts listed below?

An image of the Queen
A glass bowl
A dress

Now consider how you might have tackled these tasks differently if you were living two hundred years ago.

Activity

Over time, the way in which printed posters have been produced has changed a lot. In the 1880s poster artwork created by artists such as Alphonse Mucha were reproduced using **lithography**, a process that involved using hand-operated presses. Now poster designers usually use computers to create their designs, and digital, mechanised presses to reproduce the work.

Write a list of the advantages and disadvantages you think digital and mechanical processes bring to poster production.

Visiting museums and galleries are an ideal way of inspecting and examining visual arts artefacts.

Case Study: Henry Moore

Charlotte has been given a grant by Arts Council England to produce a piece of work to stand in a new area of parkland in the heart of her local town.

As she knew the piece was to be placed in an outdoor environment, Charlotte began her research by looking at some examples of other outdoor sculpture pieces. She visited the Yorkshire Sculpture Park and took time examining the permanent pieces in the park, many of which had been outdoors for some time. She admired the pieces by Henry Moore and found that he often worked in bronze. Charlotte liked the way that this material had aged and decided she would use a similar medium for her work.

When she got home Charlotte gathered a collection of library books about Henry Moore and other sculptors who had worked in bronze. She read about the ideas behind Moore's work and learned a little about the process of **casting** bronze sculptures.

From her research, Charlotte learned not only of the successful methods used by other artists, but also what her finished work might look like after some time has passed. The decisions she made showed her that she needed to gain some further skills before completing her piece and she enrolled on a beginners' course in bronze casting to ensure she was able to put her plans in place successfully.

What is your research plan for your artefact? Where will you begin? Charlotte was inspired in the first place she began, but this is not always the case; what can you do to ensure you get the most out of your research opportunities?

Case Study: William Morris

Jenna is planning to produce a cushion for use on the set of a play which is set in the early 1900s. When using the internet to research this period of time, and the textiles that were popular then, Jenna found out about a designer called William Morris. She discovered that Morris was part of the Arts and Crafts Movement, which was the name given to a group of artists and designers who all believed in using hand crafts rather than machinery to produce their work.

She found that the Industrial Revolution had made Morris worry that everything would be factory made because machines made things faster and for less money. He didn't want hand crafts to be forgotten so he always used them in his work. From her research, Jenna noted down that Morris often used plant based fabric dyes in his designs and had his fabrics printed by hand. She investigated this further then when she planned to produce her product, Jenna felt confident to print her own fabric using vegetable dyes and wood blocks cut to her design.

Your research may take you in unexpected directions – Jenna was investigating design but ended up with valuable knowledge of a production process.

How fixed are your plans? Is there scope to improve them as you work?

Planning a piece of visual art

In this topic, we will look at planning artefacts in the context of visual arts. Successful visual artists work carefully through the stages of coming up with ideas, developing those ideas and planning their time. You will need to make sure that you do the same to ensure that you can work effectively during the production stage of your project.

Generating and developing ideas

Visual artists always store all of their planning work in one place to allow them to remain organised and so that they can refer back to the records they have of their thinking. A sketchbook or visual diary is the best place for this when working on visual arts projects. In it, you can record your ideas for how your finished artefact may look or operate in your book. You should also use it to store things that have inspired you as you have been developing your ideas; to make notes of decisions you have made and to test out the materials and media you are thinking of using.

Activity

See if you can identify what problems the creators of these artefacts may have when they begin production of their pieces.

* Ellie has been given three days to produce a textile throw as a prop for a stage play. She plans to decorate the three-metre-long throw with detailed hand-embroidery.

* David is making some ceramic pots for use in the garden of a local children's nursery. He chooses to finish the pots by embedding fragments of shells and pebbles into the surface of the clay.

* Pria has a very small grant of £50 from a local charity to produce a piece of sculpture for the entrance hall of their local office. She has chosen to produce the piece in bronze using a hired bronze-casting workshop.

Case Study: Aaron

Aaron has chosen to create a piece of artwork for an exhibition being held locally to raise money for the charity Water Aid.

He has begun some research into the theme of water in art and has found that he is attracted to the seascapes that he has seen other artists produce. Aaron takes his sketchbook with him on a family trip to the seaside and uses it to record some of the things he experiences while he is there. He includes found items such as seagull feathers, photographs he has taken, written notes and his own sketches. Recording all these things and keeping them together gives Aaron a visual reminder of the colours, themes, shapes and features he finds appealing about the sea. When he returns home, Aaron begins to experiment with different kinds of media and stores the results in his sketchbook too, **annotating** his work with comments and thoughts on the results of his experiments. Aaron's sketchbook can be seen on pages 218-219.

If you do not have access to the inspiration for your artefact then objects that evoke memories and emotions relating to that inspiration are invaluable. What objects could you collect that would help you relate closely to your own planned artefact?

Making plans

Visual artists need to plan carefully if they are to meet deadlines and produce work within a budget. If you were to work on your artefact a lesson at a time, your plan may look something like this:

Date	Activity	Complete by:
28th September	Receive task to create a sculpture on the theme of 'Identity' for upcoming exhibition.	Deadline date – 2nd November
28th September	Research the theme of 'Identity' using the internet, newspapers, CD-ROMs and journals. Find examples of sculptural work from different periods using books from the library.	29th September
30th September	Collect research work together and mount in sketchbook, noting what I have found and why I have included it.	1st October
1st October	Begin working on different ideas, using my research to help me.	8th October
8th October	Choose which idea will work best, discussing with others which ideas they prefer. Note the reasons for my choices down in my sketchbook.	9th October
9th October	Decide which materials I may need to use and find out how I will source them. Book some time in the specialist workshops to work on my artefact.	10th October
10th October	Gather my materials and begin making the wire frame for my sculpture.	15th October
15th October	Make the papier-mâché mixture I will be using to coat the wire frame.	16th October
16th October	Apply the papier-mâché to the wire frame, letting it set layer by layer.	20th October
20th October	Begin to paint my dried papier-mâché coated frame.	23rd October
24th October	Finish sculpture and prepare to present it.	25th October
25th October	Build process portfolio with all of the evidence I need to show stored in it.	1st November
1st November	Present my finished sculpture and process portfolio.	2nd November

Case Study: Jan

Jan is a professional jewellery maker who often works for clients who commission her to make pieces for weddings and special occasions. If a client asks her to produce a piece for a particular date, she cannot miss that deadline as it may lead to her not getting paid. If she does not complete the work on time she will not only have wasted her own time, but the materials she has used to work on the project.

Professionals cannot afford to miss deadlines, and therefore always carefully plan their work out and schedule their time efficiently.

Look at your own work schedule. Have you built in contingency? If not, now is a good time to consider doing so – it's always better to finish early than spoil a good piece of work by rushing.

Annotating – Adding comments and notes to a visual artist's own work and findings.

Just checking

* Is your working schedule realistic?
* Have you included contingency time?

Creating a piece of visual art

Visual artists often find that a variety of challenges arise when they are working on the production stage of their projects.

Preparing to work

Gathering your materials and equipment together and preparing the space you are going to work in is very important. If you are going to work efficiently and make good use of your time, then making sure you can work without worry about practical concerns is helpful.

You will also need to consider how you are going to ensure you will be working safely.

Working safely

It is always important to *use* the plans you have made about working safely with the materials and methods you have chosen.

OVER TO YOU!

The materials and processes used by visual artists can often be dangerous. Consider the following examples of materials and equipment used by visual artists and make a list of the potential dangers associated with each one.

A computer
Adhesives
Craft knife
Pencil

Case Study: Liam

Liam is working with ceramic materials for the first time. He has been carefully sculpting a figure using clay and, having finished this stage of the process, he needs to **fire** his work at a high temperature in a **kiln**. He has asked a technician who is skilled at using this equipment for his help.

The technician asks Liam to stand well away from the area. The technician wears protective clothing and goggles to shield himself from the intense heat coming from the kiln. After the time the figure needs to fire has passed, the technician puts the protective clothing back on. This time he gives Liam goggles to wear, in case the ceramic figure in the kiln has fragmented and pieces fly out of the kiln when the door is opened. He advises Liam to let the figure cool and rest before painting it.

Identify all the things Liam has done correctly to avoid any risk of being hurt during this dangerous process.

Activity

What would you need to do to make sure you are prepared to work in the following situations?

* You are going to be painting and the acrylic paints are in the store cupboard, your best brushes in your bag and the water jars by the sink.
* You are going to be using a hot glue gun in your work and there are bags and coats all over the desks.
* You have just finished sawing some wood for the construction of your piece and are preparing to varnish it.
* You need to use a can of spray glue to mount some paper to card for your project and you are in a small, busy classroom.

Making changes

Even when you have made careful plans and thought through your ideas, you may find that you need to make changes as you progress. Visual arts practitioners constantly review what they are doing and how they are doing it to make sure they are achieving their goals. Recording what changes you have made and why you made them is important later on in the project, when you must demonstrate that you have monitored your own work.

Case Study: Ben

Ben creates illustrations for a lifestyle magazine. He uses a digital illustration package on an Apple Mac computer. He is given briefs by the magazine's Editor to create images for use in particular sections of the magazine. Ben will often email rough drafts of his work over to the Editor for her to consider and make comments on. By asking for the opinions of those he is working with, as well as regularly examining his own work and making sure it meets the brief he has been given, Ben makes sure he is on track throughout a project. If Ben did not review his work or ask for the Editor's opinion he might find that he had spent a week working on an idea that the Editor didn't like.

When was the last time you asked for someone's opinion of your artefact? If it wasn't recently, make an effort to ask a teacher or another student to look at your work. If you have received feedback, what did you do with it? Make sure you keep notes of any feedback – good or bad – and more importantly, the action you took in light of that feedback.

> **Firing** – The process of heating, baking and setting artefacts made out of clay.
>
> **Kiln** – The oven in which pottery is fired.

Problem solving

Sometimes, even when visual artists have planned things carefully, unexpected things happen during the creation of artefacts. Whatever the problem, stay calm and consider your options carefully. Checking what alternative resources are available if you have a problem with the material you are working with is always a good starting point. Sometimes going back to research alternative methods or materials is the best thing to do if you find your plans aren't working.

Asking your teachers or other people for advice or help is also a good idea, as they may have had similar experiences to you. They may be able to share what they have learned to help you to make progress.

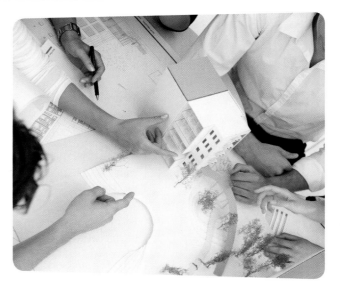

Sharing your experiences with others and seeking advice will benefit your work greatly.

Activity

Look at the problems that these visual artists are encountering in their work. Read each one carefully and consider the methodology and resources described. Can you suggest a solution for the problems?

* Luke is working on a project using images of flowers he has sourced from the internet. He realises he cannot legally use these images as they belong to someone else. What should he do?

* Kiara is producing a sculpture using plastic bags as one of her materials. She finds that the glue stick she has used to attach card and paper to her sculpture does not work with the plastic. What should she do?

* Amy is creating an artefact using textiles. She finds that the thread she has chosen keeps snapping as she uses it. What should she do?

Now consider how these problems might have been avoided at the planning stage. What should these visual artists have done before beginning work that they didn't do?

Just checking

* Have you considered the dangers your working processes and materials could pose to you and others?

* Who could you ask for help if things start to go wrong?

* What precautions could you take to help avoid as many problems as possible?

Preparation for assessment

In this unit you have taken part in the creation of an artefact from planning through to production. You may have worked on your own planning and creating, for example, a piece of sculpture or set of photographs, or you may have been part of a team of designers creating costumes for a theatrical production; in either situation, you must bring together two or more disciplines, for example textiles and 3D visual art.

Your portfolio

Your process portfolio will be expected to contain evidence of your involvement in your assignments. Your teacher may tell you what form your portfolio should take and how to present your work.

You will be assessed on...	This will be evidenced in your portfolio by...
...your understanding of the process of creating artefacts.	Your research notes. These may be notes taken in class as well as articles found in books and magazines or on the internet. You may also collect information by talking to professional artists about their work. Your presentation of your findings. This could be in written form or a talk, perhaps using PowerPoint slides. If you give a talk, remember to include the notes you use in your portfolio. **Tips for success:** • Keep a note of the title, author and publisher of any books or magazine articles you use. • Reference any passages from published works you use.
...your ability to plan the creation of an artefact.	A log or diary giving details of the work you undertook when planning the creation of your artefact. This should include notes on ideas and all rough work including drafts, sketches, ideas boards, etc. You should also include a production plan, which must give details of the materials and resources you intend to use, along with a schedule showing deadlines for each stage of the process. **Tips for success:** • Include all planning materials, even details about ideas that you eventually rejected.
...your ability to create an artefact.	The final artefact you have created. You should also include any prototypes or other experimental work you produce, as well as a log or diary giving details of the processes you undertook when creating your artefact. You may wish to include photographs taken at each stage of the process. **Tips for success:** • Write up a log entry at the end of every session, giving details of what you have done.
...your ability to monitor your creative work throughout the unit.	The documents in your portfolio. As well as providing evidence of your ability to plan and create an artefact, your log will also be used to assess your ability to monitor your own creative work during the unit. You may also be asked to complete a written evaluation of your work. **Tips for success:** • If you are working as part of a group, remember to personalise all documents that go into your portfolio to show your own contribution to the group's work.

The assessment of the unit

This unit is assessed by your teachers.

You must show that you:	Guidance	To gain higher marks:
…can undertake an investigation into the processes involved in the creation of a given type of artefact. …understand how artefacts are produced and the factors that influence their creation.	Think carefully about the topic you choose to research (your teacher will help). Try to use a range of resources when carrying out your investigations (not just the internet). You should think carefully about examples you use to illustrate your arguments.	Your research must be well-focused and your findings must be relevant. You must be able to explain the processes involved in the creation of artefacts, referring to well chosen examples. You should show that you have a good understanding of a wide range of factors that can influence the production of your chosen artefacts.
…can come up with ideas for the planning of the creation of an artefact. Can keep a record of the planning process.	Plan your work with care. Remember to check that all the resources and materials required will be available to you. Be prepared to make changes to your plans if you need to.	You must demonstrate a well-disciplined approach to planning your artefact. You must be able to come up with imaginative ideas and be able to explore them thoughtfully. Your must be able to plan the creation of your artefact with only occasional help from your teachers.
…can gather the resources and materials required and carry out your plans to create an artefact. …can follow safe working practices when working. …can work to schedules.	Make sure you have all the resources and materials you need before you begin working. Work safely. Check any health and safety guidance you have been given before beginning a task or operating a piece of equipment. Use your planning schedule as a checklist. This will ensure you keep your work on track and complete your artefact on time.	You must use your resources and materials with imagination, attention to detail and confidence. You must create an artefact to a high standard. Follow safe working practices at all times. Manage your time to make sure you meet all deadlines. You must be able to work with only occasional help from your teachers.
…know how to monitor your own creative work.	Review your progress regularly, not just at the end of the project. When describing the strengths and weaknesses of your work, give examples to illustrate your comments and try to include ideas for how you might be able to improve.	You must show that you have monitored your progress throughout the planning and creation of your work. You must show that you have used the monitoring process to improve your work and refine your ideas. You must show that you understand the strengths and weaknesses of your work.

4 RECORD

Introduction

A **record** can take many forms. From a diary to a photograph, an interview to a film, the success of a record depends on the appropriateness of the **medium** you choose. Whatever type of record you make, similar activities take place. You need to understand the medium you will be using and plan carefully to ensure the recording is successful. You should take an active part in the recording process and check that you have achieved what you planned to do.

The purpose of a record will influence the most appropriate medium to use.

Personal, learning and thinking skills

Monitoring your own activity as you plan and create your record, then shaping your ideas and modifying your work, are the skills of a Reflective Learner.

Your learning

In this unit, you should work across at least two of the disciplines on page 4 to cover the four main topics.

Understand how a specified medium is used to create a record

People use resources every day to record. For example:

✳ journalists use **shorthand** to record interviews

✳ sound recordists use microphones and recorders

✳ web designers use software tools to record images, text and graphics.

You must understand the medium you choose as your recording tool. This means studying examples of recordings in that medium from different periods in time. Your research also needs to consider recent stylistic and technological developments in your medium.

Ensure your technical skills are competent. If you want to use a camera you must be sure you can use it correctly. If you decide to record using a sketch, do you have the skill to make it accurate? If you decide to record an interview using a digital recorder, can you operate it?

Be able to plan the creation of a record in a chosen medium

Careful planning is an integral part of making a record. Professionals in the creative and media sector understand that planning can take up a major part of the time available for a project.

You will need to develop possible ideas and research them, choose the most suitable medium for your record, plan how you will make your record, prepare schedules and **contingency plans**, as well as considering copyright issues and keeping records of all your meetings, discussions and plans for your process portfolio. If you are working in a group you will also need to demonstrate good team skills and involve others at every stage of the planning process.

Be able to take part in or complete the creation of a record in a chosen medium

Once you are ready to begin creating your record, you will have to manage your resources carefully in line with your plans. If you are working in a group, everyone needs to do their job well and to communicate with each other. Keeping everyone up-to-speed on the making of the record is vital. A good team will talk to each other, discuss issues, find solutions and then put them into practice.

Working safely is also a key element of taking part, so you must be aware of relevant health and safety guidelines. It is essential to undertake a **risk assessment** before starting work.

Be able to monitor the creation of a record

Imagine writing a review for a major film magazine. You watch the film and then write your review. You do not read through your review before sending it by email to your editor. There are numerous spelling mistakes and you have the name of the male lead wrong!

You need to monitor what you are doing at regular intervals throughout the planning and production process, planned by you or your teacher. If you find that you are not achieving your aims, you must be prepared to make adjustments to your plans.

This topic is covered in the Monitoring and Reviewing unit.

Process portfolio

In your process portfolio for this unit you should make sure you have recorded and carefully stored evidence from all stages of your work.

You will need to make sure your portfolio includes:

✳ Your research and investigations – document what you find out about the medium you have studied. Include examples and notes on recordings in that medium, information about how the medium has changed over the years and how developing technology has affected it. You should also evaluate your own skills and identify areas in which you would like to develop.

✳ Your planning – you must keep a record of all activities undertaken during the planning phase of the project. This may include developing ideas, selecting a suitable medium to work in, working as a team and preparing schedules and plans. A personal log detailing your own contribution should also be included in your portfolio.

✳ Your record itself – if you are part of the performance team, e.g. a reporter or dancer, you will be part of the recording. If you are part of the production team, e.g. a sound recordist, you will be making the recording. You need to work together as a group and to document your activities during the recording by completing a personal production diary or logbook.

Record – Information set down in permanent form, e.g. a film, a music CD or a book.

Medium – In media, the presentation form in which something is created.

Shorthand – An abbreviated, symbolic writing method, used for speed.

Contingency plan – A plan that anticipates every eventuality or unforeseen circumstance and details solutions.

Risk assessment – A pre-production assessment of potential risks associated with the production and how these can be overcome.

Activity

List the recording resources you have in your school or college, for example: cameras – still and moving image; digital recorders; laptops and personal digital recorders (PDRs); desktop publishing software.

Add to this list:

✳ where the resources can be found

✳ if you need to book them

✳ how you book them and when they are available.

Keep this list in an appropriate format – this is your first record!

Remember!

✳ It is important to understand the medium you will use for recording.

✳ Careful planning is vital.

✳ Teamwork and reviewing work are essential.

✳ Health and safety must be considered when making a record.

4.1 Understanding different media

You can keep a record in many ways, for example, using the written word, a camera or an audio recorder. Keeping a record could also involve making a sketch, painting, completing a form or interviewing someone. These are all examples of a 'medium'.

Choosing a medium

Your teacher may decide what medium you are going to use to make your record, or they may leave the decision up to you. Either way, you should ask yourself these questions:

* Do I have the necessary skills to use a particular medium, for example, using a camera?
* How can I gain new skills if I need them?
* Will I have access to the equipment, materials and resources I need to create my record?

Investigating a medium

An important part of preparing to plan a record is investigating how others have tackled similar projects. Researching the work of others will help you gather ideas on how your finished record might look and help you when making decisions about methods and materials.

You can research other examples of records by:

* searching books, newspapers, magazines and journals for records of events similar to that which you will be recording
* using the internet to find the names of practitioners working in the field that you have chosen, for example, if you are going to be producing a photographic record of a gig, you could investigate music photographers
* talking to practitioners who use the materials and methods you have chosen and asking for their advice.

OVER TO YOU!

Thought shower – think of all the different types of media that you can use to make a record. Try to find examples of each one, and make a note of when and where it was used.

Use these ideas to make a shortlist of the media that you would like to use to create your record.

Personal, learning and thinking skills

You need to be able to demonstrate your skills as an Independent Enquirer. You can do this by investigating specific examples of records, then showing you understand these records through your notes and in discussion. You must also be able to explain and understand recent developments in your chosen medium.

Mark-making techniques – Artistic methods that involve making a mark on a surface using a tool or medium, e.g. pencil sketches, oil painting, pastel drawing.

Developments over time

In your investigations you should make sure that you are looking at examples from the past as well as the present day. The methods used to record have developed and changed over time, and understanding how things have changed and the impact this has had is important to your work on this project.

Use of visual records

Since very early times, humans have used visual images to record the changes that happen in their lives and events or things that are important to them. Cave paintings dating back to pre-historic times depict animals, which some believe may have had religious or ceremonial meaning to those who created them. This suggests that at a very early stage in human evolution people were creating visual images not just for decoration but to record things. Until the invention of photography in the early 1800s, all visual records were recorded using **mark-making** techniques. Throughout history we can see records of important events such as the coronation of royalty recorded by artists using media such as oil paint. Now many major events are captured using moving-image techniques or photography. However, there are still many uses for traditional visual art recording methods and some practitioners choose to use such methods as they believe they convey more of the mood and emotion of a situation.

The purpose of cave paintings is still a mystery, but they demonstrate the early use of visual images as a record.

Developments in technology

Developments in technology have broadened the variety and scope of record media. You can record and view using digital technology or through the internet. TV programmes are no longer available only through a television set, but as on-demand downloadable media files on the internet. The development of personal recording systems such as video, CD and DVD added a whole new dimension to the process of recording. For example, a film director can now show, not only his/her feature film on a DVD, but cinema trailers, interviews with the actors and mini-documentaries on production techniques to expand the 'record'. Audiences have become more demanding and more sophisticated in their use of technology, so it has never been easier to access a huge variety of records, through digital video players, home computers, mobile phones and the humble television set.

Functional skills

Using English…

Use your literacy skills to present your individual action plan and targets in written form. Make sure you write clearly and use organisational features such as bullet points and headings, where appropriate.

For your project

When you present your research findings you will have to summarise your information on creative and media activity and to demonstrate you are a good Independent Enquirer.

Improving your skills

You should undertake an audit of the skills you already have and the skills you would like to improve on. You can then create and carry out an **action plan** to make sure you are ready for your task. Use a **personal skills audit** like this to assess your skills:

	What can I do?	**What skills will I need to practise or improve when making my record?**
What skills do I already have in my chosen medium?	I have used a stills camera that used 35mm film.	I will need to practise using a digital camera and find out how to download the photographs on to a computer.
What experience have I had of working in this environment?	I've been involved in drama projects and staging performances, but I've always been behind the scenes.	I'll need to practise working with different lighting conditions. I'll need to have a list of all the important things to record.
What experience have I had of working on this subject or theme?	None	I need to find out what happens before the performance – how we get a good audience, what about reviews?

If you have not used this medium very much before then spend some time experimenting.

* Practise using different functions over a period of time, so that you are really familiar with them when it comes to making your final record.

You may be producing your record in a situation you haven't worked in before.

* If you are going to be based outdoors, have you considered what effect this may have on how you work?

* Spend some time practising your skills in similar environments to be sure you are aware of the preparations you may need to make and issues that might arise.

If you haven't produced records on a similar theme before, investigate what others have produced when faced with a similar task.

* Practise recording similar events or things and make notes of the techniques that work and those that don't.

* Ask others for their opinions so you can evaluate your work and consider constructive wcomments when carrying out your piece later.

Working in a group

If you choose to work in a group to produce your record you must:

* work together to explore a chosen medium
* produce evidence of your own collection of examples of records
* discuss and agree with your group the medium you want to use to create your record
* communicate with your group members

If you are working in a group remember to keep copies of all your own work and make sure that they have your name on them. Your process portfolio should reflect your personal contribution to the group work.

Action plan – A personal plan identifying skills to improve or learn, and how you intend to do so.

Personal skills audit – A list identifying the skills you already have and the skills you need to develop.

For your project

Find examples of recordings for your chosen area. To do this you should:

* find a range of examples of recordings and store them safely
* find examples from the past as well as the present
* look for examples of how the technology of producing these recordings might have changed.

You should put these recordings in a file and annotate them with your notes on:

* how these recordings were produced
* your thoughts on the quality, style and content of the recordings
* how you could produce your own recordings using these as a starting point.

Functional skills

Using ICT…

* Organise your work into logical files and folders on your computer or a data stick, and name your documents clearly. This will help you to find your work quickly.

* If you use images or text sourced from the internet or an interactive CD-ROM, make sure they aren't under copyright – or if they are that you ask permission to use them.

Activity

As a group, compile a list of the skills that will be needed to create a record using your chosen medium, e.g. the ability to use a camera and/or sound equipment; the ability to direct performers.

On your own, consider each of the skills and identify those that are new skills that you will need to learn, as well as those that are existing skills you will need to improve.

Draw up an individual action plan listing the skills you need to learn and those you need to improve, then set yourself a series of targets that show how you intend to develop your skills.

Just checking

* Have you researched how other practitioners have used different media to make recordings?
* Have you looked at how your chosen medium has developed over time? Has technology made a difference?
* Have you assessed your own skills and identified what you can do, along with skills you need to learn or improve?

Performing Arts Records

Music, drama and dance are 'live' forms of art. Today, however, the performance arts are primarily watched and listened to in recorded forms. When making a record of a performance it is important to understand the performance itself: the context and the creator's intentions, as well as the medium you are going to use to record it.

Changes in technology

Changes in technology have had a dramatic effect on how performance arts are recorded, and there has been a revolution in recent years in how we all access them.

OVER TO YOU!

Thought shower – think of as many ways as you can in which music, drama and dance productions and products can be recorded. Make a **mind-map** of all the media that you can think of. Group together the media you have identified that use technology and those that do not.

Radio drama

The first way in which drama was broadcast to the public was through the medium of radio. BBC Radio 4 still broadcasts regular plays, drama serials and comedy programmes. *The Archers*, a serial set in a rural farming community, is the longest running radio soap in the world at over 50 years.

Recording a piece of drama for radio is a very different process for the performers than recording a piece for television or film. Settings have to be suggested by sound and/or the dialogue of a scene. Writers and directors of radio drama need to take into account the fact that listeners cannot see the actors or the settings. If two characters are playing a scene in a kitchen, for example, the writer might begin the scene by having one character ask the other if he/she wants a cup of tea. The sound of the filling of a kettle and the clinking of cups added in the studio, along with the opening dialogue, will set the scene.

In the early days of radio drama, sound effects were created manually by someone with a table laden with materials that rattled, crunched and banged. Although live sound effects are still used in modern programmes they are commonly used side by side with pre-recorded effects.

✳ Listen to an extract from a piece of radio drama. How well do the sound effects 'set the scene'?

Live sound effects are still used in radio drama

Case Study: The rise and rise of the music video

In 1975 the group Queen released a single from their album *A Night at the Opera*. 'Bohemian Rhapsody' was a huge commercial success and is still regularly placed in surveys of favourite tracks of all time. It was promoted by what is considered to be a **pioneering** music video that went much further than merely filming the band performing the song: it created a series of visual images that complemented the style and feeling of the song.

By the early 1980s the music video had become a vital tool for popular music artists in the promotion of their work. Specialist music channels such as MTV revolutionised the music industry by **providing a platform** for the videos. Videos soon became art forms in their own right, rather than simply **promotional materials**, using a wide range of film-making techniques. The 1985 video for 'Take on Me' by a-ha, for example, used a mixture of live action and animation with a technique called **rotoscoping**.

Many successful film directors began their careers making music videos. Peter Gabriel's award-winning video for the track 'Sledgehammer' for example, was made at the Aardman Animation studio, the company that went on make the 'Wallace & Gromit' films.

Why do you think the music video became, and remains, so popular?

Can you think of a recently-made music video made that makes use of newer developments in technology?

Mind-map – A diagram used to display potential ideas.

Pioneering – New and original, never done before.

Provide a platform – To enable media to reach an audience.

Promotional materials – Materials that are designed to promote and advertise a product to the public.

Rotoscoping – An animation technique in which the live action frames are traced over by an animator, frame by frame.

Bluescreen – A technique for blending two images by making a colour in one of the images transparent so you can see what's behind it, as used in TV weather forecast reports.

Activity

Imagine you are intending to make a music video. As part of your research you need to view a range of examples from different periods, noting their key features. Choose three music videos from the last 30 years and write a report on them and their use of technology. Examine each one by asking the following questions:

* How do the visual images relate to the style of the music and the lyrics of the song?
* Does the video 'tell a story' or does it simply show the musicians performing the song?
* Has the video been shot in a studio or on location?
* Is dance featured in the video?
* Are any special effects used, e.g. animation or **bluescreen**?
* Who directed the video?
* Are you aware of any other work the director has done?

Functional Skills

Using ICT…
Your research could be presented using presentation software, such as PowerPoint.

Just checking

* Do you understand the medium you intend to use to record your performance?
* Have you researched a range of examples of recordings made in your chosen medium?
* Have you investigated recent developments in the medium you have selected?

Media Records

For the media arts in particular, technology has had a dramatic effect on creating records. Developments mean that you can now use a wide range of materials and tools to record your event.

OVER TO YOU!

Working with your group, identify a range of ways in which you could create a media arts recording. Put all these on a wall chart and include some illustrative examples to show how these records were created.

Choosing a medium

Choosing the medium you are going to use to create a record might seem easy. There are straightforward decisions to make, such as ensuring you can get hold of the equipment you need and determining if you can use it, but there is more to consider than this.

If you choose to make a video record, for example, you need to think about **cinematography**: you will need to plan a whole series of shots to tell your story, to understand the effect of camera angles and techniques, to write script and to edit your footage. A photographic record requires well-composed photographs, a technical understanding of lighting and the ability to create atmosphere through your shots. A sound recording requires attention to audio detail – being able to pick up differences in sound quality, considering the effects that recording in different locations, such as outside, might have. The best way to make a good decision is to investigate your preferred medium thoroughly at the beginning.

Looking at the medium

A great photograph requires careful thought and skill.

Case Study: Media Productions

Media Productions were approached by a company that wanted them to produce a documentary record of the traditional techniques they used to produce pottery. They still used the same techniques developed when the company started 100 years ago, and made all their pottery by hand.

The researcher at Media Productions looked at film archives, film libraries and the internet. She was then able to go back to the client with clear ideas about how their documentary record should be made.

If you were asked to produce a photographic record of your school, what would you do? Would you start by looking at current images or would you look for old images? Where would you begin your research?

Developments in technology

When you consider the best way to produce your record, you should think about the technology you will use to make it, but also the technology you could use to display or distribute it. For example, you could distribute your recordings on CD, DVD, hardcopy or on the internet.

Improving your skills

It's important to undertake an audit of the skills you already have and the skills you would like to improve on. You could use a personal skills audit form, such as the one on the facing page, to do this.

PERSONAL SKILLS AUDIT

Name: Jack Bundy

Project: British fashion designers – changing styles of male clothing since 1950

Medium: Photography exhibition

What skills do I already have in my chosen medium?	What skills will I need to practice or improve when making my record?
I have used a stills camera that needs 35mm film.	I will need to practice using a digital camera and find out how to download the photographs onto a computer

Working as a team

Case Study: Media Productions

The team at Media Productions hold regular production meetings and discuss the work that they have to produce.

Everyone has a voice in these meetings. In this way everyone feels they have a part to play in the production of the product. In the recent documentary for the pottery manufacturer, the client requested a shot of the pottery being fired/baked in a kiln. At the production meeting it was decided that the temperature in the kiln would be too high for a camera. However, one of the team had recently read an article about a camera that could withstand high temperatures. He was given the job of researching this and where one of these cameras could be hired.

How will you ensure that each member of your group has a chance to take part?

How will you communicate with your group members?

Why is it important to work together as a team?

Activity

Choose two one-minute clips from different films. Try to choose one new film and one older than 40 years. For each clip, write out a list of the shots it contains, the characters in each shot, what they are doing and what they are saying.

Compare your two lists. What differences can you see in the styles of the film-makers? What similarities are there?

How has this activity made you feel about the medium of film?

Cinematography – Everything involved in the process of making a film.

Activity

* In order to understand the medium you have chosen you must:
* Find examples of media records, e.g. videos/DVD/audio recordings/websites.
* Create a file of these media records and annotate them with your notes on:
  a) the date these media records were made
  b) how you think they were produced (e.g. by an individual or team, the technology used)
  c) your thoughts on the media records (e.g. quality, style, content, colour)
  d) what constraints might have affected their creation (e.g. technology used, time they were made, social issues, etc.)
  e) how you might use these as examples for your own media record creation.
* Your file must be collated and presented with an index.
* You could show some or all of your evidence in a presentation. If so, you must create a presentation for an audience, produce handouts, prepare presenter notes and be prepared to answer questions at the end.
* You may be able to present some or all of your research work in a video or audio format.

Just checking

* Have you considered past and present examples from the medium you have chosen?
* Have you identified the skills you have and the skills you need to gain to use your chosen medium?
* What developments in technology has your chosen medium seen?
* Do you understand the requirements of teamwork and individual work within a team?

Visual Arts Records

There are many ways that visual artists use their skills to make a record of events, people, places and objects. Using visual arts techniques to create a visual record of something that has happened is something that has been done throughout history.

Choosing a medium

Whether your teacher decides which medium you will use in creating your visual record, or whether you decide for yourself, you must consider carefully *how* you will need to use this medium whilst you are working. The media used by visual artists can often be messy and require specialist materials and equipment. Think carefully about the environment you will be working in and consider whether you have chosen the most suitable method to create your record.

OVER TO YOU!

In many situations visual images are used to record things that are actually happening. Look at the list of events below and see if you can identify how many different methods might be used to record what is going on.

The growth of a flower
A street performance
Motor-racing

Case Study: Paula

Paula works as a sketch artist for a news agency and attends court cases to produce a visual record of the proceedings.

Many high-profile court cases are held in a closed court, which means that television and stills cameras are not allowed in to the courtroom itself. Paula attends and makes sketches in pencil and pastels to make a visual record of what is happening for use in newspapers and in television news programmes. These are then used to provide some visual information for viewers and readers, to accompany the information given about the case.

A good artist can create a very realistic record of a suspect. Why then not just take a photo? Debate the reasons for and against each of the media of sketch, photography and film for use in the courtroom.

Court sketches are used to portray scenes that can't be captured using photography or film for legal reasons.

Investigating other examples of records

Finding out what other artists and designers have done in the past to create records similar to yours will help develop your own skills. You should think carefully about what may help you as you search:

* Consider looking at the work of visual artists who have worked in media similar to those you might use. Even if they have chosen a different theme or situation to record, it will help to look carefully at how they have worked.

* Consider scenes or themes similar to those you are looking at, as well as those exactly the same. For example, if you are intending to create a record of a garden at a particular time of year, it might be wise to look at the ways in which other artists have captured gardens in different seasons too.

* Make sure you make good use of all research opportunities. The image search on an internet search engine might seem like the easiest route to take, but often looking through a book on a similar theme to the one you are looking at will give you a much more varied range of images more quickly.

Developments in visual arts records

The history of visual arts offers enormous scope for research; visual arts have been around for thousands of years, methods have grown and changed, died out then been reincarnated, and of course brand new media have been created. Enjoy the voyage of discovery as you carry out your investigations. If you choose to use photography, explore how the method of capturing photographic methods has changed from the early use of **glass plates** right through to modern digital cameras and image processing. Those using mark-making techniques should consider the developments that have shaped the way images are recorded. You could look at how the developments in paint production in the mid-1800s allowed **Impressionist** artists to work outside for the first time, and how modern 3D imaging software can be used to turn a sketched record into a digital recreation of a place.

Improving your skills

Once you have chosen the medium for your records, you will need to evaluate your practical skills. Consider all aspects of this and take the action necessary to make sure you are ready for your task.

Developing your skills with a medium	Spend some time experimenting with your chosen medium in a sketchbook. See what effects and different looks you can achieve by applying it in different ways, see how it develops over time, seeing how well it sticks to different types of paper, card and other materials.
Producing a record in an environment new to you	Practise using your medium in a range of different environments, including the one you think you will be working in when you create your record. This will not only improve your skills of using this media, but also prepare you for the challenges you may face when producing your record.
Broadening your experience	The more experience you have of working on creating visual records, the better the quality of your finished record will be. Practise using the medium and methods you have chosen to create visual records of other objects, people or situations, as this will develop your own skills and abilities.

Activity

Imagine you have been given the following briefs. Using suitable research methods, find three examples of visual records on the following topics made by other people that would help you develop your ideas for this project:

* someone laying the foundation stone for a building
* the skyline of a local city
* a family on holiday.

Personal, learning and thinking skills

Make sure you support the conclusions you draw from your research into the history and development of a medium by making clear arguments and providing sound evidence. This will demonstrate your skills as an Independent Enquirer.

Glass plates – The glass plate process was used in early photography. Glass plates were coated with chemicals, known as silver salts, that were sensitive to light.

Impressionist – An artistic movement in the nineteenth century.

Just checking

* Have you thought about the many ways to use visual imagery to record events and objects before making your final choice of medium?
* Have you found out what other artists and designers have done in the past to create records similar to yours?

OVER TO YOU!

Thought shower – your group has decided what is being recorded and the medium to be used, but what decisions need to be made before you can begin work?

Making careful plans will help to ensure that your record of an event or object is clear and accurate. Planning can reduce the risk of things going wrong when you are in the process of creating a record, allowing you to concentrate on effectively capturing the essential information.

Where do you get your ideas from?

When working on a creative project, it is important to begin with a number of ideas. Collecting images or records that have inspired you, or helped you consider how you will approach this project, also helps you stay focused on what you are working towards. Find subjects similar to the one you will be recording and develop different ideas for how you could produce the record. This will allow you to explore a range of possibilities before deciding which one will be the most appropriate for your work.

Researching and choosing ideas

When you are researching a few ideas, consider the purpose of the record and the skills that you (and your group) already have or would like to learn. You will have to consider the resources that are available to you and the time you have to complete the work. Try using a mind-map to help you plan all the things that you need to capture. This will help you to decide whether you will be able to achieve a workable and accurate record.

Personal, learning and thinking skills

As you generate and develop ideas for your record you will be showing your skills as a Creative Thinker. The better you plan and document your record creation, the easier it will be to see your creative thinking skills.

Budget – A planned account of what you will be spending, including the things you plan to buy or hire and any money that you have to pay to others for their time.

Audit document – Lists of materials and resources you need to make your record.

Portraits · Fashion show · School play · A day in the life of a school · Photograph of head teacher · Still life · Wildlife · **RECORD USING A DIGITAL CAMERA**

When you have constructed your mind-map, you can then begin to look at each idea. Try to see if each one is feasible and sensible. Discount ideas that would be ineffective, cost too much or are not happening when you need to complete your work. Try to come up with one idea that would really work as a record.

Developing ideas

You should practise using the materials you have chosen and the methods you will be employing. Record your experimentations, as well as your thoughts on what you find, perhaps within a diary or log. Consider looking at subjects from different angles, in different lighting and, where appropriate, different surroundings and make note of what you think about your ideas.

Time is money

Creative and media projects can run on huge **budgets** or very small budgets, but they always seem to be on a tight schedule. Making sure that you know what you need, how much things cost and when you need to do things will really help you.

Don't forget to think about all the things that could go wrong and plan for them in advance in a contingency plan!

Don't leave it too late to book resources or you might miss the opportunity to make your record!

Planning

The first thing you need to do is ensure that you have the materials and resources to produce your record. You should undertake an audit to check that you have these available. You could use an **audit document** like the one below that will allow you to write down where materials are stored and if you need to obtain resources.

Materials required	Resources required	Where they can be found or do I need to buy them?
Digital camera memory card		Might need to buy own – check with Mr Roberts, IT department
	Photo printer	Located in IT lab – ask Mr Roberts for a booking form

Royalties – Payments to an author or creator, usually a percentage of your profits.

Artists have the right to control the way their work is used.

Preparing a schedule

Producing a schedule that shows what will happen, and when, is highly advisable. If you are working in a group then you should also add who is doing what so there is no confusion. It is important that you are fully prepared as, when making a record of something that is actually happening, you may not get a second chance to capture the event. If you are ill-prepared you may be surprised by events that will stop you being able to capture the record you wanted to.

Preparing a budget

You'll need to think about the money that you have available for making your record. Consider:

* the cost of materials
* labour or hire costs
* fees you may need to pay to others, such as copyright permissions fees.

Contingency plans

When working in situations where things may happen that are beyond their control, all creative and media practitioners make careful arrangements for how they will deal with changes to their plans. Working outdoors may mean you have to make alternative arrangements in case of bad weather. Rain in particular could damage equipment, spoil any paper-based work you have with you and, if it is also cold, may be damaging to your health. Making plans for what you will do if something that could happen actually does, is key to ensuring success in your project.

Legal and ethical considerations

Copyright laws protect those who create music and lyrics, dramatic works such as plays and musicals, sound recordings, as well as books, magazines and TV programmes. Whoever creates a published work has the right to control the way in which their material is performed, recorded, adapted and broadcast to the public.

Ethical considerations mean thinking about things which may be considered unfair or unjust to other people. It would be unethical to copy someone else's work very closely without giving them any credit for their work.

It is therefore vital that if you intend to use a copyright piece during a public performance or broadcast, you seek permission before using it. Permission is normally applied for through the Rights department of the publisher of the work. This should be done early in the planning process to ensure permission is granted before production begins. A fee or **royalties** may have to be paid, particularly if the project will make money.

Keeping everyone on track

The planning stages of a project will inevitably involve meetings and discussions. It is vital that all meetings are well organised to make the best use of the available time and to ensure that all the important issues are discussed and actioned. A good way to keep a meeting on track is by producing an agenda in advance and distributing it to those involved. This ensures that everyone comes to the meeting with the necessary materials needed, knowing what is and isn't going to be discussed.

Communicating with others

Regular communication with the others involved in the subject of your record is very important in helping you plan effectively.

If you are recording an event you will need to know:

* who is to be involved
* the dates and times of events happening
* how other people are travelling to and from the event
* what the organisers or those involved in the event feel it is important for you to capture
* where you will be able to work and how this might affect others around you
* what health and safety considerations you may need to make in order to work in this way.

Activity

Think about the audio recording of the school debate on healthy eating discussed on page 121.

* Draw up a schedule showing each stage of the process of planning and developing such a record.
* Make a list of individual roles and responsibilities during the planning and development phase of the project.
* Include deadlines for completion of individual tasks.

For your project

The project: Once you have decided what you are going to make a record of, you need to be clear as a group about the aims of your record. These aims will influence the way you plan and style your project and affect all the decisions you make. Think carefully about what you are trying to achieve. Is your record intended to entertain, educate and/or inform?

Your role: You should be clear about what is required of you individually. You will have identified the skills you need to work on, so make sure you fulfil the requirements of your action plan. If you are part of the record, you should research your role carefully. If you are taking on a role such as director then you must also be clear about what your duties are and what you are responsible for. A good team member is able to carry out their own role but is also aware of what is going on elsewhere, helping to make sure that everything is running smoothly.

Just checking

* Have you thought of a range of ideas?
* Did you decide as a group which idea would be most appropriate?
* Have you begun to create your schedules and budget carefully?
* Are you keeping accurate planning documentation safe in your project portfolio?

Planning a performing arts record

The creation of any record of a performance activity, from a play to a music video, must begin with development and planning activities. If you are intending to work in a group you must decide who you are working with so you can begin developing your ideas.

Developing your ideas

It is important to contribute ideas as individuals to your group, but you must discuss them with the best interests of the group at heart. Disagreeing on and debating ideas is all part of group work but, once a group decision has been made, then everyone needs to accept and support that decision wholeheartedly.

Communicating with others

OVER TO YOU!

What roles and responsibilities are associated with creating a record of a performance activity on film or through sound recording?

Narrative – A story.

Abstract – Not intended to tell a story or to represent particular ideas.

AOB – Any Other Business – a final agenda item that allows people to raise last-minute issues.

Minutes – A record of what is said and by whom in meetings.

Case Study: Seafarer

Our group, Seafarer, has been together for three years and we have just released a three-track CD with a small independent record label. We were keen to make a video to accompany one of the tracks and were lucky to be given a small budget to produce one for the title track, 'Never Say Goodbye'.

The song is a slow ballad about the feeling of regret when a relationship has ended. Before we began to work on the video we met with the Director and discussed three possible ideas:

* Using an empty windswept beach as a setting with the band playing on the sand and shots of a girl walking in the dunes under a stormy sky.

* A **narrative** video featuring the development of the relationship and the eventual break-up using members of the group as actors.

* A more **abstract** approach with a mix of images of people moving away from each other.

* In the end we opted for the first idea for the following reasons:

* It could be made within the budget we had been given.

* We felt it was important for the band to feature prominently in our first ever video.

* The beach setting links with the name of the band.

* The stormy sky illustrates the way the singer is feeling inside.

Do you think the band have chosen the most suitable idea for their video?

Now that the band have made this decision what should be their next steps?

Production meetings

In the performance arts disciplines, production meetings are often used throughout the life of a project to make sure that everyone knows what is going on, and what needs to be done.

The more 'takes' required, the more it will cost you.

Memo

To: Radio Drama Production Team

From: Radio Drama Production Manager

Subject: Production Meeting Fri 7th Sept 10 a.m.

Would all members of the Production Team please ensure they prepare for next week's production meeting.

Agenda

- Discussion of script: Writers please have final draft ready to show us so we can distribute it to cast in time for a read through on Tues 11th Sept.
- Sound effects: Sound Designers please report on work carried out so far – please bring all samples collected for discussion.
- Incidental music: Composers please bring examples for group to listen to.
- Recording schedule: we need to finalise the schedule so we can book the college studio.
- AOB

It is also vital that records of decisions made during meetings are kept. You could take turns to write **minutes** during each meeting.

Time is money

For the performers involved in the creation of a record, the planning phase of the process will include rehearsals. It is vital that whatever is to be recorded is well-rehearsed before the recording process begins. Recording schedules in the performance arts industry are often tight, and producing a film, video or audio recording is expensive; often involving the hire of costly equipment and facilities, as well as the employment of artists and technicians who will be paid by the hour. It is therefore important that time is not wasted by performers who are under-rehearsed. Make sure that the piece of drama, dance and/ or music that you are planning to record is rehearsed to performance standard before the recording process begins.

You can make sure you have had enough time to rehearse by drawing up a detailed production schedule well in advance. This needs to include what should happen, who is needed, what they should do and when this should happen. You will also need to think about the materials and resources you will need.

Functional skills

Using English…

* Use your speaking and listening skills in order to contribute successfully during production meetings.

* You can also use your literacy skills to produce clear, organised agendas, and for writing up decisions made at meetings.

Activity

The Production team and the Performance team both need to be equally organised.

* Thought shower a list of every possible stage for your chosen type of record for each team.

* Cross out anything that your particular record won't be doing.

* Add in anything extra or unusual that your record will be doing.

* Prepare a draft schedule with two columns – one for Performance and one for Production

Just checking

* Did you consider several ideas before choosing the one that was most appropriate to your project?
* Have you considered any copyright permission you may need?
* Have all your meetings and discussions been properly documented?
* Have you drawn up a production schedule?

Planning a media record

Careful planning of a media record is essential. You will be using valuable equipment and expensive resources to make your record. You must be sure that you have everything you need when you need it. It would not be good practice to decide to make a media record and then not make plans for producing it in the most effective way.

Choosing an idea

You should think carefully about the media record you intend to make. A good place to start is by recording a range of ideas in a mind-map. You have seen how a mind-map works earlier in this topic. Discuss and discount your ideas until you have one that you think will really work.

Working to a commission

Case Study: Media Productions

The team at Media Productions have been **commissioned** by a national charity that works with young people with a drug habit. The charity has a range of publicity material that is out-of-date. They need to make this material appropriate for young people. Media Productions have to think of suitable ideas for the publicity material and **pitch** their ideas to the client.

What questions would you need to ask the client before you could decide:

✱ What medium would be most suitable for the publicity material?

✱ What kind of images to use?

What kind of media record do you think would be best for this publicity material?

Applying techniques

Once you've chosen an idea you can begin to plan the creative detail, including the different techniques you might use when producing your record. This could involve:

✱ using a range of different equipment

✱ choosing a range of shots, angles, text or graphics

✱ producing work in black and white and colour

✱ using **flashbacks**, fade to black, **montage**, sound effects

✱ producing **diegetic** and **non-diegetic** sound.

You should consider a wide range of possibilities when choosing the techniques you will use for the production of your record. This will help your record to be innovative and creative. Think carefully about the techniques you know about and the techniques you would like to learn about and use.

Commissioned – To be asked to create or do something.

Pitch – The process of selling a proposed idea to a client.

Flashbacks – Shots that take you out of the main story and back in time to show an important event.

Montage – Selecting and joining sections of film to make a continuous whole.

Diegetic sound – Sound whose source is visible on the screen or implied by the action of the film, e.g. the voices of characters or a door slamming.

Non-diegetic sound – Sound whose source is neither visible on the screen nor implied by the action, e.g. a narrator's voice or the musical score.

Proposal – A document that outlines an idea to client.

Treatment – A document that develops the proposal and provides more detail about the production, e.g. timescale for production, budget and script/storyboard.

Planning for production

Case Study: Media Productions

The team have agreed on the type of media product they are going to suggest to the client. They have written a **proposal** that sells the idea and are now going to pitch this to the client.

A pitch is the media process of convincing your client that you can produce the media product they want. To do this media companies make a presentation to the client. The pitch will be accompanied by a proposal that the client has seen before the pitch takes place. Once the client has agreed to the proposal, then they may ask for a **treatment**. The treatment is a development of the proposal and contains all the details about how the product will be produced.

In this case the team at Media Productions successfully pitch their proposal and develop a treatment. The treatment will allow the production team to think about the resources they will need and how they plan to make the product.

For the type of media record you chose in the case study activity above, create the pitch that Media Productions might have made to secure the commission. What persuasive techniques might they have used? Try to apply the persuasive skills you learnt in your English lessons.

Personal, learning and thinking skills

By asking questions you are extending your thinking. This makes you a Creative Thinker.

Pitching an idea successfully requires skill.

When you are drafting your production plans, make sure you consider things like whether you will want to get some feedback on your record during the production process. You might find it useful to show a scene of your film, or play a few minutes of your audio to a small group of your target audience. You can then make sure you're creating the right kind of record, or make adjustments if their feedback isn't entirely positive. This type of activity needs to be factored into your plans right from the beginning so you can make sure you film/record the right part first.

Budget

An important part of your record, whether you need to pitch the idea or not, is how much it will cost to create. It is not sensible to try to pursue an idea that will cost more money than you have available. You will need to consider:

* the cost of resources, e.g. hiring cameras
* the cost of materials, e.g. DVDs
* copyright costs, e.g. using a song as a soundtrack to your film.

You must carefully budget for the production of your record. It would also be sensible to include a 10 per cent contingency fund in your costs.

Activity

Think about a media product that you could video record. This could be a school production, a special event or a promotional video for your school. Make an audit document to list the materials and resources you would need to produce a media video record and identify where they can be found.

Just checking

* Have you considered a range of media before choosing one which best fits the record you want to make
* Could you confidently justify and explain your choice of medium and record topic?
* Have you calculated the costs of your project accurately?

Planning a visual arts record

Visual records of events, people, places, objects or situations can happen in many different situations and environments. One of the key stages of creating a visual record is the planning of your activity and preparation of yourself, your materials and equipment.

OVER TO YOU!

Make a mind-map of the things you may need to consider if you are going to be working outside. Think carefully about how it might be different to working in a studio and what impact these factors might have on how you work and what you produce.

Developing your ideas

You may find it helpful when developing your ideas to practise using your chosen materials and the methods you think you will be employing. You could record your experimentations, as well as your thoughts, in a sketchbook; include anything that inspires you: visual images, artefacts, sample materials, etc. It's also a good place for your research on other similar records or subjects, and for analysing how this research affects – and helps to develop – your ideas.

Communicating with others

It may be that you are making a record of what a place or person looks like at a particular time. You will still need to make arrangements about when you will carry out your activity and inform those involved what your work will demand of them. If you are intending to make a record of something that is the private property of someone else, then you may need to ask for permission to make that record. If your subject is a person, you will need to communicate with them about the way you will use their image and what their expectations of the project may be.

Selecting materials

When considering the event, situation or objects you intend to make a record of, you need to consider what will be the most practical technique to use. If you are going to be outside with restricted space, you may want to keep the kit you take with you to a minimum, so using a wide variety of coloured paints may not be practical. Likewise, if you are attempting to capture photographs of a high-speed event, you will need to consider what kind of camera you will use, perhaps choosing one with a fast **shutter speed** or a burst mode which will take several shots very quickly, one after another.

Visual artists need to be prepared in order to capture what might be 'one-off' moments.

Case Study: Saskia

Saskia hears that a local art group have planned a trip to a sculpture park. The group want to make a record of their visit and ask Saskia to come along and make a visual diary of the event. The diary is to include sketches of the members of the group as they admire the sculptural work. Saskia initially plans to work in charcoal, knowing that she has used that in the studio and can work quickly using it. However, when she does a test run, sketching passers-by in her town, she discovers that the charcoal transfers off the paper easily, causing smudges when she transports her work between the location and her studio. She decides instead to use pencils of different grades for her work, possibly adding colour with oil pastels where time allows.

What alternative materials could you consider using if your planned medium doesn't work?

Contingency plans

You should always try to be prepared for unexpected events when working on creating a record. Visual artists must ensure that they have the following areas covered when making their contingency plans:

* Medium – have you got spare, back-up or alternative forms of the medium you have chosen to use in place, should you encounter any practical problems with it?

* Equipment – do you have spare or alternative forms of the equipment you will need? Alternatively, do you need to bring any tools to fix or alter the equipment you are going to use, should you need to?

* Environment – do you have plans and the right resources to deal with changes to your expected environment? Are you prepared for bad weather, poor light or a hot/cold climate?

Case Study: Daniel

Daniel works for a local newspaper and has been asked to photograph a street carnival happening in the town. When making arrangements with the organisers he makes sure he has all the details about where the event will take place, what time the processions are expected to happen and which floats may be the most interesting to shoot. Daniel checks the weather forecast the day before the carnival and sees that light rain showers are expected throughout the day. Aware that his expensive camera could be damaged by water, and keen not to risk getting wet himself, Daniel packs a large umbrella and a waterproof coat, and makes sure his kit bag is waterproof before setting off for the day. Later, as the procession is in full swing, a short burst of rain falls to halt the carnival as those involved continue to dance through the rain. Daniel and his camera, however, are fully protected by the kit he had prepared during his contingency planning.

The weather can really affect your project – and your spirits – think about how you could plan for different weather scenarios.

Shutter speed – The speed at which a camera takes a photo.

Activity

Make a contingency plan for each of the following scenarios. Consider what you would need to prepare in advance to make sure you could deal with this situation effectively:

* You are going to produce a drawing of a glass-blower working in his workshop. When you arrange the session the craftsman tells you that he works in an outhouse without central heating.

* You are working on a painting of a local park. The weather forecast is for rain.

* You are photographing actors in a three-hour variety performance. You know your camera battery will last about three hours, but you aren't sure.

Just checking

* Have you considered the part communication needs to play in your project?

* Are your materials and equipment the most appropriate for the task you have to fulfil?

* Do your plans include contingency arrangements??

4.3 Taking part in the creation of a record

After investigating how other practitioners have worked on similar projects and planning out your activity, you're actually ready to make your record. It's important that you follow your plans carefully and that you use the information you have gathered from others involved in the project.

Getting ready

Gathering resources

First, make sure that the materials you have identified within your planning are ready for you to take with you when you begin work on your record. Next, make sure you have arranged suitable methods of carrying your materials or equipment. If you need someone to help you transport your materials, you should organise this in advance.

Pre-production meeting

You may find it helpful to have a pre-production meeting and run through your schedule to ensure everyone knows what they are doing and when. Even if you are working on an individual project, it is a good idea to go through your plans step-by-step.

Working in a group

Communicating and cooperating with others

If you are working in a group to produce your record, you need to communicate effectively with your group members. If you plan to produce your record on a particular day then everyone should have made themselves available to be involved in the production process. You must think about:

* the way that you talk to each other
* how you work together to produce the record
* considering other people's views
* being able to take direction from other people.

Teamwork is all about working together to produce a finished record. It is also an opportunity to share experiences, discuss issues and review work in a **collaborative** way.

Liaising with others

It's a good idea to make contact with the people you have been communicating with during your planning when you start recording. If it is an event, introduce yourself to the organisers and explain or confirm the arrangements you have previously made. Making sure that the people involved in the event are aware of who you are and what you are doing will avoid any confusion as you work. It will also give them an opportunity to notify you of any last-minute changes that might affect your work.

If you are making a record of a person, you will need to make sure they are aware of what you are expecting them to do and what they can expect from you.

When working on recording something that belongs to someone else, you will have obtained permission to do so. When arriving at the place you have arranged to work, make sure you alert anyone in charge to your presence and can show him or her details of the arrangements you have made.

Health and safety

Being aware of what you need to do and how you need to behave in order to be safe in your work is very important. It is of particular importance that you check the health and safety requirements of your location before you begin work. Being aware of your own safety and the safety of others around you will help you to ensure you are successful in completing your task.

You may have to wear protective equipment in some locations. Some people will require you to talk to them about your plans to work safely before they give you permission to attend.

In industrial locations or places where heavy equipment or machinery is in use, protective and high-visibility clothing must be worn.

> ## Functional skills
>
> ### Using English...
>
> Use your speaking and listening skills in order to be an effective group member. Give others opportunity to speak and listen to what they have to say. Make sure you respond in a constructive way with your own point of view. Don't be afraid to join in discussions and debate – your view is important.

> ## Personal, learning and thinking skills
>
> Once you have created your planned record, and in doing so have shown that you can work to schedule and follow safe working procedures, then you have demonstrated Self Motivator skills.

> ## Activity
>
> What are the possible health and safety issues associated with each of these tasks? What action could you take to prevent accidents or injury?
>
> Using a computer
>
> Working with a ladder
>
> Attending an archaeological dig.

> ## Just checking
>
> ✳ Have you gathered all your resources together?
> ✳ Does everybody know their role, and what's expected of them?
> ✳ What are the demands of health and safety requirements on your location and your methods?

Creating a performing arts record

The plans have been made and the equipment is ready. The performance has been prepared and rehearsed. It will now take the collaboration of both the performers and the production team to ensure a positive outcome.

Managing and using your chosen resources

The creation of a record often involves the use of technical resources that must be carefully managed to ensure a good end product.

OVER TO YOU!

How might performing to a camera differ from performing in front of a live audience? Do you think it might be easier or more difficult?

Jobbing actor – An actor who is not necessarily paid for their work – the companies they work often offer a share of the profits instead.

Read through – An initial rehearsal in which the actors sit (usually in a circle) and read the script in character. This happens in the theatre as well as in TV, film and radio drama.

Take – The recording of an individual scene or part of a scene is known as a 'take'. Several takes of each scene may be recorded so the best version can be chosen by the editor.

Personal, learning and thinking skills

Don't be afraid to try out alternatives or new solutions when issues crop up in the making of your record. By following ideas through using innovative solutions you are showing yourself to be a Creative Thinker.

Case Study: Travis

I have worked at a national talk radio station for twelve years and I am the Panel Studio Manager for drama serials. My main role is to ensure the sound is balanced whilst we record. I coordinate the work of two other members of staff: the Spot Studio Manager and the Grams Studio Manager.

The Spot SM creates live sound effects 'on the spot'. These are generally the sound effects the actors would produce of if they were performing the scene on a real set, e.g. opening and closing doors, chinking glasses, rustling a newspaper, etc. The Spot SM also manages the studio floor during recording, setting the microphones, organising the actors and making sure everyone is safe.

The Grams SM is in charge of actually recording the show as well as playing pre-recorded sound effects, e.g. a car driving by. Like me, he sits in the control room and is in charge of a bank of machines such as CD players and synthesisers.

My job is to make sure everything sounds realistic so the listeners can believe that the characters are sitting on a beach on a summer's day, for example, rather than standing in a studio in the middle of November.

I enjoy my job as I like being part of a team and don't mind the pressure of tight deadlines. At the end of the day we have to get each show recorded on time. If we didn't the listeners would wonder what had happened to the next episode!

What checks do you think Travis and his team might need to make before a recording session begins?

What will you need to do to ensure that the resources you intend to use are available to you and are well-managed throughout the process?

The Panel Studio Manager is responsible for making sure the sound is balanced.

Communicating and cooperating with others

Creating a record in the field of performance often involves people with very different skills. It is vital that they work together as a team in order to produce the record. Good communication skills are always important and the interaction and cooperation within the group will play a large part in the success of the project.

Case Study: Erin

I have been a **jobbing actor** for ten years and in that time I've performed with a touring theatre company as well as in the West End. I recently got a role in a six-episode radio drama, my first radio role! The experience is very different from the theatre work I've done in the past. The first time I went into the studio I was nervous as I wasn't sure what to expect. Thankfully the Studio Manager was really helpful and showed me where to stand and how close to the microphone I needed to be.

The rehearsal period in radio drama is really short compared to the theatre. To begin with the Director talked us through the scene and we did a **read through**. Once we were in the studio we had a quick rehearsal of the scene and then we went for a **take**.

I was relieved that my first day in the studio went without a hitch. This was mainly down to the fact that everyone worked so well as a team.

Why do you think good communication skills and strong teamwork were important to the success of Erin's first day in the studio?

To what extent will teamwork be important in your project?

For your project

If your project includes working in a studio, a disciplined approach is vital.

* Performers must be prepared to 'hang around' whilst the technical team work, e.g. placing microphones, setting levels, etc. They must not distract those who are working but should wait quietly until they are needed.

* If you are working over several days, produce a daily schedule indicating when people are needed and where they have to be. This could be posted on a production notice board. You could choose to alert the group to check the board by texting them when a new notice goes up.

* Health and safety should always be considered in a studio setting, e.g. loose wires must be taped down and no eating or drinking allowed.

Activity

Draw up a list of group rules for use when creating your record.

Your list should include descriptions of roles and responsibilities for group members during the making of your record as well as required standards of behaviour. Include safe behaviour as well as courteous and professional standards.

The list could be used as the basis of a group contract that every member signs and agrees to.

Just checking

* Have you gathered the resources you will need?
* Have you considered the importance of teamwork and good communication skills?

Creating a media record

Creating a record involves putting your plans into action. All your planning production schedules, budgets and risk assessments – now allows you to concentrate on making an innovative media record!

Creating your record

You now have to create your media record using the resources identified and sourced earlier in this unit. Creating a record is all about using your imagination and skill and managing your time carefully.

The creative process began with your first idea and it does not end until you have written the final sentence of your project assessment. It is quite likely that you will have new ideas, or realise that planned items aren't going to work. This is fine! If you were making a black and white film but observed a beautiful sunset, it might really add atmosphere to include that shot in colour. Just make sure you keep good notes on why you are making changes, and continue with your work.

For your project

To create your record successfully you will need to:

Create your media record using innovative techniques.

Demonstrate that you can effectively work with little assistance from your teacher.

Pay attention to detail, making sure that your finished record is accurate and complete.

Reflect on your on-going work and make changes when you need to.

Ask someone else to comment on your record and make changes, if necessary.

Analyse your record to ensure that it is fit for purpose.

Produce a final version of your media record.

Remember, your record will be viewed by an audience. You should make sure that it is the best work you can do.

Working in a group

It is important to meet regularly to discuss the record production and to check on progress. You should take minutes of these production meetings so that you can see what needs to be done and by when.

Making changes during production can make your record even better than you planned.

Case Study: Media Productions

The team at Media Productions work closely together. The Producer controls the team, hires equipment, books resources and lets all the team know when they are needed for the production. The Director works with the team to create the scenes and coordinate the actors.

Think about the group that you will be working with. Consider:

– Communicating – notifying others of meetings, or changes to schedules

– Working together – discussing plans, highlighting problems, carrying out your roles, asking for help

– Responsibility – who will be in charge of what, who will make final decisions.

Testing your record

You will need to test your record to make sure that it is fit for purpose. This is essential as you would not want to have a record that an audience will not want to read or view. You should:

* prepare a short part of your media record and show this to a sample of the target audience
* ask them to comment on the effectiveness of your record
* make changes, where necessary.

Remember: you should continue to refer back to your plans and the original aims of your project regularly as you create your record.

Inviting comment from a focus group will help you hit your target audience.

Case Study: Media Productions

The team at Media Productions always test their products before they are released to the client. This might be with a focus group that consists of a sample of the target audience. If the focus group likes the product then it is presented to the client with the data from the focus group. If the focus group does not like the product the team will meet and discuss how they can change the product in the light of the feedback.

A recent production, for a pottery manufacturer, was shown to a target audience focus group, and they felt that they wanted to see more footage of the pottery being made by hand. The client agreed, so a second version was produced with more shots of the hand-made process included. This was then shown to the focus group again and they were happy, as was the client.

Look back at the original aims/purpose of your own project. Now you have begun to create your record, have you accidentally strayed away from them? If you have, make revisions to ensure you produce what you originally intended to.

Health and safety

Working safely means considering potential risks before you begin. You should always undertake a risk assessment to identify any potential problems. Once you have carried out this assessment, you must refer back to it during the creation of your record. For example, if you are going to be working at night, make sure you take torches and spare batteries with you. If you are going to be spending a lot of time on the computer, ensure you take regular breaks and don't work for more than one hour at a time. Refer back to the table on page 73.

Activity

Think about the production of the audio record of the school debate on healthy canteen food from page 121. What health and safety issues would you have to consider when making such a film? For example:

* people appearing in the debate – could they be injured by your equipment?
* crew – will they have to work in hazardous conditions, e.g. in the cold or heat, using hot lights, working with long cables?
* yourself – will you be working long hours at a video editing suite monitor, using a keyboard or working alone at night?

These are just some of the issues to risk assess when creating your media record.

Just checking

* Are you working innovatively and with independence?
* Are you regularly reviewing your work and making changes where necessary?
* Have you considered how you will test your record?
* Are you working safely?

Creating a visual arts record

When actually preparing to produce your visual arts record you need to ensure that you have everything you need, that you've liaised with everyone you should and that you can work safely and within your time constraints. Only then can you be on your creative way.

Gathering resources

Making sure that you have the right tools and resources to create your record is vital before you begin work. If you are going to be working in an environment away from a studio or classroom, you will need to ensure that you have everything with you. In your planning you should have made clear notes on what you will need to take with you. Having a checklist to make sure that you gather what you need not only before you leave for a location, but also to check you have collected everything before you leave to return would be useful.

Case Study: Deniz

Deniz has been given the task of creating some sketches of athletes competing at a local athletics tournament. The sports complex is across town from his studio. Before he leaves, he checks his plans – including his contingency plan – to ensure that he has what he needs. As he will be working using different grades of pencil and recording his work in a sketchbook, he ensures that he has a waterproof bag to carry his materials in, in case it rains on his journey to or from the sports complex. He may also have to work in a damp environment such as at the side of a swimming pool, so he makes sure he has a pencil case to store his tools in.

During a key race, Deniz breaks his 2B pencil, which he needs to capture the event he is recording accurately. Luckily he has built into his contingency plan both the need for a pencil sharpener and a replacement pencil for each grade he is using. As he is in a hurry to carry on capturing the action, Deniz chooses to use the replacement, sharpening both 2B pencils later on after the race has finished.

It is important to remember to plan for simple things that can go wrong, as well as the bigger issues. Think about the most simple tasks that need to be done in your project. How could they go wrong and what could you do about them?

Liaising with your subjects

Ensuring that you have the permission of people you are to be working with is very important. Also important, particularly for visual artists, is the need to work carefully with the people you may be recording in your image. If you are going to be taking photographs of actors or musicians at a performance, for example, it is wise to introduce yourself to them before you begin work. This will mean that they are not startled or distracted by the use of a **flash gun**, for example, and they may be willing to work with you should you need to take more images at a later date.

If you choose to capture an event or something involving many people it is also a good idea to let those in charge know who you are and what you are doing.

Flash gun – A powerful flash used with a camera to help illuminate a scene and improve the photo taken.

Portfolio – A large folder, usually hard-backed, which allows artists to transport, display and present their work.

Stanley knife – A craft knife with a retractable blade.

Health and safety

As with all your practical work, you should be aware of your own safety and that of those around you when working on making visual records. If you are to be working away from an environment that you are used to, it is easy to forget your usual safe working methods. Be alert and make sure you have planned to include health and safety considerations in your actions.

Case Study: Tom

Tom has decided that he is going to make a visual record of an abandoned building which is near to his home. During his research into his subject he discovers that the building used to be an old church. Tom wants to capture a record of the building as it is now, using a detailed sketch. Outside the building is a sign that says that a development company owns the building and that it is dangerous to enter. Tom contacts the development company to ask if he may be given access to the building to complete his work. Unfortunately, the company tells Tom that it is too unsafe for members of the public to be given access inside the building. However, the Foreman of the site informs him that he would be welcome to work outside the structure as long as he wears a hard hat and a member of the work crew is present. Tom arranges to meet the Foreman the next day and he completes some sketches of the outside of the building from a safe distance.

What might have happened if Tom has ignored the sign, gone in and had an accident? Think about the consequences for Tom, his college, the Foreman of the site and the development company.

Storing your work

When working away from a studio, you will need to make sure that you store the work you have produced carefully before travelling back to your workspace.

* Smaller paper-based work, such as sketches on A4 paper, should be put into a hard-backed protective cover like a waterproof folder or **portfolio** and carried carefully.

* Larger paper-based pieces, such as work on A2 paper, should be rolled and stored in a protective tube for you to carry back. Folding your work will damage the paper and could cause the medium you have used to transfer onto areas of the sheet you did not want it to.

* Photography work on 35mm film should be wound carefully back into the film case inside the camera when you have finished a roll. Storing the rolls of film back in their canisters, labelling them and putting them in a secure place to transport is also important.

* Photography work on a digital camera should be checked on site, to ensure that all of the shots you intended to take are stored and the card containing the images is either left in the camera as you travel back, or taken out and stored in a secure, dry place.

Ensuring that the materials you have used are securely stored and kept away from finished pieces will also ensure you return from your activity successfully.

Activity

Discuss what potential health and safety risks you can identify in the following situations with a partner.

* An easel that has been set up for an artist to work on at a live music event has the cables of a nearby camera crew curled around its supports.

* A **stanley knife** which an artist has included in their toolkit to sharpen mark-making tools has been put into a kitbag without a protective shield.

* A photographer recording the creation of products in a factory refuses to wear the protective clothing that her guide at the factory has asked her to.

Now draw up a table with two columns. In the first, list what safety issues might occur in this situation, and in the second explain how this could have been avoided.

Just checking

* Have you prepared your resources well in advance of your production start date?

* Have you communicated with others involved with the subject of your record?

* Are you fully briefed on the health and safety requirements of your project locations?

Preparation for assessment

In this unit you may have been involved in the process of recording or you may have played a part in the creation of whatever was being recorded. You should ensure that your record enables you to work across at least two disciplines, combining animation packages with film, for example.

Your portfolio

Your process portfolio will be expected to contain evidence of your involvement in your assignments. Your teacher may tell you what form your portfolio should take and how to present your work.

You will be assessed on…	This will be evidenced in your portfolio by…
…your understanding of how a particular medium can be used to create a record.	Your research notes. These may be notes taken in class as well as articles found on the internet, in books and magazines. You may be able to talk to someone who uses the medium professionally. A presentation of your research materials. This could be in written form or a talk, perhaps using PowerPoint slides. If you give a talk, remember to include the notes you use in your portfolio. **Tips for success:** • Print out useful articles from the internet; annotate them and highlight useful passages.
…your ability to plan the creation of a record.	A log or diary giving details of the work you undertake when planning the creation of your record. You should keep notes on your ideas for the creation of the record, along with any research you have done into the suitability of your ideas. You should also include notes from meetings and documents such as schedules. Remember to annotate these, for example by writing comments in the margins to show your own contribution. If you are taking on a role in the creation of a piece of work that is being recorded, you should include notes made during rehearsals and practice sessions. Your teachers may also produce observation reports on how well you carry out practical tasks. **Tips for success:** • Make sure you have blank copies of forms and documents you may need, e.g. production schedules, meeting records. • Spend a short time at the end of each session writing up what has been done while it is fresh in your mind.
…your ability to take part in the creation of a record.	A copy of the record. You should also keep a log of the processes undertaken in the production of your record. This should include any production schedules used, along with a personal log giving details of your contribution to the process. **Tips for success:** • You could keep a photo diary of the processes undertaken in the making of your record.
…your ability to monitor the creation of a record.	The documents in your portfolio. As well as providing evidence of your ability to plan and create a record, your log will also be used to assess your ability to monitor your own contribution to the work. You may also be asked to complete a written evaluation of your work and/or take part in a de-brief meeting with your teacher and other members of your group. **Tips for success:** • If you are working as part of a group remember to personalise all documents that go into your portfolio to show your own contribution to the group's work.

The assessment of the unit

This unit is assessed internally by your teachers. Remember, you'll be assessed on **what** you submit as part of your process portfolio and your teacher's observations of **how** you've worked.

You must show that you:	Guidance	To gain higher marks:
...can undertake an investigation into particular examples of records. ...can explain recent developments in the medium you have chosen to investigate.	You should focus your investigations on a particular medium, e.g. video recording. Remember to look into how the medium you are investigating has changed and developed over time. You could also look at how it has been used at different times and in different cultures.	Your research must be well-focused and your findings must be relevant. Your findings should demonstrate that you have a good understanding of a wide range of records produced using your chosen medium. You should explain recent developments in the use of your chosen medium.
...can come up with ideas for the creation of a record and plan how you will create the record. ...can document the planning process.	Explore and research your ideas carefully to assess how workable they are. Be prepared to make changes or reject ideas that are not practical. Consider the resources and materials that are available to you as well as the skills of the group. This will help you assess the viability of your ideas. You should also consider the time you have available. Remember that you should seek permission to record anything that is copyright. You need to do this <u>before</u> moving to the next stage of the project. You may need to make contingency plans, e.g. if you plan to film outdoors, what will you do if it rains?	You must show that you can plan the creation of a record in a disciplined and organised way, using planning documents efficiently. You should come up with inventive ideas and be able to explore them thoughtfully. You must be able to carry out planning tasks with only occasional help from your teachers.
...are able to take part in the creation of a record.	You may be assigned a particular role in the creation of the record. If this is the case you must make sure you understand exactly what your role requires you to do. Make a checklist of all your duties and refer to it regularly, taking particular care to work to deadlines. Always work safely. Check any health and safety guidance you have been given before beginning a task and/or operating a piece of equipment.	You must make an effective contribution to the creation of the record. When working you must select and use a range of different techniques. You must manage your time to make sure you meet deadlines. Follow safe working practices at all times. You must be able to work with only occasional help from your teachers.
...know how to monitor the creation of the record.	Review your progress regularly (not just at the end of the project.) Use your reviews to make changes and/ or modify your work if necessary.	You must show that you have monitored your progress regularly and carefully. You must show that you have used monitoring to improve your ideas. You must show that you have an understanding of the strengths and weaknesses of your work.

5 CAMPAIGN

Introduction

A **campaign** is a way of raising awareness using the creative and media arts. Many people produce campaigns, from charities wanting to make people aware of their work to producers who want to sell a product. The campaign normally involves an organised series of activities that lead to a message being received by a **target audience**.

Campaigns are normally produced by an advertising agency or a public relations company. They use creative personnel to think of ideas, plan their campaigns and produce material for the campaign.

Your learning

In this unit, you should work across at least two of the disciplines on page 4 to cover the four main topics.

The nature and purpose of campaigns

All campaigns focus on communicating information to an audience. What varies is how they do this – what methods and media they use, and why they do this – what their purpose and objectives are.

Before you can plan and create your own campaign, you need to understand what makes a campaign and how it can be conducted. To do this you will have to find an example of a campaign and investigate it thoroughly. You will then evaluate how successful the campaign was at achieving its aims. These activities will inform your own campaign.

Preparing a campaign

At the heart of every successful campaign is a clear, well-thought through message or idea. Once you have decided your message, you can set out your **aims for the campaign**, then begin to consider your target audience. Using your research skills you will investigate your chosen audience to make sure your campaign is as targeted as possible. You will then begin to consider the materials and resources you will need to prepare and run your campaign. It is important to consider the media you will use for your campaign as you will need to use more than one form.

Your preparation stage will also include thinking ahead to the end of your campaign – how will you know it's been successful? You may need to do extra research to find a measurement method that suits your particular campaign.

Conducting a campaign

Failing to organise and check your resources can jeopardise your whole campaign. As well as planning and creating your materials, it's important

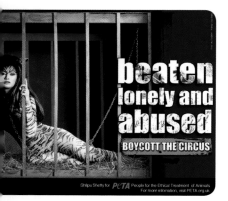

Charitable campaigns can raise awareness of an issue.

to keep in regular contact with everyone involved. You need to know when items are being delivered, when rehearsals are taking place and to confirm arrangements with **venues** and volunteers.

Monitoring the preparation and conduct of a campaign

Throughout the planning, preparation and conduct of your campaign you will have to review your plans and activities.

Once your campaign is over you will have to reflect on your work and ask yourself where you succeeded and where you could have worked more effectively. By keeping notes of all your planning and preparation work, the decisions you made and the reasons why things changed, you will be able to consider in detail where you could have improved your work and if there are any changes you could make to your campaign.

You will also carry out your evaluation of the success of the actual campaign aims and objectives, perhaps by gathering feedback from your target audience with a questionnaire or **focus groups**.

Process portfolio

In your process portfolio for this unit you must make sure that you have recorded and carefully stored evidence from all stages of your work.

You will need to make sure your portfolio includes:

✳ Your research and investigations – document what you find out about the campaign you have investigated. This should include examples of the campaign materials, **critical analysis** of the images and forms used in it, information on the target audience and analysis of how successful the campaign was. If you have presented your findings in a report or a presentation form such as PowerPoint, a copy should be included.

✳ Your campaign preparations – you must keep a record of all activities undertaken during the planning and preparation phase of the campaign. This may include development of your message and aims, research on your target audience, how you selected suitable media to work in, examples of teamwork and preparation of schedules and plans. A personal log detailing your own contribution should also be included.

✳ Your campaign materials – include hard copies of posters and leaflets, print outs of e-newsletters and website pages, any transcripts of interviews or advertisements. Radio/TV advertisements should be supplied on CD or DVD, and any performances, rallies or public events recorded.

✳ Campaign log – you need to document your activities both during the campaign preparations and during the campaign itself. Keep a personal diary or logbook of what you do and how the campaign is progressing.

Campaign – The process of promoting a message or issue using creative and media techniques.

Target audience – The audience that your campaign is aiming to reach.

Campaign aims – The things you hope to achieve through or at the end of your campaign.

Venues – Places where you can hold your campaign activities.

Focus groups – A gathering of people from your target audience who are asked to discuss certain issues or opinions or to evaluate materials. These discussions are then recorded.

Critical analysis – Detailed investigation where you give your opinion, positive or negative.

Just checking

✳ Investigating another campaign will help you to prepare your own.

✳ A campaign will not work without a clear aim or message.

✳ Organisation is key when conducting a campaign.

✳ Reviewing your campaign whilst you prepare it will make it better.

5.1 Understanding campaigns

Campaigns are used by companies, individuals or organisations to promote their message or product, or to raise awareness of issues. They reach their audience through a variety of media, including radio, dramatic performance and poster campaigns. They will have carefully targeted their audience and identified the best ways of reaching them. They may also have considered using a multi-media approach combining a mix of performance, design and media.

For your projects

In order to understand campaigns you must look at a range of campaigns and choose one to investigate. You should carefully consider your choice of campaign with the following questions:

* Can I find information and examples of this campaign easily?
* Will I be able to identify the target audience?
* Will I be able to find out the methods used in this campaign?
* Will I be able to find out if the campaign was successful?

What are campaigns for?

Campaigns are produced for many reasons, including to:

* promote a product, e.g. a magazine advert for a new computer console
* publicise an event, e.g. a poster giving the dates for the digital TV switchover
* raise awareness of an issue, e.g. a short docu-advert on the melting polar ice caps
* educate people, e.g. a dramatic performance on the dangers of taking drugs
* provide a public service, e.g. a radio advert explaining why the local council has closed roads for repairs.

They can also be run using a variety of forms, for example:

* television or radio advertisements
* posters or **billboards**
* advertisements in magazines or newspapers
* flyers or brochures
* printed material such as pens, pencils, notepads or balloons with the campaign message printed on them
* campaign meetings or rallies
* **press releases**
* dramatic or musical performance.

XBOX 360

xboxevolved.com

The main message

Campaigns convey their messages in different ways. The message might be **overt**, for example someone stating 'Eating too much saturated fat is bad for you' or **subliminal**, for example a picture of a presidential candidate in the background of an advert about how wonderful people are who tell the truth (the subliminal message being that the candidate is a person who tells the truth so you should vote for them).

What you have to work out is what the campaign is about, who is it aimed at and what they are expecting the audience to do in response to the campaign. There is a term used in marketing called AIDA. It stands for a process of four steps that campaign designers use to make their campaigns as effective as possible:

A – Awareness: make the customer aware of your product or message.

I – Interest: make the customer interested by explaining features and benefits or justifying opinions.

D – Desire: convince the customer they want the product or that they agree with you.

A – Action: lead customers to purchase your product or take action, e.g. donate money.

The AIDA model has been used in the RSPCA poster above:

A – Bold heading 'A love that will not die'. RSPCA organisation name also features prominently.

I – Subheading text and the reassuring assurance that the RSPCA will 'find a <u>loving new home</u> for a <u>bereaved pet</u>'.

D – Appealing photo of kitten looking sad and vulnerable.

A – Information hotline given, plus coupon for a free information pack.

Target audience

Campaigns have been around for a long time. Campaigners may have become more sophisticated about the ways in which they try to reach their target audiences, but the bottom line is always the same: if you miss your target your campaign will fail. When you are considering your target audience you need to ask yourself a number of questions:

∗ Who do I want to reach? Think about age, gender, race, religion, political persuasion, social class.

∗ How can I phrase my message to get their attention? Think about words, phrases, tone and style.

Billboards – Very large adverts that are mounted on boards around towns and cities, near roads and busy areas.

Press releases – Information given to the press and media about your campaign.

Main message – The most important message of the campaign, the one thing people should remember.

Overt message – A message that can clearly be seen and understood by the viewer.

Subliminal message – A message that is not spoken but is implied through action or circumstances.

Activity

Look at some of the campaign examples you obtained in the Over to you! activity.

Explain how they follow the AIDA model detailed above.

Activity

The posters on the right are examples of a campaign from the last hundred years. Answer these questions:

Who is the target audience? Give as much detail as you can.

How do you know that is the intended audience? What clues does the poster give you?

What is the message?

Do you think the poster was effective in reaching its target audience? Why/why not?

* What images will appeal to this audience? Think about the style, medium and contents of images.
* What are their interests, what activities are they involved in? Think about how you can relate your message or product to your audience's lifestyle.
* What will put this audience off? Think about what might annoy, repulse or irritate your audience.

Methods used to reach the target audience

Whatever method they use, campaigners always carefully research their target audience and the place the campaign will be best seen. They have traditionally used a range of methods and techniques to reach their audiences, such as:

* poster campaigns – these can be put up in appropriate places that the target audience might visit
* leaflets or brochures – these could be available in a place the target audience might visit, or be posted through letterboxes/placed on cars in a targeted area
* a video or DVD – these could be sent out or requested by the target audience
* a performance – this could be toured to venues that the target audience might use.

Activity

* What does this image mean to you? Where have you seen it before?
* List all the different media and creative forms it has been used in.
* Identify the target audience for each form, do they vary?
* What is the core message that the campaign is trying to get across? How successful do you think it is being?

Activity

Increasingly, campaigners are using more innovative ways to reach their audience as well. Developments in media technology such as **podcasts**, e-newsletters and **social networking websites** have added a new 'immediate' dimension to campaigns, helping organisations and individuals get in touch with their target audience more quickly and more precisely. Crucial additional information about the audience can be gained by tracking the websites they visit from, which helps future campaigns to be even more closely targeted.

Podcasts – Digital media text files downloadable from the internet for personal media players such as MP3 players or iPods.

Social networking websites – Websites where individuals connect, chat and share photos and information.

Was the campaign successful?

You will have to analyse whether or not your chosen research campaign was effective. All good campaigns are designed from the beginning with measurable success criteria, for example the NSPCC's 2007 campaign 'Be the FULL STOP' invites people to take action and register the good deeds they do to prevent child cruelty on a website. They will be able to examine these deeds to show exactly how their audience were inspired by their campaign.

When you undertake research into a campaign's effectiveness, you may have to contact the organisation or company that ran the campaign and ask them directly if and how it was effective. If they are a charitable organisation they may be tell you how much money was donated after the campaign. You could also use your own thoughts on its effectiveness if the campaign was aimed at you.

You could undertake a questionnaire to find out if a campaign has been effective by identifying the target audience, then approaching them for feedback on the campaign, and finding out how they were influenced.

If you are approaching companies, organisations or individuals about a campaign they have run, try to remember that these are often businesspeople with busy schedules. They may have only a limited amount of time to spare you, so make sure you are well prepared. Write out your questions clearly and make sure your tone is unbiased. You may not agree with their campaign message, or even like it, but it would be unprofessional to say this.

Functional skills

Using ICT…

* When researching campaigns you could use ICT systems to find and store the information you find that is useful, then present it with software such as PowerPoint.

* Your presentation could use images sourced from the internet or an interactive CD-ROM.

Personal, learning and thinking skills

By carrying out independent research into a specific campaign and explaining the nature and purpose of that campaign, you will be improving your skills in Independent Enquiry.

Just checking

* Can you describe the target audience for a campaign?
* Have you considered the different messages that campaigns are trying to get across?
* Have you thought about the different methods that campaigns might use?
* How would you evaluate the success of a campaign?

How performing arts are used in campaigns

Performing arts are important tools for organisations that produce campaigns. Drama and music in particular are often used to communicate quite strong or unpleasant messages. Think of the short dramatic scenes presented in the NSPCC's 'FULL STOP' campaign.

THINK! Drink Drive campaigns

On average 3,000 people are killed or seriously injured in alcohol-related road accidents. The Department of Transport run Drink Drive campaigns at certain times each year, e.g. in the summer months and in the run-up to Christmas, to raise awareness of the dangers and consequences of driving whilst drunk.

The main messages

The 2007 summer campaign highlighted the ways in which a drink driving conviction could ruin your life. The consequences of a conviction could include a 12-month driving ban, a large fine, a criminal record and potential loss of job or even relationships.

The target audience

Although the campaign set out to target all drivers, young men aged 17–29 were its particular focus. This is the group most likely to be involved in alcohol related accidents and most likely to produce positive breath tests.

Methods used to reach the target audience

The campaign included a powerful TV ad that told the story of Matt, a young man out for a drink with friends. He is deciding whether to have a second pint before driving home when the action freezes and the barman transforms into a series of characters he would meet if he was caught drink driving. They include a policeman asking him to step out of his car, a solicitor explaining that he'll get a 12-month ban, his boss telling him his company cannot employ someone with a Drink Drive conviction and his partner upset and angry because he's lost his job. The scene ends when the barman reappears and asks Matt 'So – what's it going to be?'.

Measuring the success of the campaign

Since the introduction of Drink Drive campaigns thirteen years ago, an estimated 20,000 lives have been saved as the numbers of accidents caused by alcohol have fallen considerably. The many campaigns have also changed people's views on drink driving, making it socially unacceptable.

Case Study: APE Theatre in Education

Drama is often used as a method of educating and informing. Theatre in Education (TiE) is a form of drama that begins with an educational topic, perhaps taken from the national curriculum. TiE is also used in schools to raise awareness of certain issues.

APE Theatre Company was launched in 1988 with a play called 'Too Much Punch for Judy'. Described as a Drink Drive documentary, Mark Wheeler's play tells the traumatic true story of a young woman who kills her sister in an alcohol-related road accident. Aimed at late teens, the play has been used by road safety groups and police authorities in campaigns promoting safer driving.

Other plays in the company's repertoire include 'Legal Weapon', a piece that tackles the issues of excessive speed and peer pressure in young drivers and 'Pills Thrills @ Automobiles', another play based on real events that warns of the dangers of Drug Driving.

Plays are often followed by interactive **workshops** designed to get the audience actively involved in exploring the issues raised in the performance.

Have you ever seen or been involved in a TiE piece?

Do you think this is a good way of getting young people to think about serious issues?

Personal, learning and thinking skills

When you are researching a campaign, consider the influence of circumstances, beliefs and feelings on campaign decisions and events. For instance, consider how an increasingly zero-tolerance attitude towards drink driving has influenced the style of Drink Drive campaign messages over the last twenty years. By investigating campaigns in a more in-depth manner you can show your skills as an Independent Enquirer.

Workshop – An activity session with a specific focus or goal.

Activity

In small groups tae an existing campaign you have looked at, devise a two-minute piece of drama that tackles the issue/subject the campaign is aiming to raise awareness of.

Share your pieces with the class and discuss the process.

'Too Much Punch for Judy' is used in road safety campaigns to raise awareness of the dangers of Drink Driving

Just checking

* Do you understand why drama can be useful in campaigns?
* Can you identify what makes a specific dramatic performance effective?

How media is used in campaigns

A campaign can use many media. It could include elements of printed media, for example posters, billboards or even images on the side of a bus. These could link to advertisements in newspapers or magazines that in turn link to advertisements on the television, radio or in the cinema.

What is the message?

There are many ways a **media campaign** can be used to get a message over to a target audience. The Improvement and Development Agency helps local councils with their campaigns. They explain how media campaigns can be used to try and explain difficult decisions a council may have had to make, or to 'soften the blow' of bad news, such as an increase in council tax. They list a number of requirements for a properly planned media campaign:

* key messages
* key audiences
* key media
* resources
* targets
* timescales and deadlines
* monitoring and evaluation.

Reaching your target audience

Media campaigns have begun to use social networking websites to help them reach their target audience. This can be particularly effective promoting good causes or issues.

The Comic Relief media campaign was innovative because it used the very latest media technology to link in with a charity that has traditionally used television as its major fundraising medium.

Media campaign – A campaign that uses a range of media forms to get a message to an audience.

Blog – A website where entries are recorded like a diary.

Recall rate – How clearly people can remember something.

Viral effect – Spreading information by word of mouth.

Qualitative research – Research to discover opinions, attitudes and preferences rather than hard facts.

Personal, learning and thinking skills

Investigating the success of a campaign allows you to identify questions to answer or problems to resolve about how you will judge the success of your own campaign, which is the mark of an Independent Enquirer.

Case Study: Red Nose Day

The organisers of the 2007 Comic Relief 'Red Nose Day' approached several social networking websites as part of their campaign strategy. They ran promotions on Bebo and MySpace, asking users to design a Red Nose Day themed homepage, upload photos and comments on fundraising events, as well as featuring quizzes, games, a **blog** and celebrity video messages. There were other promotions with moblogUK and ebay.

Hitwise, a company that tracks how people access websites noted that the site for Walkers Crisps, which was donating money to Comic Relief, became the number one online charity destination, with many more visits coming from Bebo users.

Who do you think is Comic Relief's target audience?

What kind of audience uses social networking sites?

What do you think are the benefits of using this kind of technology in your campaign?

Organisations research their target audiences carefully, to ensure that they get the best response and results possible.

Was it successful?

In this topic you will have investigated a media campaign in detail. Before the start of any campaign, the organisers will have thought through how they will measure its success. If they are running an advertising campaign for a product they may look at whether their sales increase. If they are raising a social issue they might record how many hits their website receives after their radio commercial airs.

Comic Relief's 'Red Nose Day' is run every two years and covered by the BBC.

Case Study: Nintendo Wii

When Nintendo launched their Wii Sports package, they decided to run the first-ever live cinema advert campaign. The campaign features two actors playing a mother and teenage son who are hiding in the cinema audience. During the normal cinema advertisements, the mother comes in, the adverts stop and she challenges her son to a game of Wii tennis. Their game is projected on to the big screen itself.

The campaign ran in cinemas to coincide with the opening weekend of *Pirates of the Caribbean 3*. Five teams of two actors operated nationally across nine different cinema sites over two weekends.

The campaign was created by CommentUK, a communications company. Before the launch their MD, Dean McKain commented: 'We expect to reach thousands of cinema goers over the next two weeks, and as we know that **recall rates** for this type of live communication are huge (as much as 89 per cent after four weeks), we feel sure that the word of mouth **viral effect** of the activity will have a positive impact for the brand.'
www.creativematch.co.uk

What effect do you think Nintendo wanted their campaign to have on the audience?

What made the Nintendo Wii Sports campaign effective?

Why is word of mouth important to a company like Nintendo?

Case Study: Barnardo's

As a leading children's charity, Barnardo's works directly with over 115,000 children, young people and their families every year, running 394 vital projects across the UK to help some of the most vulnerable children and young people believe in themselves, transform their lives and fulfil their potential. Barnardo's explain how they have organised ways to assess the success of their nationwide advertising campaigns: 'Each year we commission an independent research agency to carry out **qualitative research** pre/post the launch of the advertising. This research involves a new sample of individuals each year which is representative of our target audience. They are each individually interviewed for approximately 30 minutes on a wide range of questions. Many of the questions remain consistent so that we can measure the shift in responses and track:

* awareness of Barnardo's (both when people are asked about us specifically and when they are asked to name charities themselves at random)

* how deserving Barnardo's is as a charity

* awareness and thoughts about the work Barnardo's does.'

What could you learn from Barnardo's about assessing the success of your campaign?

www.barnardos.org.uk

Activity

Find other examples of games console advertising campaigns. What variety of media tools and media do companies use to promote their products? What messages are they trying to convey to their audiences. How successful do you think they are?

Just checking

* Have you investigated how different messages are conveyed in campaigns?

* Have you considered the range of media forms that campaigns can use?

* Can you identify the target audiences in campaigns you have investigated?

* Do you understand how the success of a campaign can be measured?

How visual arts are used in campaigns

Visual artists and designers play a key role in successful campaigns. By looking at the way that other campaigns have been created you will gain a much clearer understanding about the way that visual arts are used in communicating a message.

OVER TO YOU!

All of these images have been used in recent campaigns. Write down five words that come to your mind when you look at the image.

Using images in campaign messages

When investigating how existing campaigns have been created, analysing how visual images have been used is often a key stage of the process.

Activity

Plan what kind of visual images you might create in response to the following campaign needs.

* A local theatre company that is promoting a brochure promoting their upcoming productions.
* A charity for the homeless that is planning a national billboard advertising campaign.
* A local council who want to produce a leaflet to tell people about their new recycling centre.

Images are recognised by the human eye before text is, so the visual elements of a campaign will be the first impression that an audience gets. It also takes the brain less time to recognise and comprehend an image than it does written information, so even if someone only sees something very briefly, they are likely to remember the image and the message it conveys even if they haven't read any of the text.

When looking at a campaign and analysing the images used, ask yourself the following questions:

* What do the images depict?
* Do these images make me feel particularly happy, sad, worried or excited?
* What methods have been used to create these images – are they drawings, photographs, etc?
* How much of the space in this promotional item (e.g. a poster) is taken up by the image?
* What colours are used in the image and how might this relate to the way it made me feel?

Target audience

Being aware of who a campaign is targeted at will help you understand why campaigners have made the creative decisions that they have. The images used in promotional products within a campaign help to attract an audience and convey the message of the campaign.

Emotive – Producing a strong emotion.

Case Study: Attracting the vote

A political party has decided to target pensioners when campaigning for the next election. An advertising agency has been hired to design billboard adverts, print adverts for inclusion in magazines and newspapers and leaflets for putting through potential voters' doors. The designers need to think carefully about how they will make the products appeal to older voters. Making sure that appropriate images are chosen for the promotional products is key both to attracting the audience they are targeting and creating the right impression of the party's intentions.

The agency decides to use colourful, but not garish, photographs of older people doing everyday things such as shopping or socialising. They shoot the clearly focused, composed photographs in pleasant surroundings such as a nicely decorated tea rooms and a park to make sure that the images create a situation the voters may themselves like to be in.

How important do you think images are to this target audience?

How would the audience be affected if no images or garish/unusually styled photographs were used in the materials?

Reaching an audience

Visual images are used in many ways to reach an audience and help communicate a message. Images may be funny, shocking or frightening.

Case Study: Barnardo's

In 2000, Barnardo's employed an advertising agency to create a series of hard-hitting adverts showing how children who were not cared for well in their early life could grow up to suffer from problems. The agency produced a series of shocking adverts centred on photographs that had been manipulated to show babies in situations that looked like they were doing things such as taking drugs. Many people found these images to be very disturbing and they were banned by the Advertising Standards Agency.

Barnardo's 2007 campaign was entitled 'Believe in Children' and aimed to: 'challenge public perceptions and demonstrate that Barnardo's has practical solutions to the problems many children and young people are facing growing up in the UK today'. The images are still striking, but now they just feature children who are representative of those Barnardo's helps.

www.barnardos.org.uk/

How do you feel about the use of shocking or **emotive** images to promote a message?

Is it suitable to use images that shock people if the message is the promotion of a charity or to make people aware of important information?

Compare the image from the 2000 campaign with the 2007 advert. What is the difference in effect that each one might have on the audience.

Which do you feel is more effective? Why?

Just checking

✱ Have you looked at a range of campaign images?

✱ Have you investigated how images relate to the target audience of a campaign?

✱ Do you understand the different purposes of images in campaigns?

5.2 Preparing a campaign

Careful planning for a campaign is essential. You will need time and resources to produce your campaign. You must be sure that you have everything you need when you need it. It would not be good practice to launch a campaign without all the materials and resources in place. The campaign will succeed because of careful and effective forward planning.

Choosing the right campaign

You will need to think carefully about the campaign you intend to conduct. It's important to get your message right from the beginning so you need to investigate potential campaign ideas exhaustively. You could start by thought-showering ideas into a mind-map, then refining your chosen idea and your campaign message in a second map. It's a good idea to choose a campaign you are passionate about, for example child protection, third world issues, Fairtrade or cruelty to animals. Consider a range of ideas in your group, then gradually work through each one until you find the idea that you all feel inspired about.

OVER TO YOU!

Look at the campaign you investigated in topic 5.1. Make a list of the different methods the campaign organisers used to get their message across to their target audience.

Targeting your campaign

Choosing your audience

Your target audience might be very obvious, or you might be unsure about who you should target. It's a good idea to use thought-shower techniques to list every possible audience then narrow it down from there. For example, if you decided that your campaign aim was to promote Fairtrade goods, you actually have quite a wide potential audience. You could target shopkeepers to stock Fairtrade goods, or cafés and restaurants to switch to Fairtrade food and drink; or your approach might be more about informing people, perhaps students in your school because you think they should think about ethical issues, young families because you think Fairtrade products might be better for you; or those who earn lots of money because they could afford to spend more.

To help you decide which of those audiences you want to target, you need to think about things like how feasible it is to reach certain groups, or how much you know about the groups.

You will also have to think a little about the resources you have at your disposal for creating your campaign at this point – if you know that you won't be able to make a radio or TV recording, then this might help you eliminate a potential target audience group if that would have been the best way to reach them. Similarly, if the skills of your group members lie with graphic design, or performance, make sure you try to use the skills available to you to make your campaign as effective and professional as it can be.

Addressing your audience

Once you have decided on your target audience, you can then consider how to approach them in more detail. Even if you know something about the group (you might be part of the target audience!), you must research your target audience carefully. Think back to the questions you asked about target audience when you were researching a campaign in topic 5.1:

* Who do I want to reach?
* How do I need to phrase my message to get their attention?
* What images will appeal to this audience?
* What are their interests, what activities are they involved in?
* What will put this audience off?

Reaching your audience

You can then consider the media that would reach your target audience most effectively. For example, it would be no good placing adverts in the local paper if your research told you your target audience of young teens hardly ever read newspapers, but a podcast or social networking website posting might get their attention immediately.

Consider your investigations about the nature and purpose of a campaign as well. Does this give you any additional ideas about the media you want to use for your campaign? You may find it useful to map out your campaign plan by preparing a flowchart.

Measuring the success of your campaign

It's important to consider how you will measure the success of your campaign from the beginning so you don't find yourself in a difficult position once the campaign is over. Often when businesses set themselves targets they use special methods such as SMART to make sure their targets are:

Specific

Measurable

Achievable

Realistic

Timely

You could apply something to your campaign aims, which will in turn make their success or failure easy to evaluate. For example, a campaign aim like 'I want to inform all teenagers about the dangers of smoking' is very broad and hard to measure, but when you apply SMART to it, it becomes much clearer:

Realistic

> **S**pecific
>
> 'I want to inform 11–16 year olds in my school about the dangers of
>
> **A**chievable
>
> smoking. I will create a film to be shown in PSHE classes, followed by a
>
> **M**easurable
>
> quick 10-question survey to evaluate their response. This will happen
>
> **T**imely
>
> during No Smoking week in January.'

A SMART approach to your campaign message also provides a useful summary of your aims for you to refer back to continually and ensure you are meeting in your work.

Producing your campaign materials

Once you have completed your planning you will need to produce the materials to conduct your campaign. You will be using more than one creative and media art form in your campaign, so you will have to think carefully about:

* the ways in which the materials you are producing are managed, e.g. time, costs and quantity
* whether you can use the same materials in every campaign product, e.g. a photograph on a poster and in a video advertisement
* how to work safely when producing your materials
* how to work with colleagues, e.g. actors, artists and production staff.

Materials and resources

You may have already briefly considered the materials and resources you will need for your campaign, but it's a good idea to consider your options thoroughly now, including the skills you and your group have. There is no point deciding on a campaign when you do not have access to the right materials and resources. If you decide to produce a DVD, will you be able to use a camera and an editing suite? Is there any training you need to undertake? If you want to use a celebrity to endorse your campaign, will you be able to contact them and arrange for them to be free on a particular day? Consider these issues and make a comprehensive list of the materials and resources you will need and where you can obtain them.

Schedules and contingency

It is essential that you have enough time to complete your work. Campaign launches often coincide with particular dates or events, for example you might want to promote Fairtrade goods during the official 'Fairtrade fortnight', or time your campaign against animal testing on the day a relevant new law comes into force. You must produce a **production schedule** that takes account of any such deadlines and indicates when you will be undertaking tasks and when you will be completing them. A schedule, such as the one opposite, will ensure that you have sufficient time to produce your campaign materials.

Contingency – A solution or alternative for a problem or unforeseen circumstance.

Production schedule – A document that allows you to plan the production effectively.

Personal, learning and thinking skills

As a Self Manager you must show you are careful in organising your resources and able to stick to a schedule and budget. Anticipating problems, preparing contingency plans and prioritising actions will also demonstrate and develop your managing skills.

Functional skills

Using Maths...

You will be able to demonstrate your mathematical skills when estimating costs and preparing production schedules.

Production Schedule

Campaign title: Fairtrade: Good for everybody!
Clients: Abbot's Stores, Robin's Den, The Health Food Shoppe
Campaign manager: Jane Wild
Date: 21st September 2008

Activity	Start date	End date
Mind-mapping exercises	24 September	26th September
Planning	28 September	4th October
Poster production	7th October	14th October
Monitoring	16th October	25th November
The campaign	21st November	25th November
Reviewing period	26th November	3rd December
Assessment date	9th December	

Contingency period: 4th–8th December

You should allow time in your campaign production schedule for unforeseen events – this is called a **contingency** plan. You also need to think about all the things that could go wrong, and record how you will deal with each issue in a contingency plan, for example:

Potential problem	Contingency plan
The computer crashes.	Back-up my work to CD or data stick every time I make changes.
One of the stall volunteers is ill.	Have a back-up group of people who are willing to step in and help in an emergency.

Budget

Whether your budget is £100 or £1 million, you still need to stick to it by planning your expenditure and accounting for everything you end up doing. Your budget will determine the media forms of your campaign and its range. Unless you are able to obtain sponsorship or a grant, it's likely the range of your campaign will be your local area. Costs you should consider when planning your budget include:

* the cost of resources, e.g. hiring cameras, using a computer, using lights, buying props
* the cost of materials, e.g. blank DVDs, printing paper, ink, fabric for costumes
* the cost of labour, e.g. specialists who assist your campaign, staff for an event
* copyright and legal costs, e.g. using someone else's images, obtaining a public performance licence.

The campaign for fairer trade has been adopted by many retail outlets and suppliers.

Just checking

* Have you thoroughly investigated your target audience?
* Have you planned how to measure the success of your campaign?
* Are your materials and resources ready?
* Have you planned your campaign to a schedule and budget?

Campaigns and theatre

Your message

The planning process of all campaigns begins with a simple idea or a message. You may be given a brief by your teacher as a starting point, or be given the opportunity to choose your own campaign. Your campaign may involve a piece of theatre, in which case it may need costumes, props, sets or even audio-visual back projection.

Activity

Imagine you have been set the theme of 'the dangers of trespassing on railway lines'. Thought-shower some ideas for a campaign about this topic. Use these facts as a starting point:

* Every year in the UK around 60 people are killed and many more are seriously injured whilst playing on railway lines. Many are children.
* Children as young as eight have been caught playing chicken on railway lines.
* A train travelling at 125 mph takes 35 seconds to stop. In that time it will travel the length of 20 football pitches.
* Many train drivers who hit people are so traumatised that they never work again.

Where might you find more information about the subject?

Your target audience

Using the research skills you developed in topic 5.1, you will need to establish the target audience for your campaign. For example, you may discover through your research that rail trespass is more common with a particular age group, say 11–16-year-olds. You may then find that boys are more likely to trespass than girls. Your target audience would therefore be 11–16-year-old boys.

Reaching the target audience

You must also think about how you will reach your target audience. and what is the most effective medium for your message. For example, for a target audience of 11–16 year olds it would be wise to show your performance at school or through a youth facility, rather than in a local shopping centre on a weekday.

Functional Skills

Using ICT...

You can surf the internet for interesting facts and figures or use electronic newspaper archives to find real stories. Make sure you use ICT appropriately, always ask yourself: 'Is this the best way to find the information I need?'.

Case Study: Healthy Eating Roadshow

A group of students are planning a campaign whose aim is to promote healthy eating habits. Their target age group is 7–9-year-olds and they have devised a 30-minute piece of drama followed by a workshop where children can make and taste some healthy snacks. They have written to the head teachers of all the primary schools in their area, explaining their campaign and offering to visit their schools with the Healthy Eating Roadshow.

What other groups and organisations could the organisers of this campaign approach?

Producing the materials for your campaign

The next step in your planning process is to produce the materials you will need for your campaign. This may involve devising a short piece of live theatre or a TV advert. Always keep your target audience in mind when devising a piece. Ask yourself:

* Is the language appropriate? (Appropriate tone, words and phrases.)
* Are the images suitable? (Not scary or too shocking for younger audiences.)
* Are our messages clear and unambiguous (for younger audiences) or sophisticated enough (for older audiences)?
* Does the action reflect the message? (Performances should be focused.)
* Will what we are doing help us achieve our aims? (Constantly refer back to your campaign aims to stay on track.)

Personal, learning and thinking skills

As a Self Manager you must show you can organise your resources in order to produce successful campaign materials.

Case Study: 999 Emergency?

The students at Cliveden College were given the issue of hoax 999 calls as the basis for their campaign. Bridget explains how her group went about their planning:

'We began by doing some research using the internet. We found out that the number of hoax calls made to the emergency services rises during school holidays. We also collected data about how much money is wasted every time a fire engine or ambulance is sent out on a hoax call.

'We decided to devise a short film for an advert to educate 11–14-years-olds about the issue. The film tells the story of a boy who keeps making 999 calls for a laugh. He learns his lesson when his friend has an accident and nearly dies when the ambulance takes a long time to get to him because it is on the other side of town answering a hoax call.'

Do you think a TV advert is a good way of promoting this issue?

How might the advert be made to appeal to the target audience?

What other materials could Bridget's group use in their campaign?

Activity

Explore the message or issue you are planning to promote in your campaign through drama by dividing into groups and creating three still images that represent an aspect of the message or issue.

Share your images with the group and discuss how well you all feel the images accurately convey your message. Develop some of the images and present them as a series of still pictures with narration.

Measuring the success of your campaign

When planning your campaign you must think about ways in which you might measure its success. The success of a campaign using theatre, for example, might be measured through an audience questionnaire or though a workshop activity in which the audience participate and give feedback. In measuring the responses of your audience you must think about the message you are trying to get across and assess how well the audience have understood it.

People attending premieres are often interviewed in the foyer or on the street straight after the show. It's important to record responses quickly as much of a performance's success is through its emotional impact, and time quickly dulls or alters your feelings about a show as your logical brain starts to re-think what you have experienced.

Just checking

* Are you confident your performance will convey your campaign message?
* Do you understand how to make your performance appropriate for your target audience?
* Have you investigated the best way to evaluate the success of a performance?

Campaigns and media

You must think carefully about the range of media forms you will use in your campaign. It is unlikely that you would choose to use just one media form. If you are preparing material for a campaign you should consider how you can use the same material to produce other media products for your campaign. This will save time and money but also add an important consistency to your campaign materials. The case study and examples below show some of the aspects of preparing and running a media campaign.

OVER TO YOU!

Take a campaign advertisement image from a magazine. Attach this to the middle of a large poster and draw mind-map segments around the advertisement. In the segments add other ways in which this image could have been used in other media forms.

Choosing your campaign and message

A campaign can start from a small beginning. Campaigns can reflect society, or try to challenge society's negative elements. A campaign for good is often the most powerful you will come across, but it also carries a serious level of responsibility to conduct that campaign sensitively.

Case Study: What's the time, Mr Wolf?

Media Productions were approached by a teacher who had worked with their students to produce a play about stranger danger after the tragic death of a young local child. They wanted all children to understand the danger of talking to a stranger.

The staff at Media Productions saw the play being performed in a local junior school. They thought that the play was really innovative and met with the teacher and students. The teacher was frustrated that they could only get their message out to a small number of schools in their local area as the students were studying for their GCSE exams and could not spend lots of time on the road.

The Media Productions team was keen to be involved as they realised the importance of the message. This was the start of a campaign to get the play seen by children and parents across the UK.

What makes the medium of filmed performance so effective for a subject like this?

Reaching your audience

You have a wide range of media forms to choose from to reach your audience in the most effective way. You should evaluate each one carefully, considering your target audience and the form they are most likely to respond to, as well as which form would best suit your message and campaign aims.

Creating your campaign

Personal, learning and thinking skills

Working as a team to create your campaign allows you to connect your own and others' ideas and experiences. As Creative Thinkers you can use this pool of ideas to make your campaign as inventive as possible.

The resources you will need if you are making a television or radio commercial require much more organisation, as well as costing more to hire, than resources for producing a poster, flyer or billboard. It's a good idea to make **audit documents** for all the materials and resources you may need – nothing is too small, list it all so you can be sure your budget calculations are accurate, and that you have absolutely everything you need when it comes to creating your materials. Don't forget to include labour!

Case Study: What's the time, Mr Wolf?

The play was filmed and edited by Media Productions. The result was a very realistic short programme about a child being abducted by a stranger in a car. The theme of the play was a children's game 'What's the time, Mr Wolf?' and this became the name of the final programme. Media Productions enlisted the help of the local police for the production of the programme. They provided a police car, and in one scene where the young actor was too young to drive a car, he was filmed driving whilst the car was being towed on a police trailer. The team at Media Productions also begin to think about other resources they could add to the campaign. The Marketing Manager suggested that they should prepare a press release for the students to send out with copies of their DVD.

What benefit would a press release add to this campaign?

What other media materials could be helpful for this campaign?

Activity

Thought-shower all the different media forms you could use in a campaign. Write down the pros and cons of each one relating to your own chosen media campaign.

Audit documents – Lists of materials and resources you need during your campaign and its production.

Getting the message out

Whatever format you decide to use for your media campaign, you will have to distribute or broadcast your promotional materials. You will need to consider this before you finalise your plans for the products.

Measuring success

You must build a checking mechanism for your media campaign material into your plans from the beginning. This means that you must consider how you will find out whether your campaign has reached the right audience and if it has made an impact on them.

Case Study: What's the time, Mr Wolf?

The success of this campaign could be counted by how many people or organisations were able to be sent the DVD, but additionally how many of them watched the DVD, which could be measured by follow-up phone research or a questionnaire. The campaign was seen to be partially successful as the programme was shown to a wider audience. It was seen by the Home Secretary and MPs. The story was covered by national and local newspapers. However, when the time came to fund the copying and distribution of the programme there was no-one willing to pay for national distribution in the UK. One sponsor was found who agreed to pay for the programme to be sent to all the schools in the East Midlands. The campaign failed in that it did not succeed in having the programme seen by children across the country.

Do you think the failure of the campaign could have been avoided? How/why not?

What might have happened if the Home Secretary and MPs had been involved earlier in the campaign process?

Just checking

* Have you considered which media form(s) is best to reach your target audience?
* Do you know how to source all the resources you need?
* Have you thought about distribution of your campaign materials?
* Are you continually checking that your work relates to your original aims?

A campaign is a collaborative activity that involves different individuals working to produce a body of promotional products and activities that all convey the same message in a consistent way. Good planning and preparation ensure that the visual arts work you produce fits well within the campaign as a whole.

Defining your audience

Defining who your target audience will be and how you will reach them is key to the planning stage of any campaign. If you do not know who you are trying to reach, then you will not be able to define the best way to appeal to your audience and your campaign will not be successful.

Reaching your audience

Understanding what your audience is used to or wants to see will help you to produce material appropriate for them. You can do this in two ways:

* talking to people who would be in your target audience, by interviews, focus groups or conducting surveys
* finding out about what your target audience already likes – look at the TV programmes, magazines, websites and fashions that your target audience finds appealing and see what they tell you about the kind of images that they like or that communicate with them most effectively.

You can then use what you find from these investigations when planning how you will reach your audience with visual imagery.

Different people – different audiences.

Case Study: Richard

Richard works for a graphic design agency that is creating a series of glossy colour leaflets to help promote healthy living amongst the teenagers in a local area. The campaign focuses on encouraging young people to participate in sports activities and use the area's leisure facilities.

When considering how the leaflets should look, Richard first thinks about the audience he is hoping to reach. Richard holds a focus group with students from a local college and asks them what would make them want to take part in sports activities. They tell him that they want it to be fun and a chance to meet up with other young people.

When Richard books a photographer and some models to shoot images for the leaflet, he asks for young people to be hired as models, with some dressed in their own casual clothes and some in sportswear. The photographs feature young people not only playing sport, but also talking and laughing outside the leisure centres.

What has Richard achieved by talking directly to his target audience?

Selecting your ideas

Once you have identified who your campaign is aimed at and the best way to reach them, it will be time to plan what you will do to promote the message at the heart of the campaign. As a visual artist, you will probably be involved in creating print-based products such as leaflets, posters, flyers and booklets to promote the message and you need to make sure that the designs and 'look' of the products you produce sit well with the other things people are working on.

Case Study: Creative skills

A group of students wanted to produce a campaign for the PDSA, a charity that provides care for sick animals. They had evaluated their group skills early on and realised there were several artists keen to contribute to the visual impact of the campaign. The group were planning to make a short film and a number of posters. They decided to work together as a large group to agree the detail of the campaign and its **'look and style'**, before splitting into two groups, one concentrating on the film and one on the posters. The four artists would be divided between the groups so they all had a chance to use their creative skills. To ensure that they maintained a link between the groups and materials they were producing, they held regular meetings at which drafts and ideas were shown and debated.

Why do you think it is important to listen to what people want to do?

Is your group using all the skills of its members? Check that everyone is happy with their job, and if not, try to organise tasks so everyone gets to do something they enjoy.

Materials and resources

You need to consider the materials and resources you will need for your campaign alongside your budget. There's no sense in planning an extravagant, time-consuming campaign if you have two weeks and £50. This is not to say that your campaign cannot be ambitious, but it must be realistic. Compiling budget sheets, preparing schedules and audit documents will help make sure your plans are sensible and achievable, as well as doubling as checklists when you come to create your materials. Making sure that the resources you need are available and accessible before beginning production work will make your practical activities much easier.

Functional skills

Using Maths...

Estimation and calculation can be used to plan the layouts of campaign materials like flyers, posters and website pages.

Using ICT...

Look for illustrative materials for your campaign, the internet or on copyright-free image CDs. Programs such as Microsoft Picture Manager can then be used to adapt them.

'Look and style' – The visual theme and feeling you want your campaign to have.

Slogan – A catchy phrase that reflects the message of the campaign and appeals to the target audience.

Activity

What kind of materials and resources would you need to gather in order to complete the following visual arts products that are needed for a campaign?

* A series of humorous cartoon-style drawings.
* The **slogan** for the campaign printed onto T-shirts.
* A selection of black and white photographs.

Just checking

* Have you defined your target audience thoroughly?
* Have you identified the most effective ways to reach your audience?
* Have you allocated roles in your group fairly?
* Can your campaign materials be produced according to your time and budget constraints?

5.3 Conducting a campaign

Once you have prepared your campaign you will have to put it into action! This means organising your resources ready for the launch of your campaign. You will need to ensure that all your contacts have been identified and that you've enlisted the help of as many people as possible to help broadcast or distribute your campaign.

OVER TO YOU!

Make a list of all the methods you intend to use to broadcast or distribute your campaign material. Put a box by the side of each one and tick off each box as you use this method.

Personal, learning and thinking skills

Managing a campaign successfully requires the skills of Self Managing and Effective Participation. What do you have to do in your campaign that could enable you to demonstrate these skills?

Campaign safety

Running your campaign may involve members of your group working outside your school or college. You could be running a stall in your local shopping centre, or approaching the public on the street offering leaflets or canvassing opinion. Make sure you work safely by:

* never working alone
* keeping to well-lit public areas at night or during darker winter months
* making sure someone knows where you will be and when
* checking in regularly with your group
* making sure you can contact someone in an emergency with a fully charged and credited mobile phone.

Organising your resources

You must ensure that all the resources needed for the successful conduct of your campaign are in place. Go through your resources and materials audit checklists. Confirm all bookings of venues and hiring of equipment – visit in person or ring and speak to people to ensure you have firm answers, do not trust to email/answerphones at this crucial stage. Collect together all your campaign materials and any miscellaneous items you will need, such as glue, drawing pins, string, sticky tape, pens, pencils, clipboards.

Contingency

Have you made contingency plans for your campaign activities? If you are handing out leaflets and asking questions on the street, have you organised umbrellas in case it rains so your audience do not get wet while talking to you? If you are performing outside, have you arranged an inside location for inclement weather, such as asking permission to move into the local shopping centre?

Making and maintaining contacts

You will have made and maintained contact with many people and organisations during the planning and production of your campaign, but double-check that everyone in the group has an updated list of names, addresses and telephone number or email address.

It's also a good idea to contact the people who will be either directly involved in your campaign, or helping you to broadcast or distribute it. It will remind them of their agreed commitment, but it also helps to maintain good relations as you can answer any queries they may have and ensure they are happy with the arrangements.

Think about anyone else who could help you with your campaign. This could be:

* a newspaper or magazine that could cover your campaign and provide publicity
* a local television or radio company who could interview you for their news broadcast
* shops where you could leave your leaflets or flyers
* people who could hand out your materials in the street
* a personality who could demonstrate their support for the campaign
* someone who could give you advice on how to conduct and monitor your campaign.

Activity

Produce your own Handbook and use this to keep careful records of the contact details you will need for the campaign. You could also use this to record the resources and materials you need, and as a personal diary about how the campaign is progressing.

The Producer's Handbook

The Producer at Media Productions has a created a Producer's Handbook. In this handbook she keeps records of the contact details her team need for the products they are producing or campaigns they are organising. It also contains useful emergency contact numbers, for example local police and emergency services. This enables the Producer to have easy and quick access to the information she needs.

Working with a group

Think about the group that you will be working with. How will you make sure you work together as a team? Think about:

* Communicating with each other – how will you keep in touch during the campaign activities?
* Working together – how will you allocate roles in the group to conduct and monitor the campaign?
* Responsibility – who will be in charge, make decisions and check that activities have been carried out?

You might think it's easier to work with people you're good friends with, or people who think the same way as you, but the best teams are often made up of diverse people with different skills and different views and experiences. A group can benefit from a variety of opinions on a subject because it will encourage debate, which in turn often sparks new ideas or solutions to problems. This is not to say you won't make a great team if you have been friends for years, but it can be easier to voice an opposing opinion to someone you don't know very well, rather than someone you've planned to go to the cinema with that night.

Personal, learning and thinking skills

Team Work skills are really important for the success of a campaign.

Collaborating with others will make sure your materials are creative and interesting.

Discussing decisions and reaching agreements will help things get done in a democratic way, particularly if everyone works as an Effective Participator, negotiating and balancing their views.

You should also be prepared to influence others, where necessary, to make sure the campaign aims are the central focus of discussions.

Functional skills

Using English...

When attending campaign meetings, make use of your speaking and listening skills to participate effectively.

Try to contribute to discussions in a thoughtful manner and make sure any information you present is done so effectively. Prepare any important points beforehand so you can explain things clearly and answer any questions.

What really makes a good team though is respect. You may disagree with another member of your team, but as long as you respect one another's opinions, give others the opportunity to speak and ensure you explain or justify any critical opinions with facts and reason, you stand a good chance of being a successful group. It is important to meet together regularly to discuss how the campaign is progressing and to maintain team spirit. If you all have individual tasks it can be easy to feel isolated, or to start to drift away from the message of the campaign.

You should also hold regular production meetings and take minutes of these meetings so that you can see what needs to done and by when. The minutes from these meetings will also be really useful later, when you undertake a review of your work and what you have learnt in this unit.

Getting your message out

The most important part of any campaign is getting your message out to the audience. However carefully you have planned, if the campaign is not seen by the audience then it will have failed.

Monitoring your campaign

Testing your materials

As part of your ongoing monitoring and assessment of your campaign you may decide to test elements of your campaign to make sure that it is fit for purpose. This can be a particularly essential activity if you have created an unusual or challenging campaign artefact, as you would not want to have material in a campaign that your target audience will not want to read or view.

Choosing the best moment in the production of your campaign to test the materials can be tricky. Too early and your draft material may not accurately reflect the intended finished piece, too late and it could be expensive or impossible to make major changes. Consider the following when you are thinking about testing your materials:

* Have you allowed time in your schedule for testing?
* Will you be able to gather together a sample group of your target audience?
* Who in your group will organise the testing?
* How will you measure and record the response of the group?
* Can you prepare a sample or draft of your campaign without compromising your other activities?
* Do you have sufficient time and budget to make changes if they are necessary?

When you undertake the broadcasting or distribution of your own campaign you must think carefully about how the distribution or broadcasting will be happening. Is there an opportunity to reflect on how things are going and how you may be able to change the campaign as it progresses? The ability to be flexible and suggest alternative methods if something goes wrong might save a campaign from failure. Make sure you are as prepared as you can be, with a detailed contingency plan and an open-minded attitude.

Case Study: Safe Surfing!

Alanya, Faye and Julia have produced a campaign aimed at teenagers to inform and advise them on safe internet surfing and chatroom participation. They worked together to plan and create a series of posters and a short film. They met regularly to discuss issues and plan how their campaign would work.

Once the film had been shot and the finished programme produced, the girls then designed a cover for the DVD that identified it was suitable for teenagers and used appropriate images and font styles.

However, when it came to distributing their finished DVD they had a problem. No one took responsibility for ensuring that it was distributed to the national and local press and broadcasters.

The group had intended for these people to have a copy of the DVD and an explanatory letter, however over coffee one morning Julia and Faye decided it would be better if the letters were personally addressed to the individual editors. Faye wrote the letters but Alanya had been tasked with sending out the DVDs. She wasn't aware of the change and mixed up the letters and addresses so the envelope was addressed to one newspaper and the letter was addressed to a different editor. This demonstrated a lack of professionalism and the editors were not keen to support their campaign.

Why would a mistake like mixing up letters and envelopes matter to media professionals?

What lessons can you learn from this group's campaign?

Alanya, Faye and Julia had worked hard to make sure their safe surfing film was appropriate for their target audience, but they still realised it would be wise to test it out by showing it to a small sample audience. They approached a youth club in the next town and asked the leaders if they could visit and show the film on a Saturday morning. Once they had received a positive response from the leader in charge, they prepared a questionnaire that contained questions that they could ask the teenagers. The questions were designed to be asked by one of the group so the audience of 11-16 year olds could ask for clarification, if necessary. The questionnaire was designed to gauge the teenagers' understanding of the personal and internet security dangers of surfing the web and giving out information in chatrooms after they had watched the film.

Once they had gathered data from the questionnaires the group were able to see if their campaign film was effective.

Why didn't the girls just show the film to a sample of students from their own school?

What kinds of questions do you think the group might have asked to gauge the film's effectiveness?

Can you think of any improvements to this testing activity?

How would you use a similar activity to test your own creative or media campaign?

Personal, learning and thinking skills

Monitoring your campaign means acting on things that go wrong or could be improved. A Reflective Learner ensures their reflective activities actually make a difference to their work, modifying it where necessary or informing the way they approach tasks.

For your project

When you are conducting your campaign, remember to think about:

* working efficiently and with imagination to solve any problems that arise
* working within the time constraints that you have identified
* pulling together as a team to conduct your campaign
* asking for help or advice from your teacher
* giving advice and assistance to others when asked.

Just checking

* Have you confirmed all bookings of venues, materials and staff?
* Have you prepared a logbook to record how the campaign goes?
* Are you prepared as a team for the campaign?
* Can you think of any extra ways to boost or distribute your materials?

Conducting a performing arts campaign

Using live drama as part of a campaign takes careful organisation. If you have planned to conduct a campaign that uses live drama, music and/or dance you will need to organise your resources carefully to ensure everything is where it should be for the performance.

OVER TO YOU!

How would conducting a campaign that uses live music, drama and/or dance differ from conducting a poster campaign?

Getting to work

Once your plans have been made and your materials produced, you will need to get to work on running your campaign. If you are using performance arts this may mean distributing a film or radio advert. If you have planned to use live materials this will involve performing your 'show' to an audience. Whether you are involved in the performance itself, or are presenting other campaign materials, it's important to take personal responsibility for your part in the campaign. Enjoy this responsibility! You've worked hard to produce your materials and you should be confident in your work and in yourself that you will play a valuable part in the success of your campaign.

Organising your resources

Touring a show

Many theatre companies who devise and perform **issue-based** pieces tour their work into schools and other community venues, sometimes visiting and performing in several venues each week. This takes careful planning and organisation.

Travelling light

Working on a touring production will be quite different to putting on a show in a single venue such as your school/college hall or drama studio. When planning and performing a touring show you should:

* keep scenery simple so it can easily be transported and set up when you arrive at each venue
* use a flexible set that can be adapted to fit different shapes and sizes of venues
* be ready as performers to be flexible. You might find yourself performing in a long narrow space one day and a larger square one the next
* keep lighting to a minimum or don't use it at all. Few primary schools have **blackouts** in their halls so any lighting effects may be lost anyway!

When you are moving equipment and materials from one venue to another, things can easily be misplaced or left behind. To ensure this doesn't happen, keep a checklist of everything you are using. Smaller items can be transported in carefully labelled boxes.

Personal, learning and thinking skills

A Team Worker doesn't stop once the campaign materials are made, they keep focus through the campaign itself, supporting their group members and accepting help from others when it is offered.

Issue-based – Performances created around an issue, e.g. giving up smoking or not wearing fur.

Blackout – A complete absence of light. In spaces with windows this is achieved by the use of thick black curtains.

Flats – Timber frames generally covered in plywood, then painted or given a textured finish as pieces of scenery.

Greenfield Community School
Healthy Eating Road Show
Checklist of equipment and materials for tour

Larger Items of Scenery
3 x **flats**
folding table
Props (to be transported in large green crate)
plastic fruit and vegetables x12
frying pan
wooden spoons x3
large (fake) chocolate bar

Sound Equipment
CD Player
Amplifier
Cable (in green crate)
Sound effects CD (in green crate)
CD of backing tracks (in green crate)
Costumes
Actors to be responsible for own costumes.

Running a workshop activity

Some Theatre in Education productions include workshop activities for the audience. Performers take part in discussion and/or practical activities and games with the audience to allow them to explore the issues raised further. Workshops can also be used to assess the success of a production in getting a message across.

Case Study: Big Wheel Theatre in Education

Big Wheel is a company that specialises in theatre for schools. They use workshop activities to allow students to explore issues from sustainable transport to drugs and alcohol in a safe environment. In their 'Get Stuffed' show, which tackles the subject of healthy eating, the audience take part in a game in which two teams try to fill their plates with a balanced meal and are challenged by the 'healthiest person in the world' in a fitness competition.

Can you think of a game, competition or interactive activity to use as part of your campaign?

Enlisting help

If your campaign features performance, it is likely you have already planned ways to advertise it within your other campaign materials. You may have considered a press release – they are an easy way to get information to a large number of people, who can then tap into a huge media audience.

You could follow up your press release by contacting a few select editors or journalists to enlist their support. It might be the thing that helps your press release stand out from the others that day, and result in a radio plug or even feature in a newspaper.

Big Wheel use games and competitions to help audiences explore issues.

Just checking

* Are your resources ready and organised for your performance?
* Are workshop activities planned and venues/staff confirmed?
* Have you drafted any press releases to promote your performance activities?

OVER TO YOU!

Produce a checklist of all the materials and resources you have planned to use to launch and distribute your campaign. Make sure that all of these are still available. Use this as an opportunity to double check that you have everything in place.

Personal, learning and thinking skills

Inviting feedback will help you to improve your campaign. However, as a Reflective Learner you must be prepared to deal positively with any criticism or setbacks – and be able to accept praise too!

Activity

There is lots of advice on testing products and materials on the internet. If you have created a website there are even free websites such as browsershots.org or webxact.watchfire.com which will test the technical elements of your web pages for free. Try using such a site on your own website and devise a plan to test the content of your pages.

Navigating – Using a website, trying to understand how it works and where things link.

Conducting a media campaign

You've planned and created your media campaign activities, now you just need to organise, deliver, distribute, circulate, turn on, log-on, sign-in, upload, email… and, if you have any energy left, enjoy the excitement of a campaign in action!

Testing your campaign

Hold on! You may need to test your media campaign before you distribute it to make sure that it is fit for purpose. It would be a disaster to have a media campaign that insulted an audience or included unsuitable images. To test your materials, you will need a group of people who fit the target audience for your media campaign. Depending on the form of the material, you could:

* distribute a physical sample, e.g. a poster or leaflet, to the target audience and ask them to comment on its effectiveness
* perform a short extract of your dramatic piece in a focus group setting and take immediate feedback and improvement suggestions
* email your e-newsletter to someone to ensure that any images appear as they should and text has not moved
* give someone access to log on to the working model of your website and practise **navigating** around it to ensure any links work and that it is easy to use.

If there are any problems, now is the time to solve them!

Organising your media resources

Organising your media resources means making sure everything you have planned to use is available at the right time and in the right place. You could use a checklist like the one opposite, which also acts as a schedule reminder.

Resources	Venue	Date	Time	Comments
Posters	Town centre	Sunday 17th October	10.30am	Group to meet by Starbucks, MAXWELL to bring posters, ABBI to bring string, tape and pins.
	School	Monday 18th October	12.30pm	Group to meet outside canteen. Same supplies as before.
E-newsletter	IT suite	Friday 22nd October	3.30pm	Make sure the IT suite is booked. Check REBECCA has finished compiling the address list.
Film projector	School hall	Saturday 23rd October	6.30pm	The projector is stored in the technician's room. It must be taken out by JOE by 5pm.

Maintaining your media contacts

It is essential that you keep up your contacts when running a media campaign. Sometimes you may think of a brilliant idea at the last moment, or a celebrity approaches you at the last minute to be in your campaign. You will need to use this to your advantage and be able to contact a local newspaper, radio station or television news desk to cover this story. It may be too late if you have to go back to your office and rummage around your desk for a couple of hours to find a telephone number.

Organise yourself from the beginning with an address book, or keep your mobile phone updated with all new numbers.

Getting your media campaign materials out to the audience

Media campaigns often have more technical requirements than campaigns relying more on paper-based materials. It is essential that you have the technical means to distribute or broadcast your media campaign materials.

* If you have produced a video product will this be in a format that everyone can access?
* If you have a radio commercial do you know which is the most commonly-used file format so everyone will be able to play the material?
* Can your website material be viewed by any browser?

You will still need to consider practical issues too, for example:

* How will you transport weighty or cumbersome boxes of flyers or posters?
* Have you arranged any necessary courier services, or checked the opening hours of your local post office?

Personal, learning and thinking skills

You are now working towards your campaign goals. You will need to show commitment, perseverance and initiative to reach them. A Self Manager continues to push themselves to do the best job possible: to find that extra bit of campaign promotion or to persuade that extra volunteer to hand out leaflets.

Just checking

* Have you tested your campaign materials to ensure they are appropriate?
* Do you have checklists for campaign activities and necessary resources?
* Are your campaign materials technically ready for distribution?
* Do you have an up-to-date list of all your media contacts?

Conducting a visual arts campaign

How you actually use the materials you have planned for and prepared will be key to the success of communicating your campaign's message.

Distributing your campaign materials

During your preparation you will have been thinking about how you will go about getting the campaign materials and promotional products to the intended audience. Now you will need to act on these plans and ensure that you can actually deliver the campaign effectively.

Organising the distribution of promotional materials

How you go about dealing with the distribution of the campaign materials you have delivered will depend on the nature of your campaign, the nature of your target audience and the budget you have to work with. Those working on campaigns focused on the local area with a small budget will approach this task in a very different way to those who are conducting national campaigns with a large budget.

National campaigns usually have a big budget and involve things like billboard advertisements.

Case Study: Maria

Maria has been working in a group who are conducting a campaign to promote a dance and drama workshop aimed at parents and toddlers. They have conducted a survey with people from their target audience, thought carefully about what their promotional materials should contain and produced leaflets and posters to promote the event.

They begin to plan how they are going to get the campaign materials to the audience and start, in their planning stages, by thought-showering where people with toddlers might regularly visit or meet. The group decides that, as many young children need check-ups at the doctor's surgery, this might be a good place to put some of their materials. Maria telephones the doctor's surgery and speaks to the receptionist about getting permission to promote the event within the surgery. After consulting with the surgery manager, the receptionist informs Maria that this would be allowed. The receptionist also says that the clinic's nurse has said that she will hand out leaflets to any parents she sees in the coming weeks. Maria returns the following day with copies of the poster to display on the walls of the surgery waiting room and a pile of leaflets both for the nurse to give out and for parents to pick up.

Where else would be suitable places for Maria to distribute their campaign materials?

What organisations might take an interest in her campaign?

Contacting organisations

Have you considered contacting existing organisations who share your campaign message, such as charities, or have undertaken similar campaigns themselves, such as advertising agencies? You may find them a valuable source of information about the best ways and places to distribute your campaign materials and reach your target audience.

Exploring opportunities

It is more than likely that there will be several different ways that your campaign can be delivered to your audience. The more ways that you find to distribute promotional materials and stage promotional activities, the more people you will reach and the more successful your campaign will be in communicating a message to the target audience.

Consider all of the following:

∗ leaving materials in prominent or suitable locations

∗ delivering or distributing material by hand

∗ displaying material in appropriate locations.

Legal and safety considerations

Whenever you are working on distributing materials or delivering campaign products you must always be aware of your own safety. If you are visiting anywhere, go in pairs or small groups. Be aware of your surroundings and make sure what you do and how you behave doesn't endanger you or those around you.

When mounting posters or leaving materials for others to pick up, ensure you have the permission of the person who owns or is in charge of that place. Placing any kind of campaign materials in locations without permission could mean your carefully produced materials are thrown away or, even worse, that you break the law. Shopkeepers, library staff, receptionists, assistants and security guards are all good people to ask for advice about getting permission when you identify somewhere you think is appropriate.

Preparation for assessment

In this unit you have taken part in the preparation and delivery of a campaign designed to promote an idea, issue or message. Your work should cover at least two of the disciplines listed in the Introduction to this book. For example, you might look at how creative writing and advertising can both be used in developing a campaign.

Your portfolio

Your process portfolio will be expected to contain evidence of your involvement in your assignments. Your teacher may tell you what form your portfolio should take and how to present your work.

You will be assessed on…	This will be evidenced in your portfolio by…
…your understanding of the nature of campaigns.	Your research notes. These may be notes taken in class as well as articles found on the internet, in books and magazines. You should also include examples of campaign materials you have investigated, annotated with your own comments and notes. Your presentation. This could be in written form or a talk, perhaps using PowerPoint slides. If you give a talk, remember to include the notes you use in your portfolio. **Tips for success:** • You may need to gather a range of materials in different formats. Posters and leaflets can be scanned if you prefer to store your materials on a computer.
…your ability to prepare a campaign.	A log or diary giving details of your planning work. This should include notes on ideas you have and all rough work including sketches, ideas boards, scripts. You must also include a campaign production plan, which should include details of your materials and resources, along with a schedule showing timings and deadlines for each stage of the process. You should also include documents such as schedules and notes taken at meetings. You must include the actual campaign materials. They could be in a number of different forms, e.g. posters, leaflets, website pages, videos. If your campaign includes live music, dance and/or drama, you should record a final rehearsal of the piece. **Tips for success:** • Make sure you have blank copies of any forms and documents you may need, e.g. production schedules, meeting records.
…your ability to conduct a campaign.	Your log or diary. You must keep a note of the processes you undertake when conducting your campaign. Your teachers will also produce observation reports on how well you carry out practical tasks **Tips for success:** • Spend a short time at the end of each session writing up what has been done while it is fresh in your mind.
…your ability to monitor the preparation and conduct of the campaign.	The documents in your portfolio. As well as providing evidence of your contribution to the planning and conduct of the campaign, your log will also be used to assess your ability to monitor your progress and contribution to the work. You will also need to include details of how successful the campaign was in achieving its aims. This could be evidenced through a written report or a presentation. **Tips for success:** • You need to monitor and review your progress at all stages. In the planning stage you should use this process to improve your work.

The assessment of the unit

This unit is assessed internally by your teachers. Remember, you'll be assessed on **what** you submit as part of your process portfolio and your teacher's observations of **how** you've worked.

You must show that you:	Guidance	To gain higher marks:
…can undertake an investigation into the nature of a particular campaign.	Use your investigations to inform the work you do later in the unit. For example; if you are intending to use drama or music in your campaign, look for examples of existing work to investigate. You should use a range of resources when carrying out your investigations (not just the internet).	Your research must be well-focused and your findings must be relevant. The presentation of your findings must include a detailed explanation of the nature and purpose of the campaigns you have investigated. Your work should make reference to a wide range of examples.
…can come up with ideas for a campaign and plan its creation. …can organise resources to produce campaign materials.	Explore ideas carefully to make sure they will work. You could start with the idea, issue or message you intend to promote. Bear in mind the amount of time you have available: an idea may be excellent, but will you have time to produce the materials? Remember to consider the purpose of your campaign at each stage of the planning process: how successful will it be in promoting your idea, issue or message? Make sure all the resources and materials you are planning to use are available and that you know how to use them.	You must come up with a number of imaginative ideas for the campaign and be able to explore them thoughtfully. You must work in a disciplined manner when planning your campaign, taking care to note any time constraints. You must make good use of planning documents and gather your resources efficiently. You must produce campaign materials that show imagination and skill. You must be able to carry out planning tasks with only occasional help from your teachers.
…can manage the conduct of the campaign. …can work well with others.	Make sure you have a clear understanding of what your responsibilities will be when conducting the campaign. Manage your time carefully by making a checklist of tasks that includes deadlines. Refer to it regularly. Teamwork will be important. Remember to listen to others and respect their views.	You must manage the campaign imaginatively and effectively. You must manage your time to make sure you meet deadlines. You must work positively with others. You must be able to carry out your role with only occasional help from your teachers.
…are able to monitor the planning and conduct of the campaign.	You need to consider how you are going to assess the effectiveness of your campaign <u>before</u> you begin to conduct it. You may, for example, decide to use audience questionnaires or collect information through interviews. Whatever you decide, you will need to find time to design and create the materials needed for this task.	You must show that you have used monitoring to improve the work you have undertaken during the planning and conduct of the campaign. You must describe your contribution to the project showing that you have a thorough understanding of the strengths and weaknesses of your work.

6 FESTIVAL

Introduction

Festivals provide a way of showcasing arts and media work in a single event. Some festivals have a particular focus, for example the Montreux Jazz Festival or the Bath Film Festival. Others celebrate a range of work across a number of different genres, for example the Brighton Festival includes a wide range of theatre, dance and music.

OVER TO YOU!

Thought shower – the British Arts Festival Association currently has over 100 annual festivals listed on its website. Why do you think festivals are so popular?

The Brighton Festival celebrates work in theatre, music and dance.

Your learning

In this unit, you should work across at least two of the disciplines on page 4 to cover the four main topics.

Understanding festivals in the creative and media industries

A festival is a celebration and should carry a feeling of vibrancy, excitement, spontaneity and innovation. To help you understand the nature of festival you will investigate a range of different kinds of arts and media festivals from the UK and around the world. You will need to find out what the **target audiences** are for these festivals as well as how they are funded. You will also need to find out their **artistic policy** then investigate their programme of events to see how closely they match. Your research will help you begin to understand the many considerations of staging your own festival.

Contributing to the planning of a festival

You will go on to use the knowledge gained during your investigations to plan your own festival, perhaps to showcase work you have created in other units of this course. No matter how relaxed a festival may seem, it is the product of meticulous planning and organisation. You will need to decide the kinds of artefacts, performances and/or products required for your festival carefully and select suitable work. Your group will also need to consider the resources you have available so you plan a festival that can realistically take place. You will need to decide who does what in terms of organising your festival and draw up a schedule of planning activities. Your plans should also include visual designs and representations as appropriate.

Contributing to the promotion of a festival

You wouldn't try to stage a family-orientated festival that began at 5pm – your target audience would be having tea and getting ready for bed! It's crucial to plan your festival with a target audience in mind and to make sure that each element of the festival is appropriate, from its timing to its content to the facilities it requires. You will need to devise and create a **publicity campaign** to suit these elements and to take part in promotional activities to raise awareness of your festival.

Contributing to the running of a festival

The success of your festival will be determined to a large part by how smoothly it runs. Depending on the nature of your festival this may involve the setting up of artefacts and/or products for exhibition, organising the viewing of recorded work or the production of performance activities. Your group will need to put the plans you made into action, making sure deadlines are met and that everyone and everything is where it is supposed to be. Teamwork and communication are the keys here, and you must plan your teamwork as thoroughly as you plan the content of your festival.

Working as a team

Success in this unit will rely on strong teamwork. Festivals, by their nature, are made up of a range of different performances, artefacts and/or products. The planning and promotional activities as well as the running of your festival will require you to work as a team. Members of the group will need to take on individual roles whilst also communicating with others to ensure everything is completed within the deadlines you are working to.

Process portfolio

In your process portfolio for this unit you will need to make sure that you have recorded and carefully stored evidence from all stages of your work.

You will need to make sure your portfolio includes:

* Your research and investigations – you should keep copies of all research materials you use during your investigations, as well as your findings. You may present the results of your investigations in written form or orally as a presentation to the class.

* Your planning documentation – keep careful notes of all ideas, plans, schedules and the decisions made during the planning of your festival. This should include records of the meetings you attend, as well as personal notes showing the reasons for decisions and your own thoughts on the planning process.

* Your promotional materials – again you should keep notes of discussions made during planning and creation of promotional materials. Any materials used to help create the publicity materials should be included along with rough work, drafts and details of decisions made along the way.

* A record of the festival itself – you should keep a journal detailing your activities during the running of the festival. Include details of your individual responsibilities and your thoughts on the success of the work.

Target audiences – The audiences that a festival is aiming to reach.

Artistic policy – The artistic policy of a festival is a set of aims and objectives that helps shape the content and inform who will be invited to contribute.

Publicity campaign – Advertising materials you distribute to make people aware of your creative or media activity.

Activity

Visit the website of the British Arts Festival Association and follow the links to three different festivals. For each one:

* Note the type of work being showcased.

* Look for evidence of funding (from local councils and/or the Arts Councils).

* Look for evidence of sponsorship (from business).

* Discuss the type of audience the events might attract.

Remember!

* Researching different kinds of festival will help you plan your own.

* You must plan and budget your festival carefully.

* Your promotional activities are vital to your festival's success.

* Teamwork is essential for a successful festival.

6.1 Understanding festivals

There is probably no such thing as a typical arts/media festival; they come in all shapes and sizes. Even the largest festivals, however, have often grown from humble beginnings. In 2005, 153,000 people paid £125 to attend the Glastonbury Music Festival – a far cry from the 1,000 people who attended the first 'Glastonbury' in 1970, when tickets cost £1 and included free milk from the farm!

Beginning your research

Your teacher may give you a theme for your festival, or they may leave the choice to you. Either way, in order to understand the possibilities for a festival, you will need to collect information about a variety of arts and media festivals that are staged in this country and around the world. You could undertake your research individually or in groups, sharing and discussing your findings as you progress.

Even a festival the size of Glastonbury had small origins.

You might begin by:

* searching books, newspapers and magazines for information about arts and media festivals in your region, nationally and internationally

* using the internet to find examples of past festivals and those planned for the future – download or send off for festival brochures will provide information about each festival's programme of events and research arts and media festivals from around the world

* watching and/or listening to performances (music, drama and/or dance) recorded at arts festivals.

You could also ask your teacher to arrange a visit to a festival in your region. This would allow you to look around and sample some of the performances and/or exhibits first hand. If possible, arrange to speak to one of the organisers about the way in which the programme of events was put together and how the festival is run.

Artistic policy

At the heart of any festival is an artistic policy that sets out the aims of the event. For some festivals the aims will include bringing high-quality arts events to the local community. For example, the Bath Film Festival includes an **outreach** programme of events that, through the use of portable equipment, brings the cinema to communities with no local access to film.

OVER TO YOU!

What do you think festivals have to offer the artist or performer? For example, if you were a professional musician, playwright, visual artist or filmmaker, what might be the advantages of showcasing your work at an arts and media festival?

Many festivals aim to include a wide range of events. The International Indian Film Academy **Fringe** Festival ran alongside the Bollywood version of the Oscars, plus there were stalls, street entertainment, dancing, a film workshop and an exhibition celebrating Indian cinema.

Some festivals may decide on a specific theme, for example a link to a historical event or period. In 2007 the annual Hebden Bridge Festival commemorated the bicentenary of the abolition of the slave trade by including events linked to the theme of 'freedom'. Events related to this theme were clearly marked in the Festival programme by the symbol of a broken chain. They included a concert by the Grand Union Orchestra, a photographic exhibition about life in a refugee camp on the Thai–Burma border and themed 'drop-in' arts sessions for children and adults.

Some festivals aim to include something for everyone.

For your project

You should focus your research on at least four festivals. Try and choose contrasting examples, for example:

* a small festival from your own region
* a large national festival that showcases a range of arts and media work
* a festival from another country e.g. Europe, India or Australia
* a festival with a particular focus, e.g. a film or literary festival.

Make an effort to consider festivals that have a particular cultural or religious emphasis that is different from your own experiences; you may well get a lot of new and interesting ideas.

Outreach – Activities or events that extend your festival out into the community.

Fringe – Alternative, not mainstream.

For your project

Finding out about a festival's aims:

* Most festivals have a brochure that includes details of the programme of events, as well as background information about the festival itself. Festival websites also include this information.
* The artistic policy or aims of the festival may appear on the homepage of their website or introductory section of the brochure. You should also look for sections such as 'about us' or 'festival history' for further information about their aims.

The 'Proms' is a festival of classical music that takes place each summer.

Festivals may also be trying to highlight a political or social issue. The Big Cuba Fiesta is organised by the Cuba Solidarity Campaign who believe in Cuba's right to independence. The Festival features performances by salsa and merengue bands, Latin American DJ-ing and salsa dance classes.

Content and audience

Once you have discovered the artistic policy of a particular festival you should find out how this matches the programme of events on offer. For example, if a festival is aiming to 'to present the widest possible range of music, performed to the highest standards' (as is the stated aim of the BBC Proms, a festival of classical music), you would expect to find a programme of events that included a rich assortment of classical music played by the best orchestras, ensembles and soloists in the world.

In any festival there will also be links between the artistic policy and the target audience. Remember to look out for these links when you are researching your chosen festivals.

For your project

Look in the brochure or on the website of each of your four chosen festivals for evidence of funding or sponsorship. The **logos** of any business sponsors will be included, as will details of public funding received from the Arts Councils and/or local councils.

For your project

✱ To find the links between the artistic policy and programme of events, you could begin by getting a feel for the range of events on offer in each of your chosen festivals by listing and categorising the different types of events included in the programme, e.g. film, drama, dance, music. If the festival policy is to promote a particular type of work, look for examples in the programme.

If the festival has a specific focus or theme, can you see how specific events and/ or activities are linked to this?

✱ What is the target audience?

The artistic policy may give information about the target audience of the festival, however, the programme of events will also provide clues.

Look to see if the programme includes events that could be described as 'popular' in their nature, e.g. pop/rock music or popular forms of theatre such as musicals and/or pantomimes.

Are there are any events that are targeted towards specific groups, e.g. children or families?

Does the festival include any events that the public can participate in, e.g. workshops, and drop-in sessions?

Are any 'outreach' events included in the programme? These may be events that take place in venues away from the main festival sites, e.g. in rural villages.

Funding

The staging of an arts and media festival can be expensive. Artists, performers and festival staff such as administrators will need to be paid. Venues will need to be hired and publicity materials produced. Some festivals operate in the commercial sector and have to cover all of these costs through ticket sales, **merchandising**, etc.

Many arts and media festivals however are **subsidised**. This means they receive **public funding** from the Arts Councils and/or local councils. Many also receive financial assistance from local, national and international businesses. In 2007, Brighton Festival, for example, received funding from Arts Council England and Brighton and Hove Council. Business sponsors included Lloyds TSB, Waitrose and First Capital Connect.

Your process portfolio

It is important that you put copies of all your research materials in a file. Make sure you annotate them with your own notes and comments on why they are relevant and what they tell you about:

* the arts and media festivals you have investigated
* how each festival is funded
* the artistic policy, target audience and programme content of each festival.

You should also present your conclusions in written form or in the form of a verbal presentation.

Activity

Why do businesses provide funding for the arts?

What do you think they receive in return?

Functional skills

Using ICT...

When choosing and researching festivals you can use ICT to find and select information. This could include:

* using the internet as a research tool
* selecting information that is useful
* keeping a record of websites accessed.

Your research could also be presented using word-processing software and/or presentation software such as PowerPoint.

Logos – Designs used by an organisation in advertising and promotional materials by which they can be easily recognised.

Merchandising – The sale of products such as T-shirts, mugs, etc.

Subsidised – Receiving financial support from government bodies.

Public Funding – Money that comes from the taxpayer and is distributed by the government via Arts Councils and/or local councils.

Activity

As a class, collate the information collected about the artistic policies of the festivals you have looked at. Break into small groups to thought-shower ideas for an 'artistic policy' for your own arts and media festival. Each group should then present their ideas to the class for discussion.

As a class, use the ideas to come up with an artistic policy for your arts/media festival.

Just checking

* Have you identified a range of different arts and media festivals from across the world?
* Have you identified how these festivals are funded?
* Have you investigated the artistic policy, target audience and programme content of each audience?

Different types of festival

In this topic we will look at some of the different types of festivals from ones that cover music and arts, to media and visual arts festivals.

OVER TO YOU!

What do you think the attraction of a music festival is? Why do you think festivals such as Glastonbury and Reading continue to be so popular?

Music and arts festivals

Festivals have been an important part of the popular music scene for nearly forty years. In 1969 a music and art fair took place at a dairy farm in New York State, USA. Over a long weekend 500,000 people watched and listened to some of the best-known musicians of that time. 'Woodstock' went down in popular music history as one of the greatest events of all time.

The Pyramid Stage at Glastonbury is the setting for world-class acts.

Functional skills

Using English…

When you are researching festivals on websites and in brochures, you will need to use your English skills to compare, select, read and understand the material. Your research should give you not only factual information, but inform you of opinions and arguments in the festival world, and help your own festival ideas to develop.

Activity

The Glastonbury Festival website states that the Festival's objective is to 'encourage and stimulate youth culture from around the world'.

* What do you understand by the term 'youth culture'?
* How might the Festival 'encourage and stimulate' youth culture?

Case Study: Glastonbury

From very small beginnings the Glastonbury Festival has grown into one of the major events in the UK music calendar. Recent Festivals have seen a diverse mix of acts playing the Festival's many settings such as the Jazz World Stage, the Dance Village, the Acoustic Tent and the Pyramid Stage.

More than merely a music festival however, Glastonbury includes in its programme dance, fringe theatre, circus and poetry performance, as well as painting, sculpture and other forms of art and design. On top of this a large area of the site is set aside for complementary and alternative medicines and marketplaces where food and crafts are sold.

Could you get other departments from your school/college involved in your festival, e.g. by providing sports activities or refreshments?

Content and audience

Festivals such as Glastonbury and Reading attract a wide range of music lovers through a diverse programme of events. Other, more specialist, music festivals may appeal to a more particular kind of audience.

Case Study: Huddersfield Contempory Music Festival (HCMF)

HCMF focuses on contemporary and **experimental music**. The Festival aims to present 'some of the most challenging and innovative contemporary classical music being written and performed today'.

In 2006 the Festival programme included 50 concerts including world premieres, specially **commissioned works** and sound **installations**.

Does the work you are planning to showcase at your festival have popular appeal?

Will some events and/or activities attract a more specific audience?

How might you address this in your publicity?

Funding

Like many of the larger festivals, Glastonbury operates in the commercial sector of the arts. This means it covers its own costs without government funding, e.g. through ticket sales. Like many smaller festivals, Huddersfield Contemporary Music Festival is a subsidised event. In 2006 it received funding from Arts Council England as well as Kirklees Council and the University of Huddersfield.

'The art of walking on water'. An installation by Jana Winderen seen at HCMF in 2005.

Experimental music – Unpredictable music that doesn't necessarily follow a score or other performance conventions.

Commissioned works – Something created to order for a particular event.

Installations – Installations use sculptural materials and other media to modify the way you experience a particular space.

Just checking

* What are the particular considerations for planning a music festival?
* How can you be sure your target audience will enjoy your festival events?
* What types of funding are available for performance festivals?
* What part does funding play in the scope of a performance festival?

Film and media festivals

You may have seen coverage in the press of film festivals such as Cannes in France or Sundance in the USA. These are opportunities for film makers and distributors to showcase their work to an audience. There are also radio and photography festivals where specialists in these media sectors can get together and show their work.

OVER TO YOU!

Find a range of media festivals that take place both in this country and abroad. Make a list of them with the venue for the festival and when they take place.

Case Study: Multimedia or single medium?

Media festivals are held across the world. They can be multimedia, or focus on a single medium. They may simply be a celebration of that medium, but more often they have a particular theme. For example, the **Hereford Photography Festival** is an annual event which adopted the theme of Contemporary Photography from South Africa for its 2007 and 2008 exhibitions. Events included a conference looking at contemporary South African photography in the post-apartheid period and a static moving-image, audio and installation feature.

Artistic policy and audience

Some festivals, such as the Hereford Photography Festival, promote the work of local, national and international practitioners. Other festivals might have links with young people in schools and colleges and promote the development of media skills with these young people. Artistic policy might be to promote the excellence of skills amongst media professionals. In some cases the aim of a festival is to sell media products.

If the festival is a long-running annual event, the organisers may well have developed a very definite artistic policy with specified goals. The **Bath Film Festival** is a registered educational charity and does much more than simply show films in cinemas. Their events include an outreach programme to take the cinema to communities which have no immediate access to film, open-air showings, silent cinema with live music accompaniments, discussions, debates and filmed art installations.

A media festival may try to challenge traditional festival wisdom. For example, you do not have to attend physically the **Third Coast International Audio Festival (TCIAF)** – it's an online radio festival broadcast from Chicago in the USA. Its goal is 'to support producers and other artists creating audio documentary and feature work of all styles and to bring this fresh and vital work to audiences throughout the world'. The Festival audience simply logs on to the website to hear and discuss audio recordings. The Festival includes a weekly radio broadcast by Chicago Public Radio, a radio documentary competition and specially commissioned documentaries. There are also some local events such as a three-day conference plus public performances and installations.

Often media professionals use festivals as an opportunity to showcase their latest products and get feedback from fellow professionals, the press and the public. You will have seen the hype that surrounds film festivals such as **Cannes** in France. Film stars and their directors invade the French town in May, as do film critics and film and television distributors.

Andrew Tshabangu's striking image 'Women before Crucifix', displayed at the Hereford Photographic Festival.

Activity

Look at the publicity for several media festivals. Can you work out the artistic policy for each festival from the work they are showing and the language they use in their publicity materials? Now find out the actual artistic policy for each event. How close were you?

Peter Cattaneo

Media festivals in particular often double as promotional opportunities. A good film made on small budget by a British film producer and director can be screened at a film festival and stand a chance of attracting interest from Hollywood distributors. A radio programme produced with a small budget in a home studio can be heard at a radio festival where there is potential for programme-commissioners to hear and be impressed by the work or the presenter.

The British director Peter Cattaneo is a great example of how to achieve success through participation in festivals. He had done some work for the BBC before he directed a short film that was shown at the Cannes Film Festival. His first full-length film was shown at the Sundance Festival and was so well-received that it enabled him to get financing for his next project: *The Full Monty'*. This film was a runaway global success and led to an Oscar nomination for Best Director.

Why do you think it is so difficult to get funding for making films?

Who funds media festivals?

Funding for media festivals can come by commercial means: the sale of tickets, programmes and sponsorship. The Radio Academy Radio Festival, for example, is sponsored by Sony and their name will feature on all the publicity material. Many companies see this as a good investment as they feel it will raise the profile of their company through public relations and branding of the festival.

Some festivals, for example The Ashland Independent Film Festival in Oregon, USA, are funded by a combination of grants from local Foundations, City and County councils and the Oregon Cultural Trust and sponsorship from companies as diverse as Starbucks and a local cheese company. Festivals often have other events taking place at the same time, such as a conference where they can charge for admission to raise additional funds.

Just checking

✱ What kind of things can you expect to see at a media festival?

✱ How might media festival audiences differ to other types of festival audiences?

Experiencing visual arts at festivals

The range of arts and media festivals around the world is very varied. You could probably find a festival celebrating any particular art or media form somewhere in the world. Whilst visual artists often produce work to complement or accompany other art or media forms, others produce work for dedicated festivals celebrating particular kinds of visual arts practices.

Visual arts festivals

Often festivals that are dedicated to one particular visual art form or practice will feature events as well as exhibitions. Conferences, where people can discuss relevant issues or development in a particular field, are regularly included. Talks from practitioners whose work is being displayed or who are doing something new in that area of the visual arts may also be arranged.

OVER TO YOU!

Imagine you are a visual artist who has been given a grant to produce a piece of work for exhibition at the following festivals:

A festival celebrating the centenary of a local park
A literature festival
A jazz music festival

Jot down some ideas for what you might produce.

Case Study: The Edinburgh Festivals

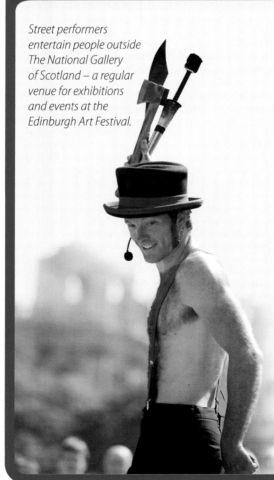

Street performers entertain people outside The National Gallery of Scotland – a regular venue for exhibitions and events at the Edinburgh Art Festival.

One of the most famous examples of an arts festival is the series of Festivals all held within August in Edinburgh. As well as an International Festival that features operatic, theatrical and dance performances from around the world, the Fringe Festival also sees venues across the city fill with thousands of different comedy, theatre and music events. Alongside this, there is now also a Book Festival, a Jazz and Blues Festival, a Television Festival and an Art Festival.

The Edinburgh Art Festival brings together the many and varied exhibitions held at the city's numerous art galleries, as well as the work being exhibited at shops, restaurants and cafés throughout Edinburgh during the Festival period. The organisers of the Festival produce promotional material that informs visitors of the various events that take place around the city. This is a major feat in itself!

The Edinburgh Art Festival is funded through the support of the Scottish Arts Council, The Heritage Lottery Fund, Edinburgh City Council and businesses such as Lloyds TSB Scotland, ScotRail and The Skinny, an arts magazine.

As a visual artist, what are the benefits of having your work featured in the Edinburgh Festivals?

What might be the stresses involved in exhibiting your work?

What are the challenges for the organisers of such a complex series of events?

The Roald Dahl Festival

The annual Roald Dahl Festival is held in Aylesbury and celebrates the life and work of the author with an array of family-focused events and exhibits. Street parades feature costumes designed and made by local children, giant puppets and characters from the books. There is live music, face-painting, storytelling, games and a range of family activities at the Roald Dahl museum and library. Local artists are involved in helping the children design the costumes and artwork.

What might the artistic policy for the Roald Dahl Festival sound like?

Who might be interested in funding such a festival?

Target audiences

Art festivals are usually targeted at as wide a group of people as possible. Very often a festival is used as a way of introducing art to people who may not usually be exposed to it. However, in some cases the target audience may be very defined and can be identified by looking at the type of work on display and who it may appeal to.

A festival celebrating children's book illustration, for example, may be of more interest to children and families than to single people in their 20s.

Funding

Very often Arts Councils, the bodies that distribute government and lottery funds to arts projects and organisations, will be involved in financing arts festivals. They support festivals because one of their main aims as an organisation is to increase people's access to art in its many different forms. Festivals are a great way to do this as they feature a short, focused period of time when lots of arts activities happen within one particular area. This gives the people in and near to this area a good chance to experience the events of the festival first-hand.

Activity

Who do you think the target audience would be for the following festivals? Note down the age and gender of the people you would most expect to be interested.

* A festival of African dance including an exhibition of photographs of African wildlife.
* A festival of computer games to include displays of game-concept art.
* A festival of Japanese culture including exhibitions of manga art.
* A festival of textile crafts.

Just checking

* Do you understand the benefits and the stresses of exhibiting in a visual arts festival?
* Have you investigated the impact the target audience has on planning and organisation?
* Have you considered how festivals inform their target audience?

6.2 Planning a festival

A festival by its very nature will include a range of performances, activities and/or displays that take place over a single day, a weekend or a longer period. The kind of planning needed to coordinate a festival is therefore likely to be more complex than that needed to organise a single performance project or exhibition.

OVER TO YOU!

Think of a small to medium arts or media festival. How do you think it is put together?

Make a list of the various jobs to be done before the festival opens.

Deciding what to put in

If you are tackling this unit towards the end of your course, you will no doubt have a range of work from projects already completed that could be used in your arts and media festival. However, it is important to remember that a festival is more than just a random collection of exhibits and performance material.

In deciding what work will be suitable you could therefore begin by considering the 'artistic policy' you might adopt. Is your festival to be a celebration of your achievements on this course, for example, or are you aiming to promote and showcase the arts and media in your school, college or even in your community?

It will also be helpful at this stage to ask yourselves the following questions:

* Is your festival going to focus on a single area of the creative and media industry, e.g. music or 3D visual art, or will it combine work for a range of media?
* Do you want your festival to have a theme that links some or all of the activities/displays?
* What work do you have that will be suitable for showing at the festival?
* What work do you have that could be adapted for showing at the festival?
* Are you intending to include work produced by others, e.g. the work of other Year groups and/or courses from your school/college, or the work of artists from your community?

Personal, learning and thinking skills

Planning a festival involves asking lots of questions to extend your Creative Thinking skills. By contributing to the pool of ideas and exploring these ideas in a group, you are also demonstrating your ability to be a Team Worker. You will also need to make sure that your discussions end in agreements to achieve results.

Working with your available resources

Once you have selected the work that will be showcased in your festival you can begin to look at the resources you have available to set up and run the festival. Organisers of any festival, no matter how large or small, must take into consideration the resources that are available. For you this will mean finding out what you have at your disposal, e.g. performance and exhibition venues and equipment. Only after considering your resources carefully can you come up with plans that are practical and realistic.

You will need to consider the types of venue that are available to you.

Begin by considering the following questions:

* What spaces/venues are available to you to use?
* How suitable are these spaces for the individual events you are planning?
* What specialist equipment do you have at your disposal?
* Do you have a budget that can be used to buy and/or hire equipment and resources?
* Do you have any specialists who can help you, e.g. your school/college technician or any of your teachers?

Plans and designs

Once decisions regarding the choice of suitable work and the use of available resources have been made, the next step will be to come up with a festival production plan.

The plan should include the following information:

* The 'name' and any theme of the festival.
* Its purpose and artistic policy.
* The target audience(s).
* When and where it is taking place.
* The programme of events, performances and/or displays to be showcased.
* The major deadlines, e.g. production and distribution of publicity materials, final rehearsals, **get-ins**.
* Financial information (where applicable), e.g. **expenditure budget**, projected ticket sales.
* Health and Safety considerations
* Any legal implications, e.g. performing rights.

Get-in – The process of delivering and taking scenery and props into the theatre.

Expenditure budget – The money you have to spend.

GATESHEAD'S FESTIVAL CELEBRATING AFRICAN & CARIBBEAN CULTURE

Gateshead's Sugar and Spice Festival had a design that reflected its African and Caribbean Theme.

You will also need to consider the design of the festival itself. This will include the **'look'** of the festival spaces and the design of promotional material. For example colours and designs used in promotional materials and brochures can be reflected in the look of performance and exhibition areas.

Make a checklist

The next stage in the planning process will be to make a detailed checklist of everything that needs to be organised. When doing so, remember that all aspects of the planning process from the setting up of displays to the serving of refreshments must be included.

Roles and responsibilities – who does what!

When your checklist of tasks, activities and procedures has been drafted you can begin to establish individual responsibilities within the group. One way of approaching the many jobs to be done is to make a member of the group (or a pair) responsible for each individual event within the festival programme. Remember that you will also need people whose role it is to liaise between the groups and any other individuals and/or organisations and to coordinate the work being carried out across the whole festival. It will also be important to establish a 'chain of command' that clearly sets out who is accountable to whom within the organisation.

Setting up a display or exhibition can be time consuming – make sure enough time is allowed in your schedule.

Deadlines

As a festival comprises several individual events it will be vital that deadlines for completion of tasks and procedures are established early in the planning process. Depending on the nature of your work it may be sensible for each event on the festival programme to have its own set of deadlines, e.g. for gathering resources, getting into the space, setting up artefacts or products for display. It is crucial that these deadlines are monitored centrally to ensure that those needed are available to undertake required tasks and no one is down to be in two places at once!

Your process portfolio

It is important that you keep copies of all documentation produced during the planning process for your portfolio. This should include:

* details of ideas discussed and decisions made during initial planning activities
* agendas, notes and/or minutes from production meetings
* your festival production plan
* other planning materials, e.g. lists and schedules, details of roles and responsibilities
* your own personal log or journal detailing your individual contribution to the planning of your festival.

Functional skills

Using English...

During planning meetings you should use your speaking and listening skills to make useful contributions to discussions. Listen to what others say and allow people time to speak. If you disagree or have a different idea, try to give reasons why you think things should be done differently – justify your opinions with facts or information from your festival research.

Collaboration – Working together with another individual or a group of people.

Activity

As a group, list the different skills needed in the planning of your festival, e.g. verbal communication skills, design skills, ICT skills.

Now on your own, consider the strengths of each member of your group, including yourself. Pair up to discuss the skills and attributes you have listed for others. Does your partner think your list is accurate.

Pool your lists and work as a group to try to match the strengths of individual members of the group to the skills required for the various roles in the planning process. Was anyone surprised by the strengths or skills the rest of the group felt they had?

Planning a performance arts festival

We will now look at some of the different aspects of planning a festival: choosing work, working to budgets and working with others.

Just checking

* Have you selected the products, artefacts and/or performances required for your festival?
* Have you carefully considered the resources that are available to you?
* Have you organised who is in charge of what within your festival group?
* Is your schedule of activities complete with the order and timings of tasks and procedures?
* Have you kept copies of plans and designs in your project portfolio?

Choosing suitable work

You should begin the planning of your festival by evaluating the suitability of all the work you have available. In doing so you should consider the quality of the work, whether it is feasible to re-rehearse pieces and, if necessary, whether work could be adapted to suit the aims of the festival.

OVER TO YOU!

Consider the arts and media profile of your school or college. Make a list of all the courses and extra curricular activities in your school or college that have an arts and/or media focus.

St Anne's Community School Possible work for inclusion in the Festival.		
Group	**Work**	**Comments and questions**
Year 8	Devised pieces on bullying (5 pieces lasting 5–10 minutes each).	Some pieces were excellent, others were less successful. Could we audition the Year 8 pieces to decide which to use?
Drama Club	*The Wizard of Oz*	We don't have the time to re-do the whole show but extracts could be performed, perhaps as street theatre.
A Level Theatre Studies	Shakespeare extracts	These were very good and could definitely be used. Check that the festival does not clash with any AS or A2 exams.
Creative and Media Diploma	Stranger Danger (Unit 5)	This was successful in the primary schools we went to and could link with the Year 8 work on bullying. Theatre in Education theme?
Creative and Media Diploma	Musical Madness showcase (Unit 2)	These would be great but some of the items were under-rehearsed first time around. Do we have time to re-rehearse all the extracts or should we choose the best ones?
Creative and Media Diploma	Radio play (Unit 4)	Could this be used as a sound installation with a display of research work undertaken for the unit?
Creative and Media Diploma	Costumes (Unit 2)	An exhibition could also include costumes produced for *The Wizard of Oz* and photos of past productions.
School Wind Band	Range of pieces	A concert could be arranged or the band could perform informally in the entrance hall.
Cheerleaders Dance Group	Range of routines	A formal exhibition could be arranged. Would be a good outdoor event.

Working with available resources

When planning your festival you will also need to consider the resources you have at your disposal. This will include venues and spaces. Deciding what goes where will be central to the planning process. Your school/college may have a range of different venues and spaces that could be used for performances, exhibitions and other activities. You may also have access to other venues in your community. You will need to consider carefully the suitability of these venues/spaces for the individual events you are planning.

St Anne's Community School Festival Survey of available venues/spaces		
Venue/Spaces	**Description**	**Comments and questions**
Drama Studio	Flexible black box space. Can seat up to 70.	Would suit Shakespeare and Theatre in Education (TiE) pieces.
School Hall	Proscenium arch stage. Can seat up to 250.	Not available on the first day of Festival (Friday). Too big for TiE pieces but would suit Musical Madness Showcase and Wind Band Concert.
Entrance Hall/ Foyer	Large space suitable for exhibitions and/or informal performances.	Would be good for costume exhibition. Could we also use for refreshments?
Sports Hall	Large open space. Could seat up to 200.	Not available on Day 2 (Saturday). Could be used for Wind Band Concert if on Friday evening.
Media Suite	Radio studio and large classroom	Classroom could be used to house radio play exhibition/installation.
Courtyard	Outdoor space at side of main building	Could be used for street theatre, cheerleaders and refreshments but what would happen if it rained?

You could invite extra curricular groups such as school bands, choirs and drama groups to contribute to your festival.

Remember!

Don't forget to keep records of all the planning you undertake and the decisions you make.

Just checking

* Have you evaluated all the work available to you for use in your festival?
* Are your plans feasible in light of the resources and materials available?
* Can your festival be carried out to budget?

OVER TO YOU!

Do you ever use budgeting skills in your daily life? If so, how do you make everyday budgeting decisions?

Working to a budget

The importance of budgeting

Case Study: Wolverton Lantern Festival

The Wolverton Lantern Festival is a community event held every year in December. The main attraction is a procession through the town lit by hundreds of home-made and professional lanterns. The Festival also includes an array of performance artists such as Morris dancers, stilt walkers, skateboarders and street performers. A live samba band accompanies the procession and the 2007 Festival featured additional live music from a bhangra band. Market stalls, games and refreshments are organised for the market square.

Sue Quinn talked about the planning of the Festival and how they worked as a small, voluntary organisation: 'We start planning in January following a debrief of the previous Festival – anything that went wrong, anything that worked really well. As a committee, everyone plays to their strengths. The hardest thing is trying to make the money stretch – we all have to get stuck in, for example we put all the lantern kits together. The best advice I can give is to plan and operate within your budget'.

The Festival is funded through the sale of their lantern kits and helped by corporate sponsorship from Tesco and grants from the local council, Milton Keynes Community Foundation, Midsummer Housing and MK Arts Association. However, funding is not guaranteed from year to year, which provides an additional challenge for Sue and her team: 'As the Festival has been going for nineteen years it is not seen as "new or innovative", so funders are less likely to contribute. The challenge for us is constantly to think of things that will add a new dimension without stretching the human resources too far.'

The committee is made up of people with a variety of skills and experience, and they decide democratically as a group on the theme for each year. They liaise with professional artists and designers for the creation of a number of huge lanterns that centrepiece the Festival.

The Festival is assisted by fifty volunteers. An extra challenge is operating a rolling roadblock as the procession makes its way round Wolverton.

What do you think are the health and safety considerations for the Wolverton Festival?

How would you approach these issues?

Budget

You may have a limited budget for running your media festival. You could investigate the possibility of someone sponsoring your media festival and approach:

* local or national companies that provide equipment or materials, e.g. a camera manufacturer if you are planning a photography festival
* local providers of media, e.g. a cinema if you are planning a film festival
* organisations that promote the arts, e.g. the Arts Councils, Yorkshire Forward
* schools and colleges that provide arts and media education.

Once you have worked out how much money you have, you can draw up a budget for your media festival, for example:

Hire of venue	1 day @ £500 per day	£500
Cost of publicity	£100	£100
Security	1day@ £300 per day	£300
Personnel	2 staff @ £50 each per day	£100
	SUB TOTAL	£1000
Contingency	@10% total	£100
	TOTAL	£1100

If you cannot find a sponsor you will need to consider the charges you will make for people to attend your media festival. You may be able to ask people to support the festival in other ways, perhaps by donating their time or giving you a discount on the cost of your materials.

Personal, learning and thinking skills

You will work as a group to make many of the decisions relating to your festival, including deciding the content. When lots of different opinions are being voiced it can sometimes be hard to reach agreements, but to do so is an important teamwork skill you must gain.

Take turns to chair your group discussions so you all have the opportunity to steer and manage the debate. Use democratic methods such as voting, if necessary, to help you reach final decisions.

Case Study: Beedale Photographic Festival

The Photographic Festival was funded by a small grant from the local council. The council wants to encourage this type of activity in the local community. However, the festival organisers found that the grant would not cover all their expenses. They decided to produce a catalogue for the Festival and invited local companies to advertise in the catalogue. These companies were not necessarily media companies but they did want to support the event and have their name associated with a photography festival.

Why might a company want to be seen to be promoting a local photography exhibition?

Activity

Make a list of all the materials and resources you need to get hold of for your festival. Your task is to get hold of as much of it for free as possible. Start with recycling and getting donations. What contacts/connections do you or your group have in the local area?

Remember to think about how you can convince people/businesses to help you: what can you give them in return that doesn't cost money?

Just checking

* Do your plans include audit documents and detailed budget plans?

Working with others

Often practitioners will have to communicate with, and work alongside, festival organisers during their planning stages to ensure that they are preparing the right kind of work for inclusion in the festival.

Different roles and responsibilities

Choosing what work will be exhibited during a festival will depend on the themes you have chosen as a group and what decisions you have made about the artistic policy you will follow when working on the festival. Often, selecting an individual, or a small group of people to be responsible for this part of the process is a good idea. It is hard as an artist or designer to make objective decisions about whether your work is appropriate for an exhibition or not.

Case Study: Jenny

Usually art exhibitions, particularly those within festivals, will be overseen by one central person. Alongside those who are making the practical arrangements for exhibitions, a Curator makes creative decisions about what work should appear and how it should be presented.

Jenny is the Curator for a gallery that often hosts exhibitions as part of the town's local arts festival in the summer. Jenny will attend the meetings held by the organisers of the arts festival and contribute to the decision-making process regarding the theme of that year's festival. She will then look carefully at the work already owned by the gallery she works for and consider what may be useful for an exhibition on that theme.

The artistic policy of the local festival includes a requirement to 'celebrate artistic talent from the local region' and 'bring contemporary work to the local area'. Therefore when Jenny begins to consider what other work may be displayed during the festival she looks at the work of local artists and designers, and also at the work of contemporary artists from elsewhere who have not had their work exhibited locally before.

Jenny must also consider whether work will fit into the space she has available in the gallery, and how it will be presented. Showing work in an appropriate way will ensure that those visiting the gallery have the best possible experience of viewing the work.

When you are deciding on what work to show you may have to make tricky decisions, for example, 'What is a local artist?'

– Someone who lives in the area?
– Someone who uses local materials or resources?
– Someone whose work reflects the local area?

Activity

How could the following problems have been solved at the planning stage?

* Both a dance performance and an art exhibition are scheduled to open at 7pm on the same night. This is the only performance of the dance piece scheduled and all tickets are sold out. However, only three people turn up to the exhibition opening.

* Whilst mounting a display of textile works, the artists working in the foyer of the theatre need a step-ladder to mount displays that hang from the ceiling. However, the step-ladder is being used to adjust the lighting on stage. The play begins at 8pm and the audience are supposed to admire the textile display before the show. It is 5pm.

* On the day of preparing for a festival, visual artists have been asked to prepare their display of eight pieces of sculpture in a large hall, whilst a theatre group have been given a small side-room in which to fit their stage and audience seating.

Personal, learning and thinking skills

Working with other people on the planning and coordination of a festival will help to strengthen your abilities as a Team Worker, Creative Thinker and an Effective Participator. Noting how others work and giving them constructive feedback and support will also help to build these skills.

Knowing your role and the role of others

Making sure that you are aware of what is expected of you and what other people will be doing is a key part of contributing to a collaborative event such as a festival. Making sure that you are aware of the deadlines that you are expected to meet is as important as fulfilling the role you have been asked to do. A festival is something that is publicised to other people and therefore if you miss deadlines, you will be disappointing all the people who have responded to the publicity.

Producing plans

When working with the rest of the group on planning your festival, those considering the exhibition of visual arts work will need to be involved at every stage.

Planning how you will stage your exhibition, what it will require and how you will go about putting your plans into practice need to be established at this stage. As a festival is likely to involve people from different fields all working at the same time, making sure that resources and personnel are shared out fairly and in an organised way is very important.

Just checking

* Have you finalised your festival's artistic policy?
* Do you understand your role and responsibilities in the planning process?
* Do your plans include contingency arrangements that may be necessary?
* Are you sharing the responsibilities of organising your festival fairly within your own group?

6.3 Promoting a festival

An audience is vital to the success of any festival. The hard work undertaken in the planning and preparation stages of the project needs to be rewarded by an appreciative audience. You therefore need to get the promotion right to get your audience through the door.

Your target audience and your campaign

When devising any publicity campaign it is important to begin by considering the people you want to reach, i.e. your target audience. As a festival comprises a number of different events you may need to go through your festival programme to identify a target audience for each event.

Glenwood Community School 3D Festival	
Event	**Target audience**
Puppet Show	Children (under-nines)
Moving Sculpture	General public
'Heavy Metal' installation	Teenagers and young adults
Junk Sculpture Family Workshop	Families

Your target audience and your campaign

Examining the target audience(s) for your festival will help you to devise suitable promotional materials that will attract the attention of those you are targeting.

OVER TO YOU!

Why do you think people should come to your festival? Make a list of your festival's best selling points?

Some of your events may have a very specific target audience.

St Anne's Community School Festival Publicity Campaign

Promotional Materials	Distribution
Posters and Flyers	Local shops Leisure centre Library Tourist information centre
Direct mailing (letter and Festival flyer)	Department mailing list School Governors Ex-arts and media students
Direct mailing (Theatre in Education events letter and Festival flyer)	Local primary schools
Press Release	Newtown Gazette Newtown FM BBC Local TV and Radio
Webpage	Link from home page of school website

Devising your campaign

Your publicity campaign must be designed to attract the attention of your target audience or audiences. It may include some or all of the following:

* Posters and leaflets – these can be very effective publicity tools but production can be expensive. Make sure you make the most of posters and leaflets by placing them where they will be seen by your target audience.

* Press releases – mailings aimed at journalists. Press releases can be sent to your local newspaper as well as regional TV and radio broadcasters.

* Direct mailing – your school/college may have a list of people who have attended previous events. If you know who your target audience is, the under-fives for example, you could also send publicity directly to appropriate organisations, e.g. playgroups and nurseries, your local children's library.

* Use of websites – you could develop a page for your school/college website promoting the festival; make sure you remember to add a link from the home page.

* Special events and stunts – a stunt can catch the public's attention as well as that of the media. A scene from a show or a musical number could be performed in your local shopping precinct. You may need to ask permission, however.

Producing publicity material

Once you have decided on the type of publicity campaign required, you will need to design and produce the actual materials to be used. Images used on materials such as posters and leaflets need to reflect the nature of your festival. You should also consider keeping to the same **palette of colours** for promotional and other materials.

Make sure any images you use are copyright free, or that you have obtained permission to use them.

You must always ensure that all the important information is included:

WHAT – what is happening?

WHO – details of performers and/or exhibitors

WHERE – details of the venues

WHEN – dates and times of specific events

WHY – reasons why people should come along, details of what is special about the festival

HOW – details of how to get more information and/or tickets.

Professional presentation is also vital, so be sure to proofread all text before it goes to print. It's usually best to get someone who hasn't written the copy to do this – fresh eyes often spot the mistakes!

For your project

Play to the strengths of the members of your team.

Use the skills of the people in your team to best effect when devising and producing publicity materials. For example, those with artistic flair should work on the design aspects of posters and flyers, whilst those with good written communication skills devise the **copy** for press releases.

Activity

Why do you think people should came to your festival? Make a list of your festival's best selling points.

Publicity material must grab the attention of anyone who sees or hears it. It must also answer the essential questions someone wanting information about the festival would ask: who, what, when where, why and how, for example:

St Anne's Community School Festival – Suggested copy for press release
St Anne's Community School will be hosting their first annual Arts and Media Festival from 11th–13th July 2007. A celebration of the achievements of students from the school, the Festival includes a host of exciting events involving street theatre, music, dance, design and media arts. The Festival opens at 7 pm on Friday 11th July with a spectacular outdoor concert by St Anne's Wind Band. Other events include a Theatre in Education event for the under 11s, a costume exhibition, a Shakespeare Showcase and appearances by the school's award-winning cheerleading team. Further details and tickets for individual events can be obtained from the school office.

Consider a publicity stunt

A very good way of attracting the attention of the general public and the press is through a publicity stunt. You could consider performing an extract from one of your events as a piece of street theatre. Make sure you have people on hand to give out leaflets promoting the festival and invite the press along!

Stunt crazy!

Richard Branson is well-known for his enthusiasm for stunts to launch new Virgin products and services. For the announcement of Virgin Festival Canada, a two-day music event, he lowered himself 75 feet from a helicopter into a reception room in the building below, through an opening in the glass ceiling!

Just checking

* Have you considered a wide range of forms and methods of publicity and marketing?
* Have you investigated how other festivals similar to yours have advertised themselves?
* Are your publicity materials eye-catching and appropriate for your target audience(s)

Making campaign materials

Making the campaign materials for your media festival is a great opportunity to have fun with design. You can experiment with a range of techniques to produce the materials, for example using print, web or audio visual media:

Print based – you could produce leaflets and flyers with examples of the content of your festival.

Web based – you could produce a website with details of the festival and clips of the content of the festival.

Audio visual – you could produce a short video or audio commercial.

Try to consider all the possibilities when choosing the techniques you will use. Think carefully about the techniques you know about, but also the techniques you would like to learn about and use.

Running the campaign

Once your publicity materials have been produced and any activities/ stunts organised, you must ensure that your message reaches the eyes and ears of the target audiences. Make sure posters and leaflets are placed where they will be noticed – research which shops and public places your audience are likely to visit. Create a mailing list for direct mailing and one for the press and ensure materials are sent out.

Promoting a festival

You may have to take part in promotional activities such as handing out material in the street, knocking on doors or being interviewed in the press or on radio and television. Remember how important it is to be professional and polite whenever you are dealing with the public. You are the public face of the festival and must take care not to put people off attending by being rude or badly informed.

Direct mailing – Targeted promotional mailing sent to specific individuals or organisations.
Copy – The written text.
Palette of colours – The selection of colours and shades you want to use in your festival

Activity

Divide into small groups and come up with ideas for a logo for your festival. Test your ideas by doing some market research by asking students from other courses and Year groups what they think about the various logos.

Use your findings to decide the logo you will use in the promotional materials.

Consider a stunt to get extra publicity but don't do anything dangerous!.

Just checking

* Have you identified the target audience for different elements of your festival?
* Is your publicity campaign planned in detail?
* Have you produced carefully targeted publicity materials for the campaign?
* Have you personally contributed to promotional and marketing events or activities?

How festivals have been promoted

OVER TO YOU!

Look at some examples of print-based promotional materials or the websites for festivals that you investigated earlier on in the project. Make a list of words you would use to describe the images used on the front cover of these materials or home page of the sites. Which words occur often?

Case Study: The Sydney Festival

The Sydney Festival in Australia is a huge event, featuring diverse performance, visual and media arts performers from all over the world, including Björk and the National Theatre of Scotland. Their marketing and publicity activities are extensive, promoting the Festival in a number of different ways. Their website is packed full of information, showing music and video clips, providing information on getting to the venues, offering links to buy tickets plus giving all the media releases they have made. You can sign up for the Festival e-news 'Festival Buzz', and order a brochure – they print over 650,000 throughout their campaign! Outdoor advertising includes bus shelters, billboards and the sides of buses. Smaller posters and postcards have been supplied to local cafés. In the lead-up to and throughout the Festival, print, radio and TV advertisements will give stories on all Festival artists and companies taking part. The publicists set up interviews for the Festival artists to give the public more history and context.

Publicity Manager, Sarah Wilson, talks about the targeted mailing they do: 'We direct-mail the Festival brochure to people who have purchased tickets before. We also do mailings to people we know are interested in specific shows (e.g. they may have bought tickets to a see a particular musician and we have a similar act which we think they'll be interested in).'

A vital part of their publicity is their media pack which is sent out 8–9 weeks before the Festival. Approximately 1000 packs including brochures and media releases are sent to different print, radio, TV and online organisations. Journalists and picture editors are sent carefully tailored weblinks to the Festival image library. They also use a media agency to distribute key media releases. The bulk of the marketing material is carefully prepared to appeal to a broad audience, alongside a smaller proportion of the material targeting special interest media.

www.sydneyfestival.org.au

Which aspects of the Festival's campaign do you think will be most effective in telling people about:

– the artists and groups taking part in the Festival

– when and where different events are taking place

– who is sponsoring the Festival

– how much tickets cost?

Restricted Service Licence
– A temporary, short-term radio licence, usually granted for festivals or one-off events.

Personal, learning and thinking skills

The purpose of publicity stunts can vary from wanting merely to capture public attention with an outrageous event, or wanting to inform the public of particular details of your festival. As a Creative Thinker you should try to use your group's ideas and experiences in inventive ways to create a stunt that achieves your chosen aim.

Case Study: Natural disaster!

The ways in which you will promote your festival will depend on the target audience for the festival. When deciding on the type of campaign you will adopt, you should consider:

* the content of the media festival
* who will be attracted to make entries to the festival
* the age of the target audience.

A local council decided to hold a film festival that would showcase the work of local filmmakers. Its theme was 'Celebrating the Natural World' and local filmmakers were invited to submit their work. However, the council's publicity department only sent out information to local primary schools and the central library. The number of entries for the festival was low as many filmmakers never saw the publicity material.

Where should the publicity have been sent?

What else could the council have done to target their audience and promote the film festival?

> ### Personal, learning and thinking skills
>
> Don't be afraid to try someting new or different when you are promoting your festival, it shows you are working as a Creative Thinker. However, if your idea doesn't work as planned then you must also be prepared to adapt it or find an alternative solution.

Case Study: Butterfield College

The media students at Butterfield College decided to hold a radio festival. They wanted to provide information on how radio shows operated under a **Restricted Service Licence** can benefit the local community. They asked for help from the Community Media Association who were able to provide advice and support. They were able to raise money for the festival by approaching local companies for funds and this was very successful.

In order to raise awareness of the festival, the students planned and took part in a one-day outdoor event in the town marketplace. They had a display all about the festival, they played music that would be available during the festival and they talked to shoppers about the festival. They were able to give flyers to the shoppers and pencils with the festival name on them to children.

What are the pros and cons of promotional gifts like pencils, or key fobs?

Have you considered using them to promote your own festival? What influenced your decision as to why or why not you might use them?

Promoting a festival

Visual arts may be used in promotional activities in a variety of ways. Inspiring and exciting imagery is one of the key ways in which you can encourage people to attend your festival. These could include:

* photographs of performers or participants during rehearsals for use in a flyer or exhibition programme
* photographs, scans or the inclusion of digital versions of art or design work to be exhibited for use in posters or printed promotional materials
* promotional photographs to accompany written press releases for inclusion in local media products such as newspapers
* the design of the flyers, posters and programmes for the event using desktop publishing or digital illustration packages.

When promoting an event such as a festival, it is important to ensure you have planned suitable publicity to promote it: have you given enough thought to reaching your audience? Have you planned to use a good variety of print, web or audio-visual media for your promotional material?

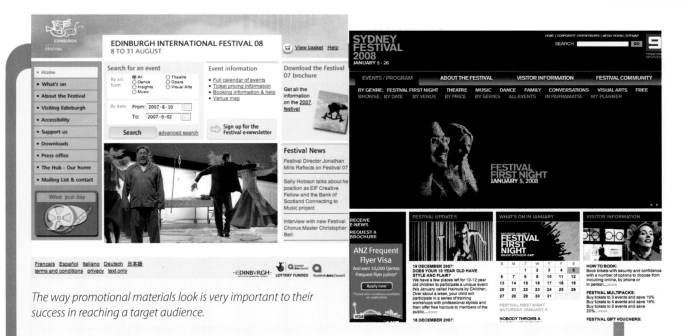

The way promotional materials look is very important to their success in reaching a target audience.

When they design the layout of the flyer they split the space they have available into different sections for the different events. They choose a colour scheme of grey and dark purple for the section about the dance and feature a black and white version of the photograph taken in rehearsal. They decide that this will help the audience understand that this will be a serious piece of work and that it may appeal to adults more than children.

✳ What differences might Aimee and Dominic make to their design if the performance was aimed at children too?

Activity

Imagine you have been given the task of producing a promotional poster for each of the events listed below. List which colours you would choose to use, what kind of images you would seek out and sketch an idea for a logo for this event for use on promotional material.

✳ A rock music festival

✳ A festival celebrating ceramic art in a village famous for its pottery

✳ A festival of circus skills and street theatre in a busy city

✳ A film festival with the theme of 'Horror'

Activity

Make a list of the events and activities included in your festival. Discuss your opinions on the target audience for each event. Then consider your festival as a whole and answer the important questions: who, what, when where, why and how. Use the answers to compose a press release. Consider what visual images you might include to encourage media organisations to report your festival.

Just checking

✳ Have you made full use of images in your promotional materials?

✳ Do you understand how visual arts in promotional materials can influence the audience?

✳ Have you considered the timing and running of your campaign carefully?

6.4 Running a festival

It is now time to put your plans into action as you set up and run your festival. You will need to check that the resources, equipment and/or materials you have planned to use are available and ready to be set up in the venues you are using.

You will also need to have a clear understanding of your own and others' roles and responsibilities during this phase of the project.

Is everything ready?

You will need to gather all the materials, artefacts and products that were identified in the planning stages of the festival and make sure that everything you need for your festival is in the right place, at the right time. For example, if you are running a film festival you must ensure that all the films that you plan to show have arrived. You must also ensure that the projector you are using to show your films is in good working order. Do you have spare projector bulbs in case one blows?

Remember that the setting up of a display or the fitting up of a performance space can be time consuming, so be sure to allow enough time.

You should have a checklist of everything needed that you can refer to during this process. You must:

* check that you have the space and, where necessary, seating for your festival
* ensure you have told everyone who needs to know, where to be and at what time
* make sure that you have a contingency plan in case equipment does not work
* ensure that personnel are available to open doors and manage **front-of-house**.

OVER TO YOU!

What do you think are the most important things to take into account when running a festival or other arts and media event (e.g. meeting deadlines)?

Make a list of the things you think will be vital to the smooth running of your festival.

Personal, learning and thinking skills

A good Self-Manager is able to anticipate problems that may arise and be prepared to act to solve them.

You may need to take some risks, but as long as you think things through and carefully manage your actions, you will be working in the best interests of the festival.

Activity

Imagine the following scenario:

You have planned to run a photographic festival. You arrive at the venue for the Festival to find that the doors are locked and there is no one available to let you in.

What might have gone wrong?

What would you do to save your Festival?

Front–of–house (FOH)– In the theatre all the areas the audience has access to are known as 'front of house', roles include checking tickets and selling programmes and refreshments.

Is everyone ready?

It is important to understand your role during the setting up and running of the festival. You should also make sure you are aware of the roles of others in your group, and how your work contributes to or affects them.

Everyone needs a copy of the most up-to-date festival agenda and you should check that any last-minute changes have been communicated to everyone who needs to know.

Teamwork is all about working together to run a successful media festival. It is also an opportunity to share experiences, discuss issues and review work in a collaborative way.

Personal, learning and thinking skills

A Team Worker and Self-Manager always takes responsibility for their own role when running a festival and makes sure they do everything that is required of them, at the time that has been agreed in the schedule.

Health and Safety

Before your festival opens you will also need to run through any health and safety issues and then ensure that you work together so all public areas are safe.

This may involve checking that:

* display boards and other products or artefacts are secure and cannot be knocked over
* fire exits are not being blocked
* there are no tripping hazards such as trailing cables.

Depending on the types of events and activities being staged, it may be necessary to undertake a risk assessment of the festival. If you have done this, it's good practice for everyone to have a copy so they can be aware of potential hazards and what your agreed solutions will be if a problem arises. Further information about risk assessments can be found in Units 2.3, 3.2.

Responding to others

When working with a group you must be able to respond to requests from your group and be able to carry out instructions. This might be a request such as 'please show these people to their seats'. Such requests might only be a simple task but it impacts upon the success of the festival. If there is no one to show people to their seats, then the showing of a film or the planned talk by a media professional will be delayed. If this event is delayed then there will be a knock-on effect with other events. Eventually the whole media festival could grind to a halt.

You must ensure that there is a clear and respectful communication network between you and your group. It is important for the public to see you treat your group members with courtesy, even when events are stressful.

Think about:

* the way you talk to each other
* how you can work cooperatively to make the media festival a success
* considering other people's views
* being able to take direction from other people.

Close contact

A local film festival was staged in a number of locations throughout the town. This meant that at any time there could be three different film events taking place. The organisers decided to invest in a state-of-the-art mobile intercom system that allowed all the team to be in constant contact. Personnel could then be diverted to other venues where necessary.

Communicating with others

As well as communicating with your group members, you may be speaking to exhibitors, sponsors, caterers, local media reporters, technicians, venue staff and your friends and family. That's a lot of different people, with a lot of different needs! Running your festival is exciting but it can also be stressful, even when you have planned it thoroughly.

It is likely that you will also come into contact with members of the public during the festival, either through front-of-house duties or during specific activities and workshops.

It is important that you are polite, helpful and approachable when dealing with the public. The audience's impression and enjoyment of your festival will be affected by their interactions with individuals, as much as by the arts and media exhibits they see.

Your process portfolio

Keep a journal of the activities you have undertaken during the run of the festival. Include any plans or drawings used to set up displays and/or equipment. You could also take photographs of any display work you have worked on. If you are working as a performer, keep a log of each performance with details of what went well and less well, in addition to notes for improvements.

When dealing with the public it is important to be polite and professional.

Activity

Compile an individual checklist of your responsibilities during the setting up and running of the festival.

Include any important timings and/or deadlines.

Personal, learning and thinking skills

As a Team Worker, you must make sure that your communication skills are appropriate at all times. When you are communicating with others consider whether you are:

* making yourself understood
* making appropriate requests.

Just checking

* Have you made sure that everything is ready for the opening of your festival?
* Are all health and safety issues dealt with?
* Does everybody involved understand their role in the running of the festival?
* Is your project portfolio up to date with all your planning and preparation materials?

Preparation for assessment

In this unit you have taken part in the planning, setting up and running of a festival. With your teacher's guidance, you will have had to work as a team to make decisions about the artefacts, products and/or performances that were showcased and you are likely to have been given a role with specific responsibilities. Your festival should have given you the opportunity to draw on a range of disciplines, from music, drama and dance, to media and the visual arts.

Your portfolio

You will be expected to present evidence of your involvement in your assignments in a process portfolio. Your teacher may tell you what form your portfolio should take and how to present your work.

You will be assessed on…	This will be evidenced in your portfolio by…
…your understanding of the nature of festivals in the creative and media industries.	Your research notes. These may be notes taken in class as well as information found on the internet, and in brochures and promotional materials for the festivals you are investigating. Your presentation. This could be in written form or a talk, perhaps using PowerPoint slides. If you give a talk, remember to include the notes you use in your portfolio. **Tips for success:** Remember to include at least one local/regional festival, one national and one international festival in your investigations.
…your contribution to the planning of a festival.	A log or diary giving details of the work you undertake when planning the festival. You should include details of decisions made with regard to the choice of artefacts, products and/or performances that will be suitable for the festival. You will also need to include any decisions about the suitability of venues and spaces. **Tips for success:** Personalise any documents produced at group planning meetings, e.g. by annotating them to show your own opinions and contributions.
…your contribution to the promotion of a festival.	Your log or diary. Give details of all decisions made during the planning and running of the publicity campaign, e.g. details about target audiences, types of publicity materials to be used and ideas for their distribution. You should also include notes on ideas you have and all your rough work including drafts and sketches as well as the final versions of the materials produced. You should also include any plans for the distribution of the materials, along with a schedule showing deadlines for each stage of the process. **Tips for success:** Get inspiration by looking at promotional materials for the festivals you investigated earlier in the unit.
…your contribution to the setting up and running of a festival.	Your log or diary. You will need to keep a log or diary giving details of your work during the setting-up and running of the festival, in which you document the tasks you undertake. You could include photographs of exhibition spaces you helped to set up and/or recordings of performances you were involved in. Your teachers may also produce observation reports on how well you carried out practical tasks. **Tips for success:** Write up the details of your contribution as soon after the festival as you can, while the experience is still fresh in your mind.

The assessment of the unit

This unit is assessed internally by your teachers. Remember, you'll be assessed on what you submit as part of your process portfolio and your teacher's observations of how you've worked.

You must show that you:	Guidance	To gain higher marks:
...can describe a number of festivals, giving details of their artistic policies, programme content, target audiences and how they are funded.	Choose the festivals you investigate carefully to make sure you include a range of examples. This will enable you to compare them.	You must give full descriptions of the festivals you have investigated. Your presentation must make comparisons between the festivals you have investigated and should make reference to their artistic policies, target audiences and programme content. You should explain how the festivals are funded.
...can work with others to plan a festival and are able to produce planning records.	Consider ideas for the festival carefully to assess their suitability. Do not be frightened to reject ideas that are not suitable: this is an important part of the planning process. Teamwork is vital to the success of the planning process. Remember to listen to others and respect their views.	You must come up with imaginative ideas for the festival and be able to explore them thoroughly. You must make a positive contribution to group work. You must produce clear and detailed planning records. You must be able to carry out planning tasks with only very occasional help from your teachers.
...can work with others to plan and produce promotional materials for a festival.	Plan your work with care. Remember to check that all the resources and materials you need are available. Consider doing some research by testing ideas for promotional materials on a sample of your target audience.	You must come up with imaginative ideas for the promotion of the festival and be able to explore them thoroughly. You must contribute to the production of imaginative promotional materials. You should collaborate with others and make a positive contribution to group work. You must be able to carry out your role with only occasional help from your teachers.
...can carry out a role in the setting-up and running of a festival, collaborating with others. ...can follow safe working practices and work to deadlines.	Make a checklist of all your duties and refer to it regularly. If you have a number of tasks to complete, prioritise them according to deadlines, i.e. begin with the one that has to be completed first. Always work safely. Check any health and safety guidance you have been given before beginning each task.	You must carry out your role confidently and efficiently. You must be able to work to deadlines consistently. Follow safe working practices consistently. You must be able to carry out your role with only occasional help from your teachers.

MONITORING AND REVIEWING

Monitoring and reviewing your progress

Throughout your course, you will be assessed on the way that you monitor and review how you work, as well as what you produce. You will need to make records of the decisions you make and explain why you have made them. Your teacher will help you decide how to present your records. Whichever way you monitor your progress, you should show that you have thought carefully about your own work throughout the whole planning and creative process. In this section, you will find some tools and techniques to help you.

Monitoring and reviewing

You will need to make sure that you are making regular records of how you have progressed, with comments about how well you are working. Make comments about:

* whether you feel you are achieving your aims
* how well you are managing your time
* what new things you are learning or discovering
* what changes you have made to your plans or ideas
* how you are going to use the comments you have made about your work to alter what you do next.

Monitoring your work means making sure that you are sticking to the plans you have put in place and staying within the time and budget constraints of your project. **Reviewing** involves making judgements about the progress you have made and evaluating the good and bad aspects of your work.

By recording how they have worked, practitioners can go back at a later date and remind themselves of how they created something, using this information to save time, money and effort in future projects.

Case Study: Ellie

Ellie has been producing a painting using mixed media. On one section she has painted a large block of colour using oil paints. Because of the kind of oil paint she used, the section is still not dry after a week and this delays Ellie from continuing with her work. In her sketchbook Ellie notes, 'I have learned that I should have experimented more with the materials I had chosen before progressing on to creating the work. I am pleased with how this section looks but I now know it will not be dry for some time. I have decided to change my plans and leave this section as a single colour and will in future check the drying times of any paint I use before starting work'.

There are several key stages at which you should make sure you have recorded an evaluation of your progress and the decisions you have made, in a way appropriate to your work. The following questions will be a good guide to doing this effectively.

When conducting research and developing your understanding
• Did you conduct enough research?
• Did you research the right subjects?
• Was the information you found useful to you?
• What kind of research do you think was particularly helpful for finding information for a unit?
• Did you find it difficult or easy to investigate the creative context for a unit?
• How could you improve your work at this stage of the project when you approach other units?
Planning your creative and media activities
• Did you think of enough ideas to give you a range of choices when selecting an activity to carry out?
• Did you enjoy the process of coming up with ideas?
• Did you find making plans difficult or easy?
• How detailed were the plans you made and could they have been more specific?
• Did you make a good plan for how you would use your time?
The creation or production stage of your project
• Did you gather all the materials you needed in plenty of time to begin your work?
• Did you encounter any problems or issues about the resources you had planned to use?
• Did you keep to your plans and schedules for using your time?
• How well did you carry out the plans you had made to work safely?
• Are you pleased with how your final product looks?
• What changes or alterations did you need to make to your plans as you worked, and why?
• What improvements or changes do you think you would make to the way you work in future?
Your finished work
• Was your product fit for purpose (i.e. was it suitable for the use you originally intended it for)?
• Were you happy with what you had created?
• What went well during your project?
• What could have been done better?
• What have you learned from completing this work?

Summary

* Making notes as you work of the decisions you make and your reasons will help you understand more about your own working practices.
* Reflecting as you work on how your work is progressing helps you make sure that you are always producing the best work you can.
* Check with your teacher how you should record your evaluations, so that you can submit them in your process portfolio. There are some examples of effective reviewing and monitoring methods on the following pages.

A performer's logbook

A performer's logbook must include a record of rehearsals and the other preparations you undertake individually or as a group. You should include anything that you feel is important in terms of the progress you make during rehearsals, including the ideas generated and the decisions made. It is important that you include evaluative comments, not just descriptions of what happened. If something went well, or not so well, try to explain why and identify possible solutions where appropriate. It is vital that your log is completed on a regular basis, not just at the end of the production process. So divide your log into sections, with one section for rehearsal notes, another for individual practice and so on.

Rehearsal notes

In your rehearsal notes section, log every session you attend. Include sketches and diagrams if they are relevant, as well as any notes you are given by the director, musical director and choreographer.

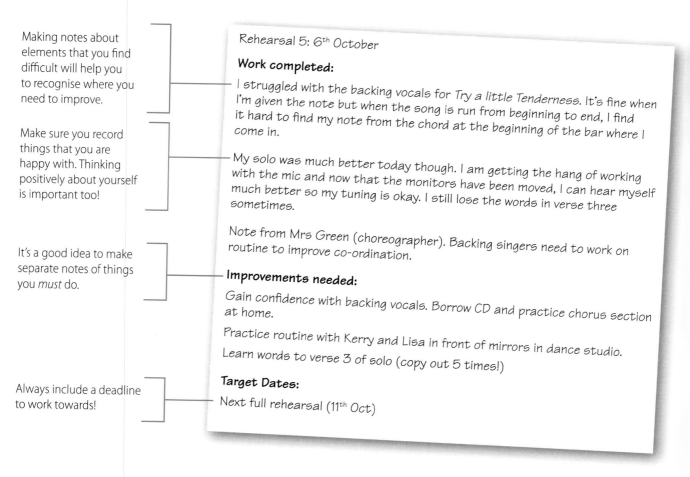

Making notes about elements that you find difficult will help you to recognise where you need to improve.

Make sure you record things that you are happy with. Thinking positively about yourself is important too!

It's a good idea to make separate notes of things you *must* do.

Always include a deadline to work towards!

Rehearsal 5: 6ᵗʰ October

Work completed:

I struggled with the backing vocals for *Try a little Tenderness*. It's fine when I'm given the note but when the song is run from beginning to end, I find it hard to find my note from the chord at the beginning of the bar where I come in.

My solo was much better today though. I am getting the hang of working with the mic and now that the monitors have been moved, I can hear myself much better so my tuning is okay. I still lose the words in verse three sometimes.

Note from Mrs Green (choreographer). Backing singers need to work on routine to improve co-ordination.

Improvements needed:

Gain confidence with backing vocals. Borrow CD and practice chorus section at home.

Practice routine with Kerry and Lisa in front of mirrors in dance studio.

Learn words to verse 3 of solo (copy out 5 times!)

Target Dates:

Next full rehearsal (11ᵗʰ Oct)

Individual practice

Your log is also a place to record individual practice and preparation. If you are performing a role in a play or musical, for example, you will need to record the methods you used to develop your character. This might include research materials, details of games and exercises used to explore your role and character maps or spidergrams like the one below.

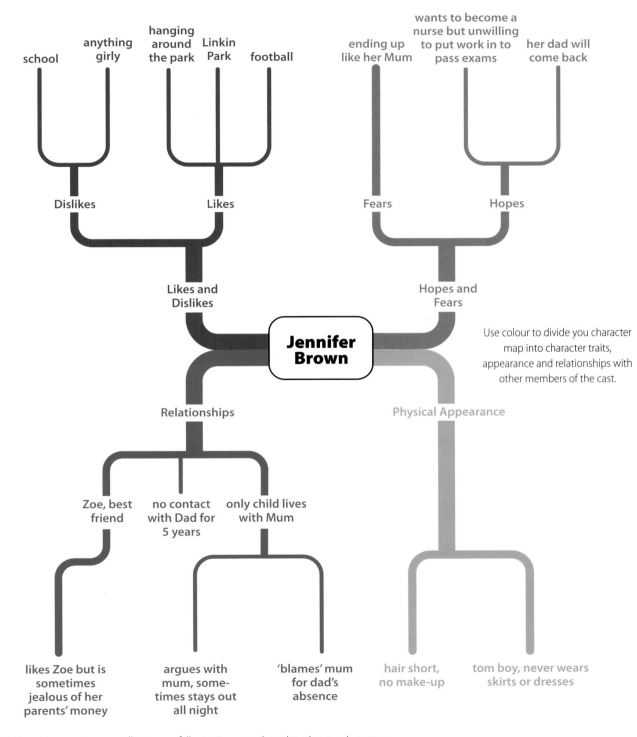

A character map is an excellent way of illustrating your thoughts about a character.

Depending on the nature of the work you are doing, you may be given very specific targets by your tutor for the improvement of your technique. You should log each of these targets in your individual practice section.

Areas for improvement	Strategies	Review 1	Comments
General Flexibility	Undertake a programme of gentle stretching after warm-up.	Flexibility of hamstrings slightly improved.	This has been hard for me but I am pleased to have improved.
Stamina	Undertake some cardiovascular work three times a week. Gradually increase length and intensity of workout.	General stamina has really improved.	I don't feel as breathless at the end of a routine now.

Performance production logs

If you are part of the production team for an event, festival or performance, there may be a number of documents that can be used to monitor the progress of your work during the production process.

Rehearsal notes and the production notice board

Rehearsal notes are an important method of communication between all those working on a production. They allow those working on, for example, the set, costumes, props, lighting and sound to monitor what is going on in rehearsals and make adjustments to the work they are doing when necessary. The note is distributed to all concerned and a copy placed on the production notice board. It helps if one person can volunteer to take detailed notes at each rehearsal.

North Street Community College
'Aladdin'
Rehearsal Notes

Thurs 22nd Nov

Divide the questions and information up so that it is clear what each department needs to do.

Construction
1. Could the door in the flat S.R. in Act 1 be fitted with a large doorknocker?
2. The Princess's coach needs to be small enough to be stored behind the backdrop when not in use.

Wardrobe
1. Could we have Widow Twankey's hooped underskirt for use in rehearsals?

Sound
1. Could the following sounds be sourced: dog barking (big dog!); doorbell; car screeching to a halt?

LX (lighting and electrics)
1. Could we have a green spot on the Genie in Act 1 scene 4?

Stage Management/Props
1. The contents of Widow Twankey's laundry basket need to include a pair of red bloomers.
2. Wishywashy needs a bunch of flowers that squirts water.

Make sure that dates and locations of rehearsals are clear to everyone.

General
1. There will be a meeting for the production team on Mon 26th Nov in room E12 to discuss progress made with costumes, props and the set.
2. There will be a full run through of Act 1 on Wed 28th Nov at 3.15pm.

Personal production logbook

If you are taking on a role that involves stage management, technical or front-of-house work, you will need to record and monitor your contribution. This can be done in a production logbook, which is essentially a diary of the day-to-day activities you complete, and should include details of decisions made and their outcomes.

Production Log

Name: Gail Jarvis   Role: LX Technician/Operator

Date: 17th October (Fit Up Day One)

Time/Work Undertaken	Activities	Required Actions
1.15pm – 4.30pm Rigged on-stage lights	Henry and I read out details of where lights were going on the rig from the plan. Mr Harper rigged them.	Front-of-house lights to be rigged tomorrow afternoon. **We have run out of green gels and need to make 3 more.
5.00pm – 5.45pm Installed rostra at back of stage.	Put up the steel deck using the plans. We did not have enough 12" legs for the back section (one short).	See Mr Brown tomorrow about getting an 18" leg cut down.

Evaluation of Contribution:

I think we all worked well today and got a lot done. Rigging the lights took a long time and I found the lighting plan confusing to begin with, but I eventually got the hang of it. I think rigging the front-of-house lights tomorrow will be easier now that I know what to do. I am also looking forward to getting on the lighting desk.

Show reports

Once the show is up and running, each performance must be monitored. Anything that goes wrong must be noted so action can be taken to make sure the error does not occur again. After each performance, a show report will be produced by the stage manager and distributed to all staff.

North Street Community College
Show Report 'Aladdin'
Performance Number 2
Wed 12th Dec

Production Team	
Stage Manager	Martin Harris
DSM (Deputy Stage Manager)	Helen Browne
ASM (Assistant Stage Manager)	Gail Jarvis
Crew	Barry Haslam, Kevin Waite, Henry Oh
Front-of-House (FOH) Team	Kari Lewis, Zoe Reeves, Lorraine Masters
Lighting Operator	Lewis Davidson
Sound Operator	Jen Ferris
Wardrobe	Kyle Barratt

Running Times
Act One Up: 7.00
Act One Down: 7.55
Act Duration: 55 minutes

Interval Duration: 20 minutes

Act Two Up: 8.15
Act Two Down: 8.58
Act Two Duration: 43 minutes

Total Running Time: (including interval): 1 hr 58 mins
Total Playing Time: 1 hr 38 mins

Notes

1. Noise from backstage areas could be heard when house lights went down at the beginning of Act 1. Cast need to be silent when off stage and crew must to keep talking to a minimum.

2. Scene change into Act 1 Scene 3 was slow and disorganised. ASM and crew please rehearse this change before next performance.

3. Aladdin arrived on stage late in Act 1 Scene 4 because the lamp was left in the dressing room and had to get it. ASM to make sure all props are returned to props table when not in use.

4. Interval overran by 5 minutes as FOH team were waiting for boiler to heat up for tea/coffee. Please switch boiler on earlier tomorrow night to avoid this delay.

5. LXQ 8 (Genie's entrance) was early. Q was called early. DSM error.

6. 'Sea' sound effect in Act 2 Scene 2 was too loud and made dialogue difficult to hear. Please check levels before next show.

7. Chorus did not stay in position for 2nd curtain call. Please do not leave the stage until told by the ASM.

For your project

* Keep a record of all rehearsal reports produced during the production process. Add you own notes and comments to show when tasks were completed and any decisions made.
* Keep a record of any show reports produced, adding your own comments.

An annotated sketchbook

A sketchbook is a great way to record comments and thoughts about your work and the progress you are making, especially if you think 'visually'. Many visual artists use sketchbooks.

Irregular lines and shapes

Some seaweed I noticed

Whilst I was at the seaside I noticed the contrast between the irregular shapes of the natural objects and the straight lines in the manmade things.

Smooth curved line in a seagull feather

Straight man-made lines

Some of the colours that I saw were surprising, like the bright orange rust on the metal within the seabreaks.

A sketchbook can be used to record things that you discover in the research and investigation stages of a project.

Annotations, or notes, are essential to both the artist and other reviewers – they help everyone to understand people's thought processes and why things have been included.

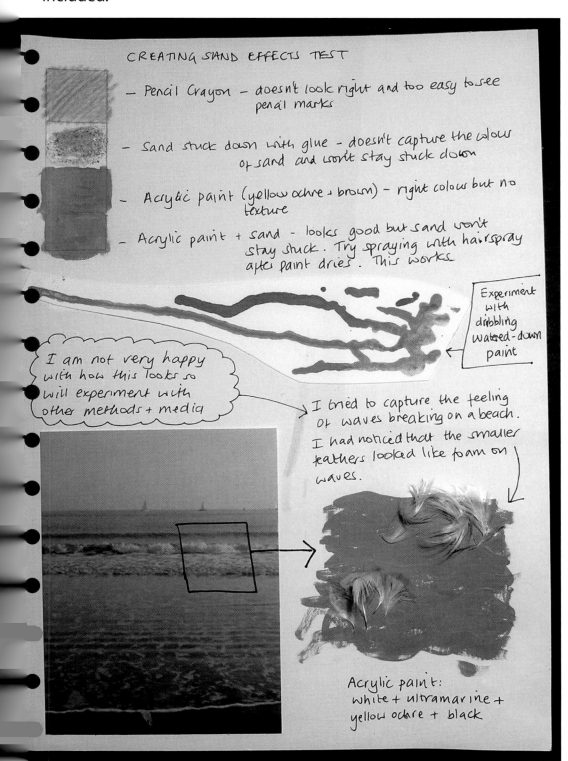

CREATING SAND EFFECTS TEST

- Pencil Crayon – doesn't look right and too easy to see pencil marks

- Sand stuck down with glue – doesn't capture the colour of sand and won't stay stuck down

- Acrylic paint (yellow ochre + brown) – right colour but no texture

- Acrylic paint + sand – looks good but sand won't stay stuck. Try spraying with hairspray after paint dries. This works

Experiment with dribbling watered-down paint

I am not very happy with how this looks so will experiment with other methods + media

I tried to capture the feeling of waves breaking on a beach. I had noticed that the smaller feathers looked like foam on waves.

Acrylic paint: white + ultramarine + yellow ochre + black

Annotations that report on your experimentations and findings show you are recording and monitoring your progress.

A diary in your sketchbook

Within your sketchbook, you may wish to keep a diary where you record what you have achieved and how well you feel you are progressing. This could be at the back of the book away from the visual materials you collect. It could be handwritten or typed and pasted in. Make regular comments, ideally at the end of each session you spend working on the project. You should always:

✳ write the date at the top of your entry

✳ explain what you have achieved since your last entry

✳ note down how you feel about your work and how well it is going

✳ explain any problems you have encountered and how you are going to solve them

✳ include notes on new things you have learned and what areas you think you need to improve in.

April 29th

Today I began work on producing the posters on the computer, using the photo-imaging software. When I came to use the shot of a rainbow that I had taken on the digital camera, I realised that it didn't look very good when I enlarged it. This was because it was taken at a low resolution. I decided to use one of the other images that I had taken, although it is not as colourful. In future, I will always check the settings on the digital camera before taking photographs for print projects.

Annotation

You can also include evidence of monitoring your work within the sketchbook itself by using annotations.

Below are some things you should consider including in your annotations in order to meet the requirements of the unit.

✳ Comments on the research you find during your initial work on any project:

✳ Refer to particular pieces and have them pasted into your book to illustrate what the points you make.

✳ Explain what you have found out about the context things were created in and note what further investigations into this area you might need to make.

✳ Highlight things that particularly inspired your ideas and explain how you are going to use the things learned from other people's work to develop your own ideas.

✳ Make notes on which particular skills or abilities you may need to develop to use the techniques you admire in the work of others.

Making regular notes helps you to keep track of your project and the progress you have made.

* The plans you have made for your work:
  – You should make notes about the good and bad points of the ideas you come up with. Store everything you work on in the sketchbook, even if you think it isn't very good. Make sure you comment on why you don't think it is useful in your annotation.
  – Paste or write in the schedules you draw up for working on your ideas and leave space to comment on whether you had allowed enough time for different tasks later on.
  – Comment on any experiments or tests you do with materials. Explain whether you are going to use these techniques or media, and if so, how you will do this. Explain the methods you used in your tests and say if you are pleased with the results.
  – Include comments on your planning before you begin practical work. Identify any areas that you think may cause you problems or issues before you begin. Then, go back once you have finished work to see if these things actually happened.

* The creation of artefacts or products:
  – During the creation process, keep regular notes about how well your work is going.
  – Examine any issues or problems that arise and refer back to your planning. Explain how you could avoid these problems in future projects.
  – If you find any part of the project particularly difficult, explain why this is and what you could do to improve your skills or knowledge in this area.

* Comments on your involvement in team work to accompany photographs of you working with others:
  – Note any problems or issues you had when working with others in a team environment.
  – Say what you do well when working with others and what you could improve.
  – List the benefits and issues surrounding working with others as opposed to working alone.

* Evaluations of finished work, either at stages in the project or at the end:
  – Comment on how happy you are with the way things look and work.
  – Consider carefully whether your finished product is fit for purpose and useable as you intended.

Some more techniques

A blog

One of the methods that you could use to document your progress and build in regular monitoring and reviewing activities is to build a blog. This will allow you to keep a note of what you do and when, and allow you to note your evaluations in a form that you and others can access.

How blogs work

'Blog' is a shortened version of the words 'web log'. It describes the use of a website to host an online diary. Blogs are usually written by one person and can be anything from their everyday thoughts on a particular topic or project to a more general diary that documents their thoughts, feelings or actions.

How to set up a blog

Some websites will let you set up a blog for free and some **social networking sites** have a blogging facility built into them. Such sites will take you through the process of setting up your blog and give you guidance about what you need to do to see your blog appear on screen.

Alternatively, your school or college might have a blog program built into their intranet or virtual learning environment. Your teacher will be able to help you find out if this is the case and tell you how to set it up.

Consider including the following in your monitoring and reviewing blog:

* links to any online resources that you used in your research (explaining carefully how they were useful)
* photographs and videos of you or those within your group working as they progress (but make sure you have their permission first!)
* links to the blogs of others in your group, to show how you have all reflected on working as a group.

Monitoring and reviewing using a blog

Use your blog to reflect on a particular project. Ensure that you keep your reviewing work for a project clearly separated from your thoughts on other projects, or indeed other subjects not related to your work.

Try to set aside a regular time to update your blog so that it doesn't get left until you have forgotten what you have done. Don't wait until you have three weeks' work to document in your blog!

Be aware

Always remember that most blogs are in the public domain as they are usually on the internet and therefore accessible by others.

* Be careful that you never give out personal details such as your home address, telephone number or email address whenever you are using internet blog sites. Those who need to read the blog such as you and your teacher already know these things. It is unwise and unsafe to give such information out on the internet.

* Be aware that if you decide to make your blog public, then others will be able to read what you put. You must not put anything on there about other people that you would not want them to read or that you wouldn't want anyone to say about you. Part of reviewing involves commenting on your work with others but using derogatory language or making accusations in a blog can be hurtful, unfair and can lead to serious issues.

* Don't post photographs on to a blog without checking with a teacher or a responsible adult that this is OK first. It is easy to forget sometimes that the images you post could be seen by anyone who chooses to access it.

You can often set a blog to have restrictions on who can see the information. Read the FAQ and help pages on all blogs sites carefully before posting anything and find out how you can control who has access to your information.

Director's commentary

Have you ever watched the 'extras features' on a DVD? One of these may have been a Director's commentary. The director may have talked about the ways in which they made the film and analysed scenes to clarify why they were included. If you are producing a recording or media product in DVD format, you could add a commentary of your own. You may be able to add further soundtracks on top of scenes, and use the menu facility for turning the commentary on and off.

A video diary or webcam

Video is a useful tool for recording your thoughts about what you have done and how you could improve your skills. The simplest form of video diary is to set up a camera or a webcam in a room and then talk about the work you have done and what you could improve. However, using your media skills, you could overlay images from your media work over your voice. In this way, you could illustrate some of the issues you found and examples of the techniques you used. You could use photographs of your work as well as examples of scanned images of your storyboards or magazine articles.

An audio diary

You could also use an audio diary to record your review. Preparing a prompt sheet beforehand will help you to plan what you want to say, so you will avoid spending time editing later.

Social networking site – A web-based service which allows a community of people to interact online in various ways, using online chatrooms, file-sharing facilities and discussion groups.

Public domain – A body of information which is considered to be for unrestricted public use or exploitation.

For your project

* Always save your work when writing online and, to be safe, it may be wise to write blog entries as a word-processing document first and then save them onto the blog, in case there are any errors when uploading.

* You will need to store your blog carefully online and give your teacher access to it digitally. It may also be wise to print out your blog at the end of a project so that you have a paper copy to store.

7 PROJECT REPORT

Introduction

Well done! By now you should have completed most of the project work for your other units. Thought that your work was brilliant? Well, this is your chance to find out what your audience *really* thought about your practical work. You will then be able to think about your work and evaluate what went well and what didn't. Finally, you will be able to present your findings in the form of a written project report.

OVER TO YOU!

On your own, think about the projects that you have completed for Units 2, 3 and 4. Which did you enjoy the most? Which did you enjoy the least? Does one stand out as being particularly interesting or challenging?

Important!

Remember that the whole project report should be no more than 1,750 words long. You will need to count all of the words carefully and make sure that you do not go over this amount.

Functional skills

Using English…

When you are discussing which project to choose for your project work, make sure you are using your listening and speaking skills to good effect.

Contribute to group discussions by giving your opinion and listening to what others have to say.

Your learning

In this unit, you should work across at least two of the disciplines on page 4 to cover the four main topics.

Gathering responses to your own work

Your written report needs to be written about project work that you have completed in one of the following units:

* Unit 2: Performance   * Unit 3: Artefact   * Unit 4: Record.

It doesn't matter which unit you choose or which project you decide to write your report on. The most important thing is to choose a project that you have a lot to say about!

Once you've chosen your project you must work alone to gather and evaluate the responses of audiences, clients and customers, as applicable to your project. You will use this information to help decide how successful your project has been. You must be able to design and carry out surveys, gather responses from audiences and clients, e.g. through focus groups and interviews, and finally to summarise your findings.

Evaluating your own work

Your report needs to be an honest evaluation of your project and identify strengths and weaknesses of both the finished product and your role in the creative and planning processes.

You need to be able to use the research you have collected to explain the creative process that you have been through, evaluate the strengths and weaknesses of your chosen piece of work and suggest ways in which it could be improved.

You should consider how well you developed your ideas, the quality of your planning and organising and how well you used your chosen materials and techniques. If you worked in a group, it is important to consider how well you worked in your group and got on with other people, and of course how effective your final piece of work was.

Presenting an evaluation of your own work in a project report

You will be writing your final report in controlled examination conditions, but remember – your report needs to be well-written, carefully structured and written in formal English. You will need to add in supporting material such as graphs and ensure you do so correctly. Finally you must stick to the word limit – a maximum of 1,750 – or you will lose marks.

The report structure

This unit will help you get all the information you need for your report and advise you on how best to structure and present it. Your final report will need to be presented in **two** sections and must have some additional material attached to it.

You need to decide which project it is best for you to write your report on.

Section A: Sources

In this section of the report you need to describe the research methods and sources of information that you used and then summarise what you found out from your research.

Section B: Evaluation

In this section you should evaluate your project work by explaining its strengths and weaknesses, and then suggest ways in which the work could have been improved. This evaluation needs to be done in the light of the information that you have gathered in your research and should be as detailed as possible.

Remember, even if your project was brilliant, there are always ways that it could be improved. There is more advice on how best to present and structure your report later in this unit.

Additional illustrative material

You must attach illustrative material such as photographs and sound and video recordings to your report to explain clearly what your project is all about. You can also attach examples of any research materials such as questionnaires, interview questions and data that you used.

This material is not included in your word limit of 1,750 words. You should discuss with your teacher what illustrative material it is best to include for your particular project.

> ### Activity
>
> Discuss the project report with the rest of your group and your teacher and make a decision as to which unit and which project you are going to base your report on. Explain why you have chosen this particular project as the focus of the report.

> ### Remember!
>
> * Choose one of your projects from Units 2, 3 or 4.
> * Gather feedback on your project.
> * Evaluate your project and your part in it in light of this feedback.
> * Produce a written project report 1,750 words in length.

> ### Presenting information
>
> Sarah included graphs, tables and charts in this section of her project report to present the information that she had gathered in a more interesting and imaginative way. She also made sure that the examples of the material used to gather her research (which included questionnaires, interview questions and focus group minutes) were attached to the report as separate files.
>
> What kind of information is best presented using each of the different techniques Sarah used – graphs, tables, charts and written text?

7.1 Finding out what people think about your work

You may have thought your project was the best thing you have ever done, or you may have thought that it was a disaster, but what do your audience and your client think? Well, this is your chance to find out!

Audience

Most of the products that are made within the creative arts and media industries are produced with a particular audience in mind. If the audience like your product then you are on to a winner. If not, then you had better make some changes, or you might end up losing money or your reputation – or both!

Of course, you should have undertaken some audience research in the pre-production stages of your project work so that you could make any necessary changes as your project developed, but it is also important to find out what they think about the final product. This will allow you to understand what went well and, perhaps more importantly, what didn't. You can then make sure that you improve things next time around.

Case Study: Blade Runner

Most major film studios show newly completed films to a small sample of the target audience to check if they like them. If they don't, they will often change parts of the film before it is released.

One example of this is the science fiction film *Blade Runner*, which was directed in 1982 by Ridley Scott. The preview screenings suggested that the audience did not understand parts of the story and didn't like the way the film ended. The studio that had paid Scott to make the film added additional voice-overs to explain certain scenes, removed the now famous 'unicorn scene' and added a happy ending.

Ridley Scott later released a 'Director's Cut' version with the additional voice-over removed, the unicorn scene restored and the original ending. It is now this version that is seen by many as the better one.

Do you think that the studio was right to make such changes to the film?

What do you think were their main reasons for doing this?

How would you have felt if somebody did this to your project work?

Try to see both versions of the film and decide which you think is the better version.

Working for a client

Before your work even reaches your audience you will probably have to make sure that your client is happy with it. Most of the products in the creative arts and media industries are commissioned or requested by a client of some kind. These might be known as a commissioning editor, producer, exhibitor, broadcaster, publisher or potential purchaser, but whatever they are called, their opinion is vital to the success of your project.

OVER TO YOU!

Think about the different ways in which you can find out what your audience thought about your project work. Which do you think are the best ones to use for this unit?

Functional skills

Using ICT...

You must be able to organise your work clearly and logically so when you come to write your report under the timed examination conditions you don't waste time looking for things. Use your ICT skills to keep your electronic data in order with clear file names and folders.

Personal, learning and thinking skills

When you gather responses to your work you will inevitably encounter some criticism as well as praise. It is important to remain positive and accept that you can't get everything right – but what you can do is learn from your mistakes by explaining how you would improve things next time. When you do this you will be demonstrating the skills of a Reflective Learner.

You can record your interviews with your client in different ways.

Gathering responses to your own work

To achieve this objective you need to gather accurate and reliable responses to your chosen project work from a range of different people. These should include a sample of your target audience or customers and your client. You should then measure and analyse these responses and use this information to help you decide how successful your chosen project has been.

Getting feedback

Sarah was keen to get as much feedback as possible about her project. To help her do this she arranged an interview with her client, organised a focus group with six members of her target audience and also produced a questionnaire for a sample of twenty people.

How could you get responses to a questionnaire? Make a list of all the possible ways you can think of to reach your target audience.

You will need to think carefully about how best to gather this information, and you will probably need to design and conduct a survey of some kind with a representative sample of your target audience. You could also undertake interviews with your client and other people involved with your project work.

The data and information that you gain will need to be recorded and stored in a secure way so that you are then able to analyse the results and summarise the findings. It's also a good idea to think about how you will organise your findings when you get them. You could set up a folder system in advance either on your computer or for paper-

Activity

Think carefully about who you need to gather information about your chosen project from. Identify:

* your target audience or customers
* your client
* any other people who may be able to provide valuable feedback to you.

How will you contact these people to gather the information you need?

Just checking

* How are you going to find out what your audience thought of your project?
* Have you identified who you need to contact to gather information from?
* Have you contacted your client and target audience to request their feedback?
* Do you have a plan for organising your research information?

Primary research – Original research to obtain original data, using such techniques as interviews, questionnaires and focus groups.

Secondary research – Research using existing data, and information that has already been gathered by other people or organisations. Often available in books, magazines or on the internet.

Quantitative data – Measurable facts and information that can be counted, producing numerical and statistical data.

Qualitative data – Opinions, attitudes and preferences rather than hard facts.

Research

You will need to undertake your own research to find out what your audience and others thought about your project work. To do this, you will need to design and conduct your own surveys, gather the responses from those who have seen your work and then analyse the data you produce and summarise the findings.

Primary and secondary research

The two main types of research are called **primary research** and **secondary research**.

Primary research is original research that is carried out for a specific purpose to obtain original data. The techniques used include: conducting a survey in the street, interviewing people over the phone and running a focus group. An example of primary research is when a film company will show a preview of their new film to a group of people (often called a focus group) and ask them what they think of it.

Secondary research involves the use of data and information that have already been published or are already available within an organisation. The techniques you might use when doing secondary research include: reading books and magazines, searching on the internet and taking notes from research studies that already exist.

Quantitative and qualitative data

The research that you undertake for this unit will be mainly primary research and it is important that you obtain both **quantitative** and **qualitative data** when undertaking your research.

Quantitative data is information that you can measure and count. The data can usually be shown as a set of numbers and is often presented in the form of tables, charts and diagrams. Quantitative data can include such things as ratings, circulation and viewing figures and market analysis, as well as the counting and measuring of items or space in a particular media product.

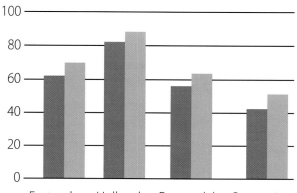

% of young people surveyed who watch soaps

Legend: Boys, Girls

Categories: Eastenders, Hollyoaks, Emmerdale, Coronation St

Readership of The Times newspaper by age

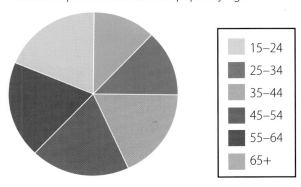

	15–24
	25–34
	35–44
	45–54
	55–64
	65+

The other main form is qualitative information about people's opinions, views and preferences about something. Both primary and secondary research techniques can produce qualitative data, and it is often very important within the creative industries, as it is used to find out what individuals and groups think and feel about a particular media product.

Depending on the nature of the research and the types of questions asked, it is not always possible to analyse the results of qualitative research statistically, particularly if the responses are personal and subjective, like the ones below:

Rob	I really liked the picture of the woman on the front of the magazine. It reminded me of an ex-girlfriend. I liked the way that she dressed, but I do not think that I would buy the magazine. I might read it if a friend of mine had already bought it.
Jane	I thought the woman on the front of the magazine looked ugly. Her make-up looked old fashioned and her hair was not very trendy. I do not think that I would buy the magazine as I don't think it would appeal to me and it is also over-priced.

A film company asking a focus group what they think about a new film is likely to produce both quantitative and qualitative data. For example:

By asking the group to fill out a short questionnaire before the film started they might discover that 55 per cent of women and only 38 per cent of men had visited the cinema in the last month. This is quantitative data.

After the film had finished, the company would have asked each individual what they thought about the film. What were their feelings about the main character? What did they understand about the storyline? What did they think about the ending? This would have provided them with qualitative information.

Conducting your primary research

You will need to undertake your own primary research to get feedback for your project. The main form of survey will probably be a questionnaire given to a sample of your target audience or customers. You could also conduct a focus group meeting and organise interviews with your client and any other people who have been involved with your project work.

Questionnaires

Questionnaires are a very popular form of primary research that can be used to survey a sample of your target audience or customers. You will almost certainly want to include at least one questionnaire when undertaking your own primary research, and you will need to think very carefully about the questions that you ask and the way in which your questionnaire is structured and presented.

Many questionnaires are conducted in the street by asking people the questions face-to-face. This can be very time-consuming, but it does allow you to choose your sample very carefully and to explain any questions that people don't understand. Another way is to send the questionnaire out to people for them to fill out on their own. You might want to post them or email them to your sample. Some people might feel happier to write down what they really think rather than tell it to your face, particularly if it is bad news!

We will look in more detail at the design and use of questionnaires on page 232.

Focus groups

Focus groups are pre-selected panels of people who are chosen to represent a particular target audience. They are often used by marketing and advertising agencies to test the likely response of the target audience towards the product that is being advertised and to the advert itself.

As you saw earlier, film studios use focus groups in preview screenings of major films to try to ensure that the audience reaction is the one that they are looking for, and that the film will be well received. Companies launching a new computer game, magazine, radio show or TV programme may also show a preview of the product to a focus group to test it out and get feedback before they launch the full product.

OVER TO YOU!

Think about what sort of primary research you will need to undertake to gather information about your project work. Will you run a focus group? Who do you need to interview? How many people do you think you will need to survey when you use your questionnaire? Make a research plan that lists everything you plan to do.

Personal, learning and thinking skills

Planning, organising and carrying out your own primary research will enable you to develop further a range of learning and thinking skills and provide you with the opportunity to have them assessed.

For example you can show that you are an Independent Enquirer by identifying questions to answer and problems to resolve, and by planning and carrying out meaningful research.

Focus groups

Sarah decided to run a focus group as part of her research. She invited six people who she thought would represent her target audience and booked a room at her school to hold the focus group meeting. She wanted to make sure that she captured the thoughts and ideas from everybody, so asked a friend to record the whole meeting on video.

Think about what you would need to do in order to organise and run a successful focus group.

Who would you invite?

Where would you hold the meeting?

What sort of questions would you ask?
How would you record the results?

Make sure your focus group contains people from the right target audience

Interviews

Conducting one-to-one interviews with your client and any other people involved with your project can be a very effective method of getting feedback, as you can respond immediately to the answers that they give and clarify or ask them to elaborate on any points that they make.

Before the interview:

* **Organise a convenient time to meet:** Do this well in advance so that your interview is not hurried, and both you and the person you are interviewing are fully prepared.
* **Choose a good location:** Meet in a quiet, relaxed place where you are not distracted by phones and other people.
* **Be prepared:** Have a set of questions ready to ask and a means of recording what is being said.

During the interview:

* **Listen carefully:** It is important to listen carefully to what is being said. Don't be afraid to ask extra questions or ask the person to explain what they are saying in a little more detail.
* **Be professional:** You might want to work with this person again in the future and you can improve your reputation by being polite and professional.

After the interview:

* **Review the responses:** Listen to the recording and make a careful note of the answers given. You might want to transcribe the whole interview.
* **Summarise the findings:** Analyse what was said and think carefully about what this says about your project work.

Planning your primary research

When planning your primary research it is important to think carefully about what you are trying to find out, and who you need to find out the information from. You may design a very professional-looking questionnaire, but if it doesn't ask the right questions then all of your efforts will be wasted.

Activity

Using the advice given above, plan, organise and undertake a focus group meeting with a sample of your target audience and an interview with your client.

You will need to analyse the results for each meeting1 so consider how best to do this. Can you make use of ICT? Summarise your findings in a written mini-report. Include any diagrams or tables that you feel are appropriate.

Just checking

* Have you made a research plan?
* Have you planned your focus group meetings or interviews?

Questionnaires

One of the main techniques used in primary research is asking people questions, and it is highly likely that you will use some form of questioning technique in the research that you carry out for this unit. The questionnaire is perhaps the most popular form of primary research, but you will need to think carefully about the way that it is presented. You also need to work out the best way to write and structure the questions so that the questionnaire makes sense.

OVER TO YOU!

Think about questionnaires or surveys that you have completed in the past. What factors encouraged you to answer truthfully, and what put you off?

Questionnaire design

If you are going to give out the questionnaire for people to complete, rather than read the questions out to them, then the questionnaire itself needs to look attractive and professional to encourage people to complete it.

An appropriate title for the study should be at the top of the page, followed by a brief introduction so that people know who you are, the purpose of the survey and what the results will be used for.

You should also make sure that all of the questions make sense and are easy to follow, as you will not be there to explain anything to them that they do not understand. Don't forget to tell them where to return it to either! You may find it useful to ask someone who does not know your project to read your questionnaire through before you print out copies – they may spot something you had missed.

Open question – This type allows the person answering to give his or her own views and opinions on a particular subject, and often start with such words such as: What, Why, When, How or Who.

Closed question – A closed question is more limited in terms of the potential answers that can be given, and are often answered with: Yes, No, Don't know, or an answer picked from a range of given options.

The questions

There are two main types of question that you can use in a questionnaire or interview. One is a **closed question** and the other is an **open question**.

As a general rule you should start your questionnaire with some simple closed questions that are easy to answer. Asking people their age, gender and occupation, for example, should get them into the process of completing the questionnaire, and will also provide you with some basic information about the people you have surveyed. It will also allow you to check that you have covered the right sample of people, and allow you to include some more people in the survey if you haven't.

When using closed questions it is often easier to include potential answers for people to select, for example:

Q1: How old are you?

☐   ☐   ☐   ☐

15 or younger   16–18   19–21   22+

Q2: What is your gender?

☐ Male ☐ Female

Q3: Which of the following TV services do you have in your home? (you can tick more than one box)

☐ Terrestrial ☐ Satellite ☐ Cable ☐ Freeview

Closed questions, where the potential number of responses is limited, are good in this form of survey as they are easy for people to complete and will provide you with quantitative data which you can easily analyse and represent in the form of graphs, charts and diagrams.

However, a more open-style question, where you might be asking people to write down a personal response to something, often provides you with qualitative information that gives a more meaningful insight, for example:

Q4: Why did you choose to take a creative arts and media qualification?

Both open and closed questions are sometimes used together in a paired question, for example:

Q5a: Do you play computer games?

☐ Yes ☐ No

Q5b: If you answered yes to 5a, please explain in the space below what you like about playing computer games.

Whatever style of question you choose, try to keep the language of your questions as simple as possible. Avoid asking confusing questions or those which direct people towards a preferred answer.

Writing question

Sarah included the following questions in her questionnaire. Her teacher was not very happy with them. Can you see any problems with them?

Q1: Why do you think game shows are good?

Q2: What do you think about the media?

Q3: Do you prefer vector-based or pixel-based image generation and manipulation software programmes and what do you think of CGI in CD-ROMs?

Using ICT...

* Using a PC to produce your questionnaires is the easiest and most professional method to use. You can also research examples of other questionnaires on the internet to give you ideas on how best to style your own.

* ICT also makes analysing your data a much simpler process. It's a good idea to think about how you will analyse your data when you are writing your questionnaire – it might influence the style of your questions.

Activity

Using the advice given above, design a questionnaire for your target audience that uses both open and closed questions.

Use the questionnaire to find out what a sample of your target audience thought about your project.

Analyse the results using a database or spreadsheet such as Excel and then summarise the main findings in a mini-report.

Just checking

* Have you decided how you will carry out your questionnaire?
* Have you included both open and closed questions?
* How will you analyse the answers you are given?

Collating and storing research material

The amount of information that is gathered when undertaking research can often be very large, particularly if it is linked to a complex production that involved many different aspects. One of the skills that you will need to learn when undertaking your own research is the ability to sift through the information that you have gathered, and to select and use only the material that is of value to you.

Don't leave it too late to get your research organised!

Organising your research material

Primary research will generate lots of material, information and data. It is important that you get yourself organised and sort through your files, folders and paperwork so that you know what you have done and where it can be found. Far too many students simply put all of their research material into a folder and expect to receive a good mark for it.

Once you have sorted the information that you require, you need to organise and store it securely. It is best if you create an electronic research folder at this stage if you haven't already got one, to keep all of your relevant research material in. You will need to attach electronic files of research material and data to your final written report, so any paper-based documents that you want to include will need to be scanned in.

Copies of your questionnaire and any questions that you used in interviews or for your focus group should also be included in your folder, together with any pictures you may have taken of the research process.

Note that photos of the performance, artefact or record go in a separate illustrative material file.

Using electronic files

Sarah had a lot of research information on paper, which she stored in an A4 folder, and she also had some electronic work saved on the computer.

She created an electronic folder called 'Research Material' and saved all of the relevant research material on her computer in this folder. She then sorted through her papers and scanned in some of the relevant material and then also saved this into the folder.

What problems might Sarah have faced when she came to write up her project report if she hadn't sorted through and scanned in her research information?

Activity

You are going to organise your research information. First, sort through your paperwork and collate the information that is important to you. Store this material in a folder.

Next, go through the electronic material you have on your computer and organise this in a logical order. Save this material in an electronic folder.

Finally, talk to your teacher about the paperwork that you will need to include with your final report and arrange for this to be electronically scanned. You can then save this to your electronic research folder.

Just checking

* Is your research collated and sorted?
* Have you organised your electronic folders?
* Does any important paper-based research need to be scanned in?

7.2 Evaluating your own work

You should now have gathered a lot of feedback from other people about your project work. Do you like what you have heard? Well, now is the time for *you* to begin to evaluate you own work. This is an important final stage before you begin to write your final project report.

Strengths and weakness

Every project has its strengths and weaknesses and now is the time for you to be very honest and try to look objectively at the work that you have produced. The feedback that you have already received should be used to support and back up what you think yourself. Of course, you might not always like what other people have told you but you need to get over this and reflect carefully on what is being said. You should say what you feel were the strengths and weaknesses of your project, and always remember to support your statements with evidence.

OVER TO YOU!

Think about the feedback you have already received. What does it tell you about your project? Has it been a success? How could it be improved?

Reflect on the strengths and weaknesses of your project.

Self-evaluation

Sarah had worked well on her project and was very pleased with the way that it had turned out. However, she could already think of a number of ways in which it could be improved.

Think about the quality of your final project. What does it look or sound like?

You are not expected to produce a professional piece of work, but how close have you come?

The project itself

The actual product or artefact that you produced in Unit 2, 3 or 4 will be the main focus of your report and you will need to judge how this has turned out, and how it compares with your original plans and ideas at the start. You will also need to comment on how the final project was presented, shown or exhibited, and how you think it could be improved.

The process

You also need to consider the creative process that you have been through. This should include the ways in which you:

* generated your initial ideas
* chose one idea to develop further
* researched your chosen idea
* went through the pre-production and production processes
* presented, showed or exhibited your final work.

You should also consider:

* the equipment, materials and technology that you have used
* the technical skills that you have learnt, used and developed.

If you worked in a group

When thinking about your role in the creative process you should consider:

* the way in which you worked with other people
* the individual contribution that you made to the project
* your planning and organisational skills
* your ability to use and apply functional skills in ICT, English and Maths.

Personal, learning and thinking skills

When you come to evaluate your own work – the part you played in your project, the processes you went through and how you worked in your group – you will be actively showing yourself to be a Reflective Learner if you can consider both your strengths and weaknesses, then outline how you would work differently next time and identify key areas for improvement.

Activity

Think about the performance, artefact or record itself. Make a list of the positive things about your final piece and then another list of the things that you don't think worked as well as they could.

Now think about your role in the creation and development of this piece. Again, write down a list of all of the things that you think you did well and then another list of the things that didn't go to plan. Include in this list how you worked with other members of your group, your client and others who were involved in the process.

Begin to identify what improvements you would make if you had the chance to start again.

Just checking

* Have you been honest in your self-evaluation?
* Have you identified both strengths and weaknesses?
* Have you considered your role in: the end product, the creative process and your team?

7.3 Writing your project report

Time for the final analysis! You have already achieved a lot by getting to this stage of the course, but you now have the chance to show what you really know by producing your project report.

OVER TO YOU!

Look through the research work and the report notes that you have already made, and gather together the important material and pieces of information that you will need to produce your final report.

External assessment

You must use a computer to type the project report directly into an electronic document that will be given to you by your teacher. This report is the only piece of work that will not be marked by your teacher. When you have written it and checked it through it will be sent off to an external examiner who will mark your work.

You should attach illustrative material to your report, such as:

* pictures
* sound clips
* video clips
* research documents.

All of these **must** be in electronic form, as your teacher will burn them onto a CD-ROM and send this on to the examiner.

Explaining your project

Sarah had taken digital photographs of her project as it was being created and had also taken some digital video clips. She was able to attach these to her report in a separate file to help the examiner understand what her project was all about.

Remember that the external examiner will not have seen any of your work from your other units and will not know anything about your project, so you will need to explain everything to them very clearly.

Your illustrative material will all be in one file, but your research materials may be in several files. Think for a moment – how clear are the file names that you have chosen? Will an examiner with no knowledge of your project be able to find everything they need easily? For example, which of these names is clearer: 'Focus group 1 – qualitative data' or '1–FG QD'?

Functional skills

Using ICT...

Writing your final project report is an excellent opportunity to demonstrate how well you can interact with and use ICT when completing a difficult task independently.

Using English...

The timed writing task also allows you to show that you can communicate information, ideas and opinions effectively and persuasively.

Report structure

Look carefully at the external assessment sheet for this unit. It was issued by the examination board, and explains that your report must be organised into two sections and that you must attach illustrative material showing your project work, as well as examples of any research material such as questionnaires, interview questions and data that you used.

Section A: Sources

This is where you describe the research methods that you used to gather the information relating to your work. You also need to describe the sources of information that you used and then summarise what you found out from your research. You might want to represent some of your data in the form of tables, graphs or charts and include copies of your original questionnaires and interview or focus group questions and answers in separate electronic files.

Section B: Evaluation

In this section you should evaluate your project work by explaining its strengths and weaknesses and then suggest ways in which the work could have been improved. Your starting point should be the information that you have gathered in your research. You should consider the final product itself, the processes that you went through and the way in which you and your group worked together.

You considered all of these points in the previous topic and now is the time to write them all up in your final report.

Remember to attach illustrative material when you write up your final project report.

Important!

Your completed report will be marked out of 60. This is broken down as follows:

10 marks are available for the presentation of your report as a whole, including any illustrative material that you attach.

20 marks are available for Section A, which should be about 750 words in length.

30 marks are available for Section B, which should be about 1,000 words in length.

Remember that your project report must not be more than 1,750 words in total, excluding any additional illustrative material.

Activity

With the help of your teacher and the rest of your group, organise the additional illustrative material such as photos, video and sound clips and any additional research documents into a separate folder and save it on your computer.

These are the only parts of the report that your teacher can help you with.

Sections A and B will need to be completed by you under controlled conditions and must be your own work without anyone else's help. You will be allowed up to **four hours** to complete your report, though this should be spread over two or more sessions.

Remember that your project report must be no more than 1,750 words in length.

Personal, learning and thinking skills

When writing a final report, a Reflective Learner aims to communicate not just information and data, but also opinion and explanation. To do this, make sure your evidence supports each point you make, and that your points follow on coherently from one another. You should also try to make your report interesting to read and use graphic material to present your findings, as well as written evidence.

Just checking

* Do you have all the information you need to write your project report?
* Do you understand the structure of the report you will be writing?
* Have you thought about the illustrative material you want to include with your report?
* Is the research information you want to include organised and saved electronically?

Here is an extract of a completed report written by a student whose group produced a video recording of their own fashion show as their final product for Unit 4. The full report was typed on a computer in two 2-hour supervised sessions and is their own individual work. The student also attached additional files to the report, including:

- a copy of the final video produced
- still photographs of the fashion show
- photographs of the research being undertaken
- copies of the questionnaires used and the questions used in the focus group
- logs of the secondary sources used and the data that the research produced.

Introduction

This report is about the group project that I completed for my Unit 4 of the Diploma, which was a video record of the fashion show that we presented.

Section A: Sources

I decided to use both primary and secondary research methods to get both quantitative and qualitative data from my client and my target audience. My target audience for the video recording were students aged between 14–18, so I made sure that I had a mixture of both males and females between these ages in my sample.

> Headings, subheading and bullet points are used to structure the report. This helps to make it clear and easy to read.

Primary Research

The primary methods I used were:

- a written questionnaire that was presented to a sample of my target audience
- a focus group with a smaller sample of my target audience
- a face-to-face interview with my client.

Written Questionnaire

This allowed me to get some feedback on my project from a large number of people fairly quickly, as 20 people completed the questionnaire. It contained a mixture of open and closed questions and gave me valuable information about what people liked and didn't like about the recording of the fashion show. Most of this information was quantitative but some was qualitative.

I kept the questionnaire to a single side of A4 so that people weren't put off by too many questions. I was very happy that all 20 handed it back to me and everybody answered all of the questions.

Focus Group

This method allowed me to ask more in-depth questions to a smaller sample of my target audience and I was able to get a lot of qualitative data from them. I invited 5 people to be in my focus group and I recorded what they said using a data recorder. I prepared the questions beforehand so that I knew what I was going to ask them.

Interview with Client

My teacher played the role of my client and I was able to interview him face to face so that I could find ou t what he thought about it and how he thought it could be improved. This was very successful and I wrote down the points that he made.

Secondary Research

The secondary sources of information that I used were:

- analysing existing fashion show videos
- searching for fashion items on the internet
- looking for ideas in fashion magazines.

I wanted to see what fashion show videos looked like and get some ideas for the types of shots and camera angles used and also the way in which they were edited to music. My teacher gave me two videos to look at. One of them was produced by some students at the school and one was a professional video.

The fashion show was aimed at 14–18 year olds and included the clothes that we had designed for different groups for going out. The internet research gave us a lot of ideas and we also looked in fashion magazines and other magazines that were aimed at the target audience.

Further details about these secondary sources can be found in the files attached to this report.

Summary of findings

The tables and graphs below show a summary of the answers from the questionnaire.

Q1: Gender	Male	Female
	50%	50%

Q2: Age	14	15	16	17	18
	10%	20%	30%	30%	10%

Q3: Would you buy some of the clothes in the fashion show?

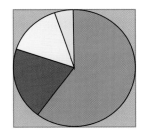

- Yes
- No
- Maybe
- Don't know

Graphs and tables summarise the findings of the research.

Q4: Is the video too long? Too short? About the right length?

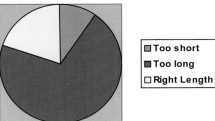

- Too short
- Too long
- Right Length

Q5: Rate the video on the scale 1 = excellent, 5 = rubbish

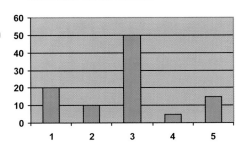

Q6: Identify the best 3 things about the video record
Most common answers were: The clothes, the music, the range of shots used, the models.

Q7: Identify the worst 3 things about the video record
Most common answers were: Too long, the editing, picture too dark, poor lighting.

For your project

* Include the title and a brief introduction that tells the examiner which unit the project was from.

* If yours was a group project rather than an individual one, make sure this is clear. Section A should be approximately 750 words and Section B (not included here) should be approximately 1,000 words.

* Make sure your report is no longer than 1,750 words.

Preparation for assessment

In this unit you were asked to write a report on a piece of work you had produced, or whose production you were involved in in one of the following units:

Unit 2 Performance
Unit 3 Artefact
Unit 4 Record.

Your report

Your report needs to be written in electronic form (on a computer) and this must be done in controlled conditions. This means you will be supervised by a teacher whilst writing the report and during this time you will not be allowed to communicate with other learners. You will be able to use notes and records you have produced, but you will not be allowed to access the internet. You will have up to four hours in which to complete your report, however this may be split over a number of sessions e.g. four 1-hour sessions.

You will be assessed on...	This will be evidenced in...
...your 'sources', which means your ability to gather information about work including audience responses.	Part A of your report. In this section you will: • describe the methods you used to gather responses about your work • describe where you got your information from • present a summary of the responses • draw conclusions from your summary about the success of your work. You are allowed to attach examples of the materials you used to gather responses, e.g. surveys. You are also allowed to include graphics, e.g. pie charts, to illustrate the findings of research and/or surveys. You should use about 750 words for this section; you will be marked out of a possible 20 marks.
...your ability to evaluate your work.	Part B of your report. In this section you will use the results of your research to evaluate your work, discussing its strengths and weaknesses. You should use about 1,000 words for this section; you will be marked out of a possible 30 marks.
...your ability to present an evaluation of your work in a written report.	Parts A and B of your report. A further 10 marks are available for the organisation and presentation of your report.

The assessment of the unit

This unit is assessed externally.

You must show that you:	Guidance	To gain higher marks:
…can gather information about and responses to your work by conducting surveys. …can use the information gathered to develop conclusions about your work.	You will need to gather responses to your work from a range of sources. You might, for example, design an audience questionnaire about a performance you have been involved in as well as interviewing members of the audience to find out what they thought about your work. Remember to consider the original aims of the work you produced when designing surveys and gathering information. You must try to find out whether or not the work achieved its aims.	You must gather information from a wide range of reliable sources. You must draw detailed conclusions that are well supported by the materials you have gathered.
…can report on the strengths and weaknesses of your work, looking at: • the way you developed ideas • your planning and organisational skills • how you used materials and techniques • how you worked as part of a team • how the work was presented.	Organise in advance the materials you intend to refer to when writing your report. This will allow you to use the time allowed to compile and write your report rather than wasting time searching through your notes. Make sure you back up every judgement you make with information and/or data from your research.	You must describe the strengths and weaknesses of your work against its aims. You must discuss in detail ways in which the work could have been improved. You must refer to the materials gathered throughout the report. You must include discussion of at least four of the following aspects of your work: • how well you developed ideas • the success of your planning and organisational skills • how well you used materials and techniques • how well you worked as part of a team • how the work was presented. You must be able to justify your conclusions.
…can compile and present a report that: • is well-organised and uses supporting material to communicate information, data and opinion • combines written work and images • is not more than 1,750 words long.	Leave time at the end of the session to read through your report and check for spelling mistakes and other errors. You should not write more than 1,750 words. Use the word count function to check the length of your report. Remember, you will lose marks if your report is too long.	Your report should be well-presented and easy to read. You should take advantage of opportunities to use graphics and images to communicate the ideas presented in your report. Any images or graphics used should be of a high quality.

What is the Project?

The Project Qualification is an important part of your Diploma. It allows you to explore topics connected to the creative and media sector in more depth. It could also be an opportunity for you to take off in a totally new direction if you have decided to change your career path. It all depends what you want to do in the future and you should think very carefully about what your choices are before you start.

Although you will have support and guidance from a teacher during the Project, it is up to you to choose a topic of interest, decide what the final outcome will be and choose what work you produce along the way. You can complete your Project over one or two years, and decide whether to work in a group or on your own; but make sure you check this with your tutor first.

It's up to you to decide on your project – but make sure that it's something you enjoy or are interested in, as you'll be spending quite some time on it!

Learning outcomes

You will need show that you can:

1) choose, plan and manage a project

2) research information and apply it to a project

3) select and apply skills to a project

4) review a project and your own performance and analyse the project outcomes.

What do I need to do to complete the Project Qualification?

At Level 2, you will need to achieve the seven objectives below.

∗ Select a topic that is either relevant to the Creative and Media principal learning, or one that will support progression into further education or your chosen career.

∗ Outline your project and its aims – *say what you are going to do and how you hope to achieve it.*

∗ Produce a plan of action for your project - *work out what you are going to do when and how these activities will help you achieve your aims and objectives.*

∗ Research your topic using appropriate techniques – *not just collecting information from the web, but conducting surveys or interviewing people, for example.*

∗ Take into account any health and safety or professional conduct issues – *make sure you work in a safe environment, that your actions don't endanger anyone else, and for example, ask for permission to use any copyright material.*

∗ Show that you can see your project through to completion – *finish your project within the deadline, and make sure you hand it in on time!*

∗ Present your project appropriately, and include an evaluation of your own learning - *this could be a performance or an exhibition, with an oral or written presentation of what you think you did well and what you would do differently.*

Remember

There is no exam at the end of this qualification. You will need to supply evidence that is in a format appropriate to your topic, such as:

∗ a video or DVD of your performance, activity or artefact

∗ written report or journal

∗ CD or presentation slides.

You will also need to submit a portfolio, so make sure you keep track of your documents!

∗ the Project Proposal Form, which you can get from your teacher

∗ tour research and activity notes

∗ tour review of your project.

Choosing your topic

All projects start with an idea. Ideas for projects come from many different sources and in many different ways. Think about the project work that you are already doing or that you know you will be starting. Do you want to develop any of this work further or do you want to try something different?

The main objective of your project is to produce a final product of some sort. This product could be a performance or an event that you have planned and run, or an actual artefact such as a video programme, musical recording, newsletter, magazine or website.

Don't worry if you can't think of something straight off – take your time and don't rush to start to something. Thought-shower ideas with other students and then talk them through with your teacher so you can get off to well thought-out start. You will have around 60 hours to plan, manage, complete and review your project work, so you need to choose an idea that is realistic for the time and resources that are available to you. You should think about how your project will enable you meet all the Learning Outcomes listed on page 244.

OVER TO YOU!

Has anything that you've done so far as part of your Diploma really sparked your interest? Make a list of the potential projects that you would be interested in developing and discuss these further with your teacher.

Capturing different people's thoughts and suggestions is a good place to start when you are trying to generate ideas and discuss the advantages and disadvantages of doing each one.

The Diploma areas

The table on the facing page shows the units, disciplines and themes that run through your Diploma, as well as a selection of jobs. Look over it and note down any areas that you have particularly enjoyed or that you can see fitting in well with your chosen career.

Units	Disciplines	Themes	Jobs
Scene Performance Artefact Record Campaign Festival	2D Visual Art 3D Visual Art Craft Graphic Design Product Design Fashion Textiles Footwear Advertising Drama Dance Music Film Television Audio and Radio Interactive Media Animation Computer Games Photo Imaging Creative Writing	Creativity in context Thinking and working creatively Principles, processes and practice Creative Business and Enterprise	Book or magazine designer/layout artist Camera person Ceramicist Choreographer Computer Games animator Copywriter Costume technician Drama teacher Fashion, textile or footwear designer Film director Journalist Marketing or advertising executive Music teacher Music technologist Photographer Sculptor

Some ideas

You might choose to: present a short piece of performance art or a multimedia show; produce a short moving image programme or a piece of music on your own; put together an exhibition of art and design or photographic work with a group of friends; develop your IT skills and decide to produce a website, or develop your business skills by marketing your own company. Whatever you decide, there are some basic things to remember:

Do:

* choose a topic you are interested in
* choose a topic that is related to your Diploma, unless you really have changed your mind about your future plans
* discuss your topic with your teacher.

Don't:

* choose a topic just because your friend is doing something similar
* choose something that is beyond the resources available to you.

Case Study: Sunil

Sunil is interested in journalism and is thinking of going on to study this at his local college. He has already done a little bit of writing, some photography and some page-layout design work on the computer. He thought that he could build upon these skills and develop them further by producing a special edition of the School Magazine. He also liked the idea of having a completed magazine at the end of the course to show at a job or college interview.

Planning your project

Aims and objectives

Once you've decided on your project topic, you will need to state your aims and objectives clearly. This means saying simply and clearly what you are going to do in your project and how you are going to achieve it.

Sunil's objectives might be:

1 *To produce three A4 pages of a student magazine. The topic for the pages will be 'School Life'. I will produce all of my own text and images for my pages.*

2 *To use at least two different research methods to find out what the target audience would like to see in my pages of the magazine.*

3 *To play an active role on the Editorial Board of the student magazine, to help design and produce a front page that will attract the target audience.*

Individual or group work?

It doesn't matter if you decide to work on this unit as an individual or as part of a small group. Some projects, such as those involving some form of performance or a complex production process, will work better as a group project; while others, such as designing a website or producing a report, might be better suited to individual work.

If you do undertake a group project, it is very important that you record and document the work that you do yourself, so that your individual contribution to the group project can be assessed accurately.

Getting started

Once you have discussed your initial ideas, one of your first tasks will be to complete a Project Proposal form so that your teacher can check that you are setting off on the right lines.

The Project Proposal form is an important document that you will hand in as evidence for this learning outcome, so you need to ensure that it is well presented and contains all of the relevant information.

OVER TO YOU!

Have you ever had to plan an event in the past? A friend's surprise birthday party? A school or college outing? What went well? Were there things that you would do differently the next time around?

Remember

If you are working in a group, each member of your team needs to produce *their own* Project Proposal form.

Activity

Get a blank Project Proposal Sheet from your teacher and begin to write out the details of your idea in the spaces provided. Think carefully about what you want to say before you start and use the guidance given above to help you. It might be a good idea to make a copy of the form before you fill it in, in case you make a mistake. Make sure that you check your spelling, punctuation and grammar, as your teacher will not be impressed by a messy, badly written form!

For Your Project

When you do your Project Proposal form, you will need to identify at least two individual objectives for the project that you are planning to undertake, as well as any additional objectives for the group as a whole (if you working as a team). Your objectives need to be realistic, achievable and written in a way that is clear and unambiguous.

When you have completed all six sections of your form and checked them through, you will need to get your teacher to sign it off. Remember, this form is a very important piece of evidence. You will need to keep it in a safe place and include it with your final portfolio of evidence.

Here's a rough draft of what Sunil is going to put in his proposal form:

Proposed title of project: *Student Magazine*
Working title: *Student Magazine*
Outcomes: *8 page A4 magazine printed in colour*

Reasons for choosing the project:
I have always been interested in writing and would like to do a journalism course at my local college. I think that it would be good experience to see the whole process of putting together a magazine .

Skills/knowledge you want to improve:
- *Creative writing skills*
- *Photographic skills*
- *Page layout and design skills*
- *Printing*

Activities:
- *Thought-showering ideas*
- *Producing an action plan*
- *Doing some readership research (primary and secondary)*
- *Taking digital photographs*
- *Writing text (called 'copy')*
- *Designing and laying-out the pages*
- *Printing*
- *Marketing and promotion*
- *Distributing the final magazine.*

Deadlines:
Complete all research into target readership.
Target date: *30th December*

Complete two A4 pages of words and images.
Target date: *28th February*

Resources:
- *Computer*
- *Colour printer*
- *Digital Camera*
- *Adobe CS3 Photoshop software*
- *Page layout and design software*

What could go wrong:
I could lose the work I have done if the computer crashes. I could prevent this by making sure that I save a back-up copy of all my work.

Some of the ideas for my articles and features might not work out. I could solve this by planning to write more material and taking more pictures than I need. This will allow me to choose the best ones and to have some spare material if something doesn't work out.

The printing might go wrong and delay the launch date. I could avoid this by building in some extra time in my action plan to allow time to catch up.

Carrying out your project

Managing your time

To ensure you can hand your project in on time, you will need to plan your time and break down your tasks into small, manageable chunks. Make sure you think about everything else that you need to get done over the coming months, and plan accordingly.

Dos and Don'ts

Do

* break each stage of your Project into smaller tasks that you know you can achieve
* think about everything else you've got on and plan time around those things too
* write a weekly action plan, and refer to it every week
* carry things that you haven't managed to do over to the following week, and do them!
* build in some 'contingency time' for when things go wrong.

Don't

* be over-ambitious about what you can achieve in a given timeframe
* leave everything to the last minute!

Activity

How well do you manage your time?

Answer these questions truthfully!

	Yes	No
Do I usually turn up to class on time?		
Do I keep appointments that I've made with friends most of the time?		
Do I regularly leave everything to the last minute?		
Do I plan time away from my assignments?		

Keeping good records

Remember that your Process Portfolio should include all of the pre-production and production paperwork that you have produced, as well as a written account and evaluation of the progress made and the decisions taken along the way. You'll also need to include examples of the final project outcome (or recordings and pictures of it) in your final portfolio of evidence for the unit.

Case Study: Sunil

Sunil had to write his own material for the magazine and spent quite a lot of the time drafting and redrafting his writing. He used a PC to write and saved drafts as he went along so that it was easy to keep track of where everything was and to improve the spelling, punctuation and grammar at each draft stage.

He also all took his own pictures using a digital camera and then uploaded the ones that he wanted to use onto the computer. He was then able to crop and resize the photographs to make then fit onto the page.

He used page layout software to combine the text and images together and to make the pages look attractive.

He had regular meetings with the other students working on the magazine, to ensure the final result was as good as possible.

Project activity records

Your activity records can be in the form of a diary or narrative account of what you did at each stage of your project. You should also include some more formal reviews with your teacher at key milestone points. When writing up your activity records, you should refer back to your original plan and monitor your own progress against this plan.

No project will ever go exactly to plan though, so be ready to respond to the problems and delays that you will inevitably face. You can gain marks by describing what problems you encountered and how you were able to overcome them. So don't get too worried if things don't go exactly as you planned!

> **Contingency plan** – This is a plan that you have in case things go wrong. For example, the students in our case study had all planned to produce more material than they needed in case something went wrong with some of the articles. This was part of their contingency plan and, as you can see below, it helped Yatin get out of a problem.

Case Study: Yatin and Shula

Yatin had planned to include a review of a gig by a local band as part of his Entertainment section of the magazine, but the gig was cancelled at the last minute and this left him with a gap. However, he had produced additional material as part of his **contingency plan** and managed to include a review of a new film that had just been released instead.

Shula faced a bigger problem when she lost her memory stick that contained some photos and text for her magazine. She had forgotten to back the files up on a more secure system and had to re-shoot the photos and rewrite the text. This was a pain but at least she learnt a valuable lesson!

Remember to back up all of your files on a secure system!

Research methods

You probably will already have done some initial research when deciding what your project was going to be, and it is likely that you will continue to research information and apply it at different stages throughout your project.

It is important that you keep a record of all of the research you do and include the details in a separate research file. This research file will be the main source of evidence for Learning Outcome 2 and will need to be handed in to be marked as part of your final portfolio of work.

You also need to use more than one type of research in your project work. The basic distinction to make is between **primary research** and **secondary research**. As well as conducting some primary research yourself, you should also conduct secondary research by gathering information from books or magazines, for example; don't just use secondary research in the form of an internet search.

Primary research – Original research carried out for a specific purpose, involving the use of particular techniques to obtain original data. These techniques could include conducting public surveys, interviews or visiting a company to observe processes.

Secondary research – The use of data and information that has already been published or is already available within an organisation. These techniques include reading books and magazines, searching on the internet and taking notes from research studies that already exist.

Quantitative data – Data based on measurable facts and information that can be counted, producing numerical and statistical information.

Qualitative data – Data based on opinions, attitudes and preferences rather than hard facts.

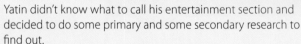

For your project

* For this project it is important that *you* choose your own research methods and sources of information.
* Describe the decisions that you made and the information that you discovered.
* Explain very clearly what you did with the findings of the research and how relevant it was to your project.

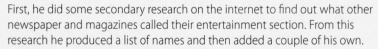

Case Study: Yatin

Yatin didn't know what to call his entertainment section and decided to do some primary and some secondary research to find out.

First, he did some secondary research on the internet to find out what other newspaper and magazines called their entertainment section. From this research he produced a list of names and then added a couple of his own.

He then composed a questionnaire (primary research) to find out what his target audience wanted to see in the magazine.

The first part of his questionnaire is shown opposite. Can you work out which questions will give him **quantitative data** and which will give him **qualitative data**?

Questionnaire

I am producing a magazine for 14–16 year old students at our school.

Please help my research by writing down the information in the spaces provided.

Q1: Name

Q2: Age **Q3: Gender** **Q4: Tutor Group**

Q5: I am producing a section on Entertainment. What would you like to see included in this section?

Q6: Please tick your favourite name for the Entertainment section.

Biz Ents Sound 'n' Vision Stage and Screen About Town What's Happening? Fun Time

Q7: Please explain why you chose this one as your favourite name.

For your project

The research activities that you decide to use will depend on the type of project that you are developing.

If, for example, you are planning to produce a video project, then you may want to conduct a survey of a sample of your target audience, or ask a focus group what they think of your ideas. You might also interview some people to find out information for your video, or to find out if they would be suitable to appear in your video.

You could visit a professional production crew to see how they operate, or research the potential locations that you might use in your video.

You may also want to search in books, magazines and on the internet for relevant information that you could include as content in your video. If the video is on global warming, for example, you would need to research the relevant issues and debates around the subject to get some up-to-date facts and figures that you can use.

Activity

You should now be in a position to plan, design and carry out a series of research activities for your project work that includes both primary and secondary research methods, and allows you to gather both qualitative and quantitative information.

Presenting your project

When you have carried out your project, you will present your review of it. You can present your review in any form that you choose. You could: present it in the form of a written report, in an audio-visual format of some kind or as an oral presentation in front of an audience. You need to discuss this with your teacher so that you can decide what is the best way for you. If you choose to present your findings in the form of an oral presentation, you should make sure that this is recorded so that your final marks can be checked by the moderator towards the end of the course.

However you decide to present your findings, you will need to think carefully about the structure and content of what you produce as well as the language that you use. Be prepared to review what went well during your project and what *didn't* go well. Learning from your mistakes is an important part of any process and will make you better at doing things next time.

The content of your review

Your review should cover the following key points:

* a clear introduction to your project in which you explain clearly what the purpose of the project was, what form it took and why you did it
* an evaluation of the extent to which your original objectives (specified in your Project Proposal Form) were met and what you have learnt through completing the project
* what skills you have used and developed through the process
* an assessment of how well you think you performed (include some primary evidence from your teacher and peers to support the points that you are making)
* how you could improve your project if you were to undertake it again.

Finally, you need to include a summary of the sources that you have used, including a **bibliography** of any published works.

The form of your review

Oral presentation

If you decide to give an oral presentation of your review, here are some things to think about:

How long have I got? Plan your presentation minute by minute, and think about what you've got to cover and what to emphasise.

Who will be there? Make sure you've got enough handouts (if you're using them), and that you feel confident about presenting in front of a group.

How much preparation have I done? Practice really does make perfect, and you'll need to have practised your presentation for timing and effect. You can do this in front of a mirror, or as a trial run in front of friends and family. Just make sure you do it!

How will I come across? Think not only about what you are going to say (your **spoken language**) but how you are going to present yourself during the presentation. Your **non-verbal communication** is just as important as what you say.

What equipment do I need? A computer? A whiteboard? A projector? You should also think about using **visual aids** to help structure your presentation. Get to the room early, and check everything is working well before you start.

For your project

Think about your own communication skills. Are you confident when speaking to other people? What can you do to improve the way in which you get your ideas across?

Written review

Of course you do not have to do an oral presentation for your review; you can choose to produce a written report instead.

You still need to make sure that your review is professional and organised – and easy for the reader to follow. There is no set way of writing up your review, but you do need to:

* make sure that it is clearly and logically laid out
* use appropriate headings and sub-headings to structure your review
* check your spelling and grammar thoroughly.

Further research

Look at the ways in which TV presenters and public speakers present themselves. Consider the way in which they use their hands and arms, the way that they move and position their body and the clothes that they wear. How do all of these things make them look?

Is there anybody you can think of who is not very good at this sort of thing? Why? How could they improve this?

Bibliography – A list of books that you have used in a particular research project. You should reference the books in the following way:

Hart, J: Storyboarding for Film, TV and Animation (Focal Press, 1999).

(The author's surname followed by his or her initial; the title of the book, which is sometimes written in italics or in bold; the publisher and year of publication)

Non-verbal communication (NVC) – This refers to all of the features of body language that occurs during a presentation. It includes such features as the clothes that you wear, your posture, facial expression and hand and arm movements. First impressions count, so make sure that you look smart, feel comfortable and act confidently.

Spoken language – This includes what you say and the way that you say it. The way that you say things is called 'paralanguage' and includes features such as voice pitch, tone, pace and volume, as well as all of the fillers and hesitations that we use in everyday language.

Visual aids – Props, objects and examples that you include in your presentation. Also includes slides, images and posters that can help to structure what you say.

Assessment tips

Your project work will be marked by your teacher and moderated by the exam board. You will receive marks for your ability to:

* manage your project
* use relevant resources
* develop and realise your ideas
* review your work.

Your teacher will use the assessment grid that is in the Edexcel specification to mark your work; it is important that you look very carefully at this grid to ensure you know what you need to do to get the best marks you can. There are two mark bands on the assessment grids and you need to try and get your work into the second band.

The tables on these two pages will give you an idea of the sort of thing you will need to do to get your work into Band 2. However make sure you obtain a copy of the official Edexcel specification assessment grid from your teacher as well.

Manage your project	
What you must do	*Aiming for higher marks*
Make sure you get and fill in all the sections of you Project Proposal form.	Be as clear and detailed as you can, and describe what you think your key activities will be and when you will be able to do them (be specific!). Give details about the resources you use and try to explain potential problems – don't just give simple descriptions of your resources.
Describe all the things you did in your Project activity records.	Describe and explain in your activity records the actual problems that you encountered and how you overcame them.

Use relevant resources	
Band 1	Band 2
Obtain a range of information from at least two sources of information for your research (internet, book, interview, questionnaire).	Use a range of both primary and secondary methods of research.
Include a bibliography that identifies your sources of information. Describe the research methods you used.	Make sure that you use a consistent format throughout your bibliography. Describe your research methods in detail.
Explain how relevant and reliable some of your research methods were.	Evaluate, rather than just explain, how relevant and reliable each of your research methods was.

Develop and realise your ideas

Band 1	Band 2
Present your written work clearly and in a logical order. Ensure your artefact or performance/event is presented appropriately and that it communicates most of your ideas successfully. Make sure you have used your resources well and with some success. Show that you considered alternative ideas or designs. Show some evidence that the processes you went through were adequate and generally successful.	Present your written work clearly and in a logical order. Ensure that your work contains very few errors. Show evidence that you have redrafted your work. Ensure your artefact or performance/event is well presented and that it communicates all your ideas clearly. Make sure you have used your resources consistently well and with success. Show that you carefully considered your alternative ideas and designs and evaluated them thoroughly. Show clear evidence that the processes you went through were well thought-out, thorough and effective.

Review your work

Band 1	Band 2
Structure your review clearly and ensure you include a conclusion. Describe the range of knowledge and skills you developed throughout the project and explain which objectives were not met and why. Describe how well you performed and suggest ways in which you could improve things. Suggest some ideas for how the skills you've learned could be transferred to other areas and projects.	Structure your review in a clear and consistent way and include a detailed conclusion. Give detailed descriptions of all the knowledge and skills you developed throughout the project and ensure you cover every objective fully. Include feedback from others in your description of how well you performed and suggest clear and realistic plans for how you could improve things. Suggest clear and realistic ideas for how the skills you've learned could be transferred to other areas and projects.

Just checking

You can always get extra marks for showing that you can begin to work more independently. This does NOT mean that you cannot ask your teacher for help; it means that once you have been given some support or advice, you can then take that and apply it to your own project work.

Index

Note: Page numbers in bold type indicate where first definition of a key term can be found

Acknowledgements

The author and publisher would like to thank the following individuals and organisations for permission to reproduce copyright material:

p. 15: With kind permission of Fabric and Bradford Council; p. 21: With kind permission of (T) Talking Voices, (B) The Community Media Association; p. 28: By permission of the Royal Shakespeare Company; p. 58: By kind permission of the Globe Theatre; p. 149 and p. 151: With kind permission from Barnardo's and BBH; p. 192: With thanks to Sue Quinn and the Wolverton Lantern Festival; p. 200: With thanks to Sarah Wilson and the Sydney Festival.

The author and publisher would like to thank the following individuals and organisations for permission to reproduce photographs:

p. 5: © Arnos Design Ltd.; p. 7: © Rex Features/Alastair Muir; p. 9: © Alamy/Simon Holdcroft; p. 12: © istockphoto/wphotos; p. 14: © istockphoto/Franky De Meyer; p. 16: © alamy/Travelshots.com; p. 19: (L) © Alamy/David Hoggett, (R) © NEC Press Office; p. 21: © Community Radio; p. 22: (L) © Rex Features/P Anastasselis, (TR) © istockphoto/Liz Leyden, (BR) With kind permission from Virgin Media; p. 29: © Julian Makey/Rex Features; p. 31: © Alamy/Simon Holdcroft; p. 33: © John Birdsall Photography; p. 34: © Rex Features/Steve Bell; p. 36: © Warner Brothers; p. 41: © Department of Health/COI/Nick Georghiou; p. 43: © Corbis/James Leynse; p. 44: © istockphoto/fotek; p. 46: © istockphoto/Chris Schmidt; p. 50: Rex Features/Trent Warner; p. 51: © Jan Tyler/iStockphoto; p. 52: © BBC Photolibrary; p. 53: © Hollywood Records; p. 54: © Rex Features/Everett Collection; p. 55: © Rex Features/Alastair Muir; p. 56: © Rex Features/Mark Mainz/Staff; p. 58: © Photostage; p. 59: © Rex Features; p. 60: © Simon Jarratt/Corbis UK Ltd.; p. 61: © Eddie Mulholland/Rex Features; p. 63: © Radius Images/Alamy; p. 66: © PhotoDisc. Steve Cole; p. 68: © istockphoto/RyanJLane; p. 70: © Arnos Design Ltd.; p. 72: © Corbis/Rick Barrentine; p. 76: © Renault; p. 77: © istockphoto/Shaun Lowe; p. 78: © Bridgeman/Sunday Afternoon on the Island of La Grande Jatte, 1884-86 (oil on canvas) (detail of 693), Seurat, Georges Pierre (1859-91) / Art Institute of Chicago, IL, USA, / The Bridgeman Art Library; p. 79: © Study for the left panel of the 'War' Triptych, 1930 (pencil, charcoal and crayon on paper), Dix, Otto (1891-1969) / Hamburger Kunsthalle, Hamburg, Germany, © DACS / The Bridgeman Art Library; p. 80: © Corbis/Edward Bock; p. 86: © iStockPhotos/Tom Young; p. 87: © istockphoto/Chris Fertnig; p. 88: © Getty/Andy Buchanan; p. 92: © Hellestad Rune/Corbis; p. 94: (T) © ITV, (B) © Rex Features Ltd.; p. 98: (T) © Blockbusters, (L) © BBC Children In Need, (R) © Rex Features Ltd/Nicholas Bailey, (B) © Rex Features Ltd.; p. 100: © Rex Features/P Anastasselis; p. 105: © PhotoDisc. Steve Cole; p. 108: © Rex Features Ltd. Newspix; p. 111: © istockphoto/Jan Derksen; p. 114: © Rex Features Ltd./TS/Keystone USA; p. 116: © Corbis/Bettmann; p. 118: © Rex Features/Canadian Press; p. 122: © istockphoto/Ken Cameron; p. 124: © istockphoto/Olivier Blondeau; p. 131: © istockphoto/Mike Clarke; p. 133: © istockphoto/Darrell Nutt; p. 134: © istockphoto/Alberto Pomares; p. 140: © Rex Features Ltd.; p. 142 (T) © Microsoft, (B) © Rex Features Ltd/Ben Osborne/Nature Picture Library; p. 143: With kind permission from the RSPCA; p. 144: (TL) © Worldaids Campaign.com, (TR) © Science and Society Picture Library, (BL) © PA Photos/Peter Byrne/PA Wire, (BR) © Alamy/Mary Evans Picture Library; p. 146: (T&B) © UK Dept for Transport; p. 147: © The Ape Theatre Company Ltd.; p. 149: © PA Photos/Stephen Kelly/PA Archive/PA Photos; p. 150: (L) © PA Photos/Unilever/PA Archive/PA Photos, (M) © Rex Features Ltd., (R) © Getty Images/China Photos; p. 151: (T) With kind permission from Nick Georghiou, BBH and Barnardo's, (B) With kind permission from Kiran Master, BBH and Barnardo's; p. 155: © Fair Trade; p. 156: © Getty; p. 159: © Corbis/ROB & SAS/Corbis; p. 160: © Corbis; p. 167: © Big Wheel; p. 170: © Department of Health/COI/Nick Georghiou; p. 174: © Alamy/Malcolm McHugh; p. 176: © Rex Features Ltd/South West News Service; p. 177: © Alamy/South West Images Scotland; p. 178: © Alamy/Homer W Sykes; p. 180: © Rex Features Ltd/Ray Tang; p. 181: © Jana Winderen; p. 183: © Andrew Tshabangu/Gallery Momo; p. 184: © Rex Features/Tina Norris; p. 186: © Alamy/Redferns Music Picture Library; p. 187: © Gateshead Festival; p. 188: © Corbis/Simon Marcus; p. 191: © Getty/Altrendo; p. 192: © PA Photos/Wally Santana/AP/PA Photos; p. 196: © Alamy/Robert Estall Photo Agency; p. 198: © Corbis/Stephane Cardinale/People Avenue; p. 199: © PA photos/David I. Andersen/AP/PA Photos; p. 200: © Rex Features Ltd/James D. Morgan; p. 203: (T) © The Edinburgh Fringe Festival, (B) © The Sydney Festival; p. 204: © Fotosearch Stock Photography; p. 207: © Arnos Design Ltd.; p. 215: © Alamy/Allstar Picture Library; p. 222: © Alamy/Glyn Ryland; p. 225: © Alamy/22Digital; p. 237: © Arnos Design Ltd ; p. 239: © Alamy/Glyn Ryland.

Every effort has been made to contact copyright holders of material reproduced in this book. Any omissions will be rectified in subsequent printings if notice is given to the publishers.